# The Development and Regulation of Non-Bank Financial Institutions

Jeffrey Carmichael

Michael Pomerleano

THE WORLD BANK

Library of Congress Cataloging-in-Publication Data has been applied for.

ISBN 0-8213-4839-6

Cover Design: James E. Quigley, World Bank Institute/Rock Creek Publishing Group.

Photo Credit: Photodisc.

# Contents

# Foreword

The past 10 years witnessed the rise of a middle class in developing countries as more and more attained a certain stage of economic growth. With the growing demand for property ownership, small-scale investment, and saving for retirement came a growing need for housing finance, contractual savings, insurance services, pension plans management, and asset management.

The World Bank Group promotes the development of nonbank financial institutions (NBFIs) because their growth leads to a virtuous cycle through which countries benefit from broader access to financial services and a more competitive, diversified financial sector that reduces systemic vulnerability. NBFIs offer individuals and small- and medium-scale enterprises a broader menu of financial services and tailored financial instruments, thereby improving access. In turn, the growth of financial services offers a mechanism for creating jobs, which strengthens the social fabric and heightens social stability.

At the microeconomic level, the growth of NBFIs promotes competition by introducing new industries that challenge the services and capacity of banks, and the ensuing competition leads to improved financial services while reducing systemic vulnerabilities. The Asian financial crisis provides ample evidence of the risks associated with the absence of a balanced financial sector with multiple channels of financial intermediation. NBFIs play an important role in a balanced and diversified financial sector that is relatively robust and stable.

The work in the NBFI sector exemplifies the synergies resulting from the complementary activities of three affiliates of the World Bank Group. The Financial Sector Vice Presidency offers policy analysis and advice. The World Bank Institute develops the capacity of NBFIs through learning programs, while the International Finance Corporation has considerable experience in transactions, technical assistance, and private sector investment. The World Bank Group is pleased to make this volume available to a wide audience.

Cesare Calari
Vice President, Financial Sector

# Preface

By distilling the empirical evidence and academic literature, this volume offers a "bird's eye" roadmap for financial policymakers seeking to promote and regulate the development of nonbank financial institutions (NBFIs). The first chapter establishes the importance of NBFIs to the financial system and the rationale for promoting their development. The second chapter lays out a framework that differentiates the various types of financial regulation in the context of regulatory objectives. The subsequent four chapters closely examine, in turn, insurance, contractual savings, securities markets, and specialized financial institutions. Each chapter points to the potential benefits that may be gained by fostering development of the industry and offers guidance for accomplishing this. The book concludes by examining the policy challenges confronting developing countries.

Two caveats are in order. Admittedly, this book cannot offer a comprehensive analysis of all NBFIs. Clearly, other NBFIs, such as microfinance institutions, credit unions, and trust companies, for instance, are equally important. In other cases, the evidence is only just emerging, as industries such as real estate investment trusts are beginning to gain acceptance in the more advanced emerging markets such as Singapore. Future study of the benefits that these industries offer may provide additional policy guidance.

Second, this book's objective is to offer a conceptual framework to think through the issues of development and regulation. However, reasonable people might reach different conclusions with regard to the policy and regulatory measures required. One should always keep in mind that there is no "one size fits all" in terms of policy and regulatory measures, and appropriate measures will always depend on unique country conditions. A case in point is the "prudent man rule" applied in pensions in the United States. This rule might not be applicable in countries with less developed equity markets.

Finally, we hope this volume proves both informative and useful.

# Acknowledgments

This volume relies extensively on the presentations at two global workshops—Nonbank Financial Institutions: Development and Regulation—jointly hosted in Washington, D.C. by the Financial Sector Vice Presidency and the World Bank Institute in January 2000 and February 2001. We would like to acknowledge the contributors to both workshops: Reena Aggarwal, Manuel Aguilera, Sally Buxton, Loic Chiquier, Patrick Conroy, Manuel Conthe, Leslie Cummins, Clemente Luis Del Valle, Gustavo Demarco, Bill Doscas, William R. Fadul, William R. Feldhaus, Michael Fleming, Jay Gillan, Patrick Goergen, Gene Gohlke, Serap Oguz Gonulal, Peter Hazell, Richard Hinz, Knut Hohlfeld, Gregorio Impavido, Estelle James, Cally Jordan, Vijay Kalavakonda, Daniel Kaufmann, Yoshihiro Kawai, Yongbeom Kim, Mark A. Kinsey, Jane Lamb, Michael J. Lea, Ruben Lee, Rodney Lester, David Lindeman, Robert E. Litan, Mike Lubrano, Donald McIsaac, Shepard Melzer, Cesar Montemayor, Alberto Roque Musalem, Robert J. Palacios, Ian Pickering, Robert Pouliot, Bertrand Renaud, Rafael Rofman, Robert Sammis, Lawrie Savage, Robert Schwartz, Anne Simpson, Harold D. Skipper Jr., P. S. Srinivas, Kim B. Staking, Benn Steil, Mark St. Giles, Robert D. Strahota, Michael Taylor, Laura S. Unger, Dimitri Vittas, and Steven A. Wechsler.

We are also indebted to participants at the NBFI workshops, whose insights enriched the discussions. In addition, we thank Dan Goldblum and Aizaz ul Haque for organizing the workshops, Dan Goldblum and Colleen Mascenik for providing research assistance, Elizabeth Forsyth for editing the manuscript, and James Quigley for designing the book.

# The Policy Framework

*Financial institutions perform a wide range of functions in the economic system. This introductory chapter explores those roles and the contributions that different types of financial institutions make to the efficiency and effectiveness of the system.*

## Financial Systems

The financial system plays a key role in the smooth and efficient functioning of the economy. The most fundamental contribution that any financial system makes is to channel resources from individuals and companies with surplus resources to those with resource deficits. In doing so, the financial system not only satisfies the savings needs of the economy but also facilitates the accumulation of investment capital that is critical to growth and development. The overall contribution of the financial system can, however, extend well beyond these primary roles by also resolving the risk preferences of individuals and companies.

Financial systems consist of markets and participants. According to the dictionary, markets are places in which "things are traded." In financial markets, these "things" are most easily characterized as "promises." Any financial claim can be viewed as a promise to deliver specified payments at specified times, under specified circumstances.[1] The promises traded in financial markets can be classified into one of three generic types: debt

---

1.  This analysis of financial claims as different types of promises draws heavily on Financial System Inquiry (1997).

**1**

promises, equity promises, and contingent promises. Of course, many promises are hybrid combinations of these three generic types.

Debt promises involve promises to pay fixed dollar (that is, cash) amounts at fixed dates in the future. The payments may be fixed in currency units or according to a formula (such as a floating-rate note indexed to three-month London Interbank Offered Rate, LIBOR). Debt promises can be subclassified further according to their maturity and the risk rating of the promisor. Debt promises include deposits, government treasury bills, commercial paper, corporate bonds, and mortgages.

Equity promises are claims over the residual earnings of a business. In most countries, residual earnings claims also carry voting rights over the operations of the business. Unlike debt promises, they make no specific promises about either the size of cash payments or their timing. Although the claim is over the residual value of the business, and therefore subordinated to the interests of holders of any debt promises made by the business, equity promises also may be subclassified by different priority rankings with respect to either cash flows or the residual assets of the business in the event of liquidation. Equity promises include common stock, partly paid shares, and preference shares.

Contingent promises are promises to make specified payments under specified circumstances. For example, a property insurance policy promises to make payments within specified parameters in the event of damage to the property indicated. Contingent promises specify trigger events to activate the promise. Typically these are tightly specified and can be independently verified. Contingent promises include all forms of insurance and warranties and guarantees.

In principle, a fourth group of promises can be distinguished. These are derivative promises to enter into transactions involving physical commodities, or debt or equity promises (or even contingent promises), at a future point in time at prices determined at the time of entering the derivative contract. In practice, however, these derivative promises mostly fulfill the definitions of either a debt promise (for example, a futures position is a commitment to deliver a fixed payment at a predetermined date in the future in exchange for a commodity or another financial claim) or a contingent promise (for example, an option is a contingent commitment to enter into such an exchange, provided the holder of the option chooses to exercise it).

The interesting feature of these generic groups of promises is that each involves fundamentally different risks. Thus a business can structure its financing by unbundling the different components of risk in its operations and selling them to different buyers with different risk preferences. In practice, there are no limits to the variations of instruments for combining different components of the generic promises to make hybrid promises.

The primary function of the financial system is to match the needs of primary issuers of financial promises (the promisors) with the ultimate holders of the promises (the promisees). Toward this end, the financial system provides the framework within which these promises are created and exchanged. In most cases, however, promisees do not hold financial promises directly (when they do, this is called "direct finance"). As financial systems have grown in sophistication, specialist financial institutions have evolved that "intermediate" the promises between issuers and holders. Most of these financial institutions fundamentally change the nature and risks of the primary promises. In addition to intermediating financial promises, financial institutions often provide services (such as conducting trades, either as principal or as agent, and providing advice).

A financial intermediary interposes its balance sheet between the ultimate suppliers and users of financial resources. Thus, for example, a bank gathers surplus resources from households and firms and channels them through to households and firms that need resources. In the process, the nature of the promise is changed. The bank typically offers its own short-term promises to depositors and, in turn, accepts longer-term individual promises from borrowers. This process of intermediation changes not only the liquidity characteristics of the promise to depositors but also the characteristics of its default risk. In cases such as banking, the nature of the promise is fundamentally altered. In other cases, such as funds management, the financial institution simply acts as an efficient vehicle for risk-pooling or divisibility purposes.

## Financial Institutions

Financial institutions can be classified in any number of ways, including by their risk characteristics, by the maturity of their assets or liabilities, and by whether or not they transform the underlying promises. For the purposes of

**1**

this book, it is most helpful to classify institutions by the particular services they provide.

The primary function of all financial institutions is to match the preferences of groups having resource surpluses with those of groups having resource deficits. They perform this primary function, however, in a wide variety of ways. In particular, they perform their primary function by providing services to some or all of the three generic categories of promises and to some or all of the participants in the financial system. Financial institutions provide core financial services such as payments services, liquidity, divisibility, maturity transformation, store of value, information economies, and risk pooling (see Financial System Inquiry 1997):

- A limited range of financial institutions provide payments services—the capacity to be used in settling transactions. To serve as an effective means of payments, a claim (or promise) must have a highly stable and reliable value, must be widely accepted in exchange, and must be linked to the arrangements for ultimate settlement of value.
- Liquidity is the ease with which an asset's full market value can be realized once a decision to sell has been made. Liquidity is often confused with, but is quite distinct from, predictability of value. For example, an equity claim may be quite liquid, even though its value may be quite unpredictable. Through both specialization and scale, financial institutions are able to enhance the liquidity of the underlying promises.
- Promisors often find it costly and inconvenient to divide their claims into the full range of denominations desired by promisees. Divisibility is the extent to which an asset can be purchased or sold in small denominations. Financial institutions are able both to break up large-denomination (lumpy) claims and to aggregate small-denomination claims to meet the preferences of the community.
- Store of value is the extent to which an asset provides a reliable store of purchasing power over time. The store of value service is fundamental to satisfying the savings preferences of the community.
- Information is costly to access and process. Providing economies of scale in processing and assessing risks is an important role of financial institutions. The informational advantage of specialized financial institutions includes their ability to resolve the unwill-

ingness of many promisors to reveal relevant information for competitive reasons.

- Risk pooling is the extent to which an asset spreads the default risk of the underlying promises by pooling. By pooling the resources of investors, financial institutions take advantage of diversification to lower risk to a much greater extent than is normally available to individual investors.

Since these services are often provided in combination, no unique classification of institutions by services provided is appropriate to all situations. The following subsections, which draw heavily on Kumar (1997), classify institutions by their major services: deposit-taking institutions, risk-pooling institutions, contractual savings institutions, market makers, specialized sectoral financiers, and financial service providers.

## Deposit-Taking Institutions

Banks and other deposit-taking financial institutions, such as thrifts (also known as building societies) and credit unions, accept call and fixed-term deposits and make loans across the breadth of the economy. Many also provide a range of ancillary services including advice, stockbrokering, and securities dealing, depending on the laws of the country involved. For convenience of notation, all of these institutions and the services they offer are referred to here as banks and banking.

Banks provide an attractive bundle of most of the core financial services. By enabling depositors to write checks and other negotiable instruments on their deposits, banks offer payments services and liquidity equal to that of currency (hence their inclusion with currency in the payments system of virtually every country in the world). Deposits also offer exceptionally high divisibility (at least to the same level as currency and usually with greater flexibility than currency). The store of value service is similar to that of other debt promises in that deposits promise repayment at (nominal) face value plus interest. Banks resolve the information conflict faced by borrowers and generally enjoy substantial economies of scale in processing and analyzing information. Finally, banks pool risk by placing borrowers' promises into a single promise by the intermediary itself.

**1**

Banks are generally accessible to all participants in the financial system. Their main limitation is that they do not cater to all three categories of financial promises. In most countries, banking activity is restricted to debt-type promises on both the asset and liability sides of the balance sheet.

## Risk-Pooling Institutions

Insurance companies specialize in providing contingent promises by under-writing economic risks associated with death, illness, damage to or loss of property, and other exposure to loss. Insurance companies issue contingent liabilities against themselves in the form of insurance policies.

Insurance companies are divided generally into life insurance and general insurance (in the United States, general insurance is known as property and casualty insurance; in some other countries, it is known simply as non-life insurance). The distinction between the two lies largely in the long-term risks that reside in life insurance (until the death of the insured) compared with the short-term nature of most other insured risks.

Within non-life insurance, a distinction is usually drawn between social and market insurance. The key feature of social insurance is that private markets typically do not exist for events such as the loss of labor income and the basic amenities of life as a result of unemployment, disability and other medical problems, and natural disasters. Private insurers do not readily provide this type of coverage for several reasons:

- Losses are difficult, if not impossible, to predict (particularly in the case of natural disaster).
- Losses, and the events that trigger them, can be difficult to define precisely (for example, the extent and nature of a disability).
- The insured is often able to withhold information important to the assessment of risks (for example, known medical conditions or tendencies).
- The existence of insurance can alter the insured's behavior (for example, unemployment insurance can create the moral hazard problem whereby the insured is less active in seeking and retaining employment than would be the case without the insurance).

For these reasons, governments have long provided social insurance. Social insurance tends to be more prevalent in Western societies where family networks and other support groups have broken down in the process of industrialization.

Insurance provided by private insurers (market insurance) is more common in areas such as casualty and property, where the problems listed above are less of a concern. General insurance companies typically take a single premium in return for the promise to make a specified payment contingent on the event that is being insured (such as fire, theft, or damage). General insurance contracts typically refer to a fixed and relatively short time period. The insurance company invests the funds (premiums) raised from the issue of the contingent promises in ways that are appropriate to meeting the financial obligations of the contingencies, should they arise.

The primary contingent promise sold by life insurance companies is insurance against economic loss arising from the premature death of the insured. The most basic form of life insurance is term insurance, under which the insurer pays a fixed sum in the event of the death of the insured during a specified period of time.[2] This pure form of life insurance is very similar in nature to general insurance. Consequently, the policy premiums from this type of insurance usually are dedicated to underwriting the assessed risks involved.

Life insurance companies, however, traditionally have extended their range of offerings beyond term life coverage. Whole life insurance (called whole of life insurance in some countries) is designed to provide long-term death benefits against an ongoing stream of fixed premiums. Since the probability of death increases with age, and since the premiums remain constant over the term of the policy, the insured tends to overpay for the insurance in the early years and (for those who survive) to underpay in the later years. The amount by which the premium exceeds the true cost of insurance during the early years contributes to what is known as the cash value of the policy. The investment of these overpayments by the life insurance company attaches an embedded investment product to the contingent promise.

In recent years, life insurance companies have tended to unbundle these two components of life insurance and to promote their investment products as a means of moving into the contractual savings sector of the financial system.

---

2. The death benefit is usually fixed either in nominal terms or according to a formula (for example, either increasing or decreasing with age).

Life insurance companies also have become the dominant sellers of annuities. Whereas life insurance provides financial security in the event of premature death, annuities provide financial security in the event of prolonged life. Annuities pay a regular income to the holders for either a specified period or, in the case of life annuities, until death. Annuities are thus another form of contingent promise.

Both the whole life and annuity businesses of life insurance companies involve long-term liabilities and therefore require corresponding long-term investments by the companies.

In terms of the core financial services, general insurance companies (and those that specialize in term life insurance) provide a high level of risk pooling and information efficiency. They also offer a high degree of divisibility. Life insurance companies also provide store of value services through their investment and annuities products.

In terms of coverage, insurance generally is available to all sectors of the community. The primary promise is a contingent promise, although the store of value services provided by life insurance companies incorporate elements of both the equity and debt promises (depending on the particular product involved).

## Contractual Savings Institutions

In general, households have three main alternatives for their savings. First, they can invest directly in debt and equity promises issued by firms and other individuals. Second, they can hold the liabilities of deposit-taking institutions or the investment products of life insurance companies. Third, they can invest in collective investment vehicles (also known as institutional investors), such as mutual funds or private pension plans. The essential nature of these vehicles is to provide contractual savings services in a fiduciary rather than a principal role.

Collective investment vehicles invest the pooled resources of individuals and firms into a wide range of equity, debt, and derivative promises. The distinguishing characteristic of these vehicles is that they transform the underlying promises into an equity promise by the vehicle. That is, the ultimate risk inherent in the underlying investment portfolio is borne by the shareholder in the vehicle.

Although there are many variations of collective investment vehicles around the world, most fall into one of two main types: either open-end or closed-end mutual funds. An investor in a mutual fund owns a pro rata share of the assets in the fund's investment portfolio. The pro rata nature of the claims has led many countries to encourage the establishment of mutual funds as unit trusts. Open-end funds issue new shares to the investing public to generate new investments. Open-end funds typically stand ready to buy back or redeem the shares (or units) at their net asset value. Closed-end funds issue a fixed number of shares only. The shareholders in a closed-end fund access the value of their investments by selling their shares on the market. Pension funds are simply mutual funds that satisfy the legislated conditions for retirement savings. These conditions typically limit the owner's ability to access the invested resources before retirement, usually in return for generous tax concessions.

Mutual funds usually distinguish themselves by the nature of their investments. Following is a typical range of mutual funds:

- Income funds that invest in assets offering a reliable stream of income
- Growth funds that focus on high-growth, low-income investments
- Tax-exempt funds that invest in tax-exempt securities
- High-yield funds that specialize in high-risk, high-yield investments
- Sectoral funds such as property trusts and bond trusts
- Hedge funds that generate their income by trading, either for arbitrage or for speculation
- Global funds that specialize in cross-border investments.

The contractual savings sector of the financial system has been the major growth area of most developed financial systems in recent decades. In terms of services, these institutions provide liquidity, divisibility, store of value services, and informational efficiencies. Unlike deposit-taking institutions, collective investment vehicles provide an equity promise rather than a debt promise on the liability side of the balance sheet, although the range of promises transformed into these liabilities can be quite wide.

**1**

## Market Makers

An important group of financial institutions encompasses institutions that make markets in financial securities such as equities, government and corporate debt, and derivatives. Securities dealers (including investment banks, stockbrokers, and other financial institutions that stand ready to buy or sell securities) make markets in new securities by underwriting their issue and facilitating their distribution to individual and institutional investors. They make secondary markets in these securities by taking principal positions as buyers and sellers of existing securities.

Securities dealers range from small firms specializing in single product lines to large diversified firms offering a broad range of services, including position-taking, brokering, margin lending to customers, investment banking services, money management, and research.

Through their dealing positions, securities dealers typically maintain large inventories of securities. The risks in these positions are substantial, and securities dealing is consequently highly capital intensive for the following reasons:

- The capital values of their portfolios are exposed to movements in market prices.
- The timing gap between securities transactions and settlement can be quite long.
- The dealers often extend credit to their customers to finance their positions.

To the extent that they add liquidity to otherwise illiquid securities, market makers can be viewed as specialists in providing liquidity services. At the same time, by making a market, they reduce the search costs involved for investors in determining the fair value of particular securities. Thus they also provide information services.

## Specialized Sectoral Financiers

A number of financial institutions provide a limited range of financial services to a specialized target group of promisors and promisees. General finance companies, for example, raise funds via debt promises from the

1

wholesale finance market and on-lend them to borrowers. Real estate finance companies specialize in channeling funds to homeownership. Leasing companies specialize in providing finance for equipment. The distinguishing characteristic of leasing companies is that they retain ownership of the leased assets. In this way, they can overcome the effects of weak collateral or enforcement laws. They also can benefit from the preferred tax treatment that is often conferred on investment equipment.

In each of these cases, financial institutions provide a highly specialized service that concentrates on informational efficiency (knowing the sector or product better than more broadly based institutions). To varying extents, these institutions may offer other combinations of services such as liquidity and divisibility. Their promises are generally of a debt nature, although equity components are not uncommon.

## Financial Service Providers

The final group of institutions in the financial system consists of the financial service providers. Unlike the other groups of institutions, service providers tend not to intermediate between promisors and promisees. Rather they provide their services (on a fee-for-service basis) in the form of advice, brokering, and so on. This group includes specialized securities brokers, mortgage brokers, management consultants, and investment advisers. In many countries, the same institutions carry out securities (and mortgage) dealing and brokering.

As with the specialized sectoral financiers, service providers primarily provide informational efficiencies and, in some cases, liquidity. In the case of brokers, there is also a transactions service, similar to (but more limited than) that of payments services.

Table 1.1 summarizes the relationship between the financial institution groupings and their provision of core financial services.

## The Role of Non-Bank Financial Institutions

The previous paragraphs outline the main types of non-bank financial institutions (NBFIs) and the roles they play in the financial system. The fact that they play a wide range of very specialized roles in practice does not,

**Table 1.1. Institutional Groups and Core Financial Services**

| Core financial services | Deposit takers | Risk poolers | Contractual savers | Market makers | Sectoral financiers | Service providers |
|---|---|---|---|---|---|---|
| Payments | ✔ | | | | | |
| Liquidity | ✔ | | ✔ | ✔ | ✔ | ✔ |
| Divisibility | ✔ | ✔ | ✔ | | ✔ | |
| Store of value | ✔ | ✔ | ✔ | | | |
| Information | ✔ | ✔ | ✔ | ✔ | ✔ | ✔ |
| Risk pooling | ✔ | ✔ | | | | |

however, establish the case that NBFIs are critical or even important to the efficient functioning of the economy. To establish this case, two additional questions must be addressed. First, do these roles genuinely make a positive contribution to economic growth and development? Second, if they do, could banks perform these roles? In other words, is the existence of NBFIs in developed financial systems a result of natural, efficient market forces, or is it an accident (or perhaps a result of regulatory interference)?

## The Relationship between Financial Development and Growth

The relationship between the development of financial sector functions and economic growth has been studied at the individual firm level as well as the national level. In a recent paper, Levine, Loayza, and Beck (1999) address two questions relevant to this subject. First, they ask whether the level of financial intermediary development exerts a causal influence on economic growth. Second, they ask whether cross-country differences in legal and accounting frameworks explain cross-country differences in the level of financial intermediary development. Their findings add to a growing literature that supports a positive relationship between financial sector functions and economic growth.

Levine, Loayza, and Beck measure the development of financial inter-mediaries in three ways:

- By the overall size of the intermediary sector
- By the extent to which commercial banks, rather than the central bank, provide intermediation
- By the extent to which intermediaries channel resources to the pri-vate sector, rather than to the government sector.

Using data from a sample of 74 developed and developing economies from 1960 to 1995, they find a substantial and significant impact of finan-cial intermediary development on economic growth. For example, accord-ing to their estimates, "If Argentina had enjoyed the level of financial inter-mediary development of the average developing country during the 1960–95 period, they would have experienced about one percentage point faster real per capita GDP [gross domestic product] growth per annum over this period" (Levine, Loayza, and Beck 1999: 5).

They also find that the three individual components of intermediary development are important. For example, in India, the extent to which intermediaries channeled resources to private sector uses was low. According to their estimates, if India had raised its percentage of finance to the private sector to the average for developing countries, it would have "accelerated real per capital GDP growth by about 0.6 percentage points per year" (Levine, Loayza, and Beck 1999: 14).

They also find that cross-country differences in legal systems and accounting standards help to explain cross-country differences in the devel-opment of financial intermediaries. These findings on legal origins are taken up further in chapter 7.

Levine, Loayza, and Beck's study provides strong evidence for the bene-fits of financial sector development. Its concentration on banking interme-diation, however, does not necessarily shed much light on the importance of NBFIs per se. The impact of different financial structures on growth, including the relative importance of bank and nonbank institutions, is addressed by, among others, Demirgüç-Kunt and Levine (1999).

To analyze the role of financial structure on economic growth, Demirgüç-Kunt and Levine compare the experiences of countries having bank-based financial systems with those having broader-based market sys-

**1**

**Table 1.2. Country Classification of Financial Structure**

| Type of economy | Financial underdeveloped economies | | Financially developed economies | |
|---|---|---|---|---|
| | Country | Structure index | Country | Structure index |
| **Bank-based economy** | Bangladesh | –0.90 | Panama | –0.92 |
| | Nepal | –0.87 | Tunisia | –0.88 |
| | Egypt | –0.82 | Cyprus | –0.77 |
| | Costa Rica | –0.79 | Portugal | –0.75 |
| | Barbados | –0.78 | Austria | –0.73 |
| | Honduras | –0.75 | Belgium | –0.66 |
| | Trinidad and Tobago | –0.74 | Italy | –0.57 |
| | Mauritius | –0.70 | Finland | –0.53 |
| | Kenya | –0.69 | Norway | –0.33 |
| | Ecuador | –0.56 | New Zealand | –0.29 |
| | Sri Lanka | –0.54 | Japan | –0.19 |
| | Indonesia | –0.50 | France | –0.17 |
| | Colombia | –0.47 | Jordan | –0.14 |
| | Pakistan | –0.38 | Germany | –0.10 |
| | Zimbabwe | –0.34 | Israel | –0.06 |
| | Greece | –0.34 | Spain | 0.02 |
| | Argentina | –0.25 | Group mean | –0.44 |
| | Venezuela | –0.15 | | |
| | India | –0.14 | | |
| | Ireland | –0.06 | | |
| | Group mean | –0.54 | | |
| **Market-based economy** | Denmark | 0.15 | Netherlands | 0.11 |
| | Peru | 0.16 | Thailand | 0.39 |
| | Chile | 0.25 | Canada | 0.41 |
| | Jamaica | 0.28 | Australia | 0.50 |
| | Brazil | 0.65 | South Africa | 0.83 |
| | Mexico | 0.68 | Korea | 0.89 |
| | Philippines | 0.71 | Sweden | 0.91 |
| | Turkey | 1.23 | Great Britain | 0.92 |
| | Group mean | 0.52 | Singapore | 1.18 |
| | | | United States | 1.96 |
| | | | Switzerland | 2.03 |
| | | | Hong Kong | 2.10 |
| | | | Malaysia | 2.93 |
| | | | Group mean | 1.17 |
| **Mean for type of economy**[a] | Financial underdeveloped countries | –0.24 | Financially developed countries | 0.28 |

a. Overall mean is 0.03.
*Source:* Demirgüç-Kunt and Levine (1999).

tems. They construct a conglomerate index of development based on size, activity, and efficiency for both the banking sector and the stock market for each country. Countries in which the ratio of the conglomerate index for banking development relative to the conglomerate index for stock market development is below the average for the group are classified as bank based. Those in which the ratio is above the average are classified as market based. In general, market-based financial systems tend to have better-developed NBFIs.

Demirgüç-Kunt and Levine further divide their sample into those with overall developed financial systems and those with underdeveloped financial systems. The latter are defined as those having below median values for both their banking and stock market conglomerate indexes of development. Table 1.2 reproduces their classification.

One of the more interesting features of Demirgüç-Kunt and Levine's classification of financial development and structure is the number of emerging markets that are classified as both market based and financially developed. The other interesting feature is that, while most emerging financial systems are bank based, many market-based systems also are in this group.

The main findings are as follows (Demirgüç-Kunt and Levine 1999: 4):

- Banks, nonbanks, and stock markets are larger, more active, and more efficient in richer countries (financial systems are, on average, better developed in richer countries).
- Stock markets are more active and efficient relative to banks in higher-income countries (there is a tendency for financial systems to become more market oriented as countries grow and become more economically developed).

Demirgüç-Kunt and Levine stress that their work simply identifies the correlation between financial structure and growth, not necessarily causality. Nevertheless, other studies support the proposition that the relationship is causal (see Levine 1999; Demirgüç-Kunt and Maksimovic 1998).

## Are Banks Sufficient for Financial Efficiency?

There is strong evidence that financial development adds to economic growth and development. There also is strong evidence that financial depth and diversity add to economic growth and development. The question remaining is whether NBFIs are essential in providing financial diversity or whether banks, if permitted, could provide all the financial services needed for growth.

The answer to this question is intuitive rather than empirical. In principle, there is no reason why a single type of financial intermediary could not provide all of the financial services: payments, liquidity, divisibility, maturity transformation, store of value, information economies, and risk pooling. The reality, however, is that such institutions inevitably would be extremely inefficient and would, in some areas, face conflicting incentives.

Although it is true that banks, as they currently are structured in most countries, provide a majority of the core financial services, they do not provide all services equally efficiently. Their main limitation is that their provision of payments services and liquidity (their main services) constrains the way in which they can provide other services. In order to provide certainty of value for payments, a bank deposit must be low risk. This limits the range and nature of assets that a bank can reasonably take onto its balance sheet.

Banks can provide some other financial services without jeopardizing their payments services. Some countries, for example, permit banks to offer securities dealer services from their balance sheets. It is no accident, however, that even where regulations allow banking and insurance to be carried out within one corporate structure (for example, through subsidiaries or under a nonoperating holding company), these services are never provided from the same balance sheet. While banks offer a limited form of risk-pooling services through their ability to diversify, the advanced risk-pooling services of insurance fundamentally conflict with the debt promises made by banks. Banks also are fundamentally limited in their ability to provide store of value services. Consistent with their efficient provision of payments services, banks tend to deal almost exclusively in debt-type promises on both sides of their balance sheets. Thus financial systems that are bank-based tend to have a smaller range of equity-type promises than those with a more broadly based structure, including a wide range of NBFIs.

More generally, NBFIs play a range of roles that are not suitable to banks:
- Through the enhancement of equity promises (by adding liquidity, divisibility, informational efficiencies, and risk-pooling services), NBFIs broaden the spectrum of risks available to investors.

## Box 1.1. The Financial Sector in Korea Before the 1997 Crisis

Korea initiated a gradual liberalization of the domestic finance sector in the early 1980s. Commercial banks were privatized and allowed to expand into retail banking services. Entry into commercial banking was liberalized, and new commercial banks were established. Similarly, entry barriers for nonbank financial institutions were lowered. By the onset of the crisis, the historical commercial bank dominance of the sector had declined to the point where banks accounted for just over half of the assets of the financial system; a large and growing number of nonbank financial institutions shared the rest.

With the benefit of hindsight, deregulation of the Korean financial system and liberalization of the capital market should have been accompanied by enhanced supervision and regulation. However, prudential regulation and supervision were not strengthened in parallel with the liberalization process. Oversight remained fragmented. Commercial banks were under the direct authority of the Bank of Korea's Office of Banking Supervision, and specialized banks and NBFIs were under the authority of the Ministry of Finance and Economy (MOFE). Weak supervision of NBFIs by the MOFE created opportunities for regulatory arbitrage and spawned an upsurge in risky practices. Three critical problems arose: the use by commercial banks of trust accounts to circumvent banking regulations, the rapid expansion of virtually unregulated merchant banks into areas traditionally dominated by banks, and the poor regulation and practices of investment trusts.

### Trust Accounts

Commercial banks in Korea had a long history of operating trust accounts on behalf of clients. In an administrative sense, these were maintained separately from their banking business, although, in practice, investments were managed as though the bank and its trust accounts were a single entity. Trust accounts were not subjected to standard prudential and supervisory practices; for example, there were no exposure limits, provisioning rules, or reserve requirements. While, in principle, trust accounts were operated on the client's behalf and therefore were not consolidated in computing a bank's capital adequacy ratio, in practice a large segment of trust accounts in Korea were effectively deposits, with both the principal and a predetermined yield guaranteed by the banks. As the competition for funds increased during the 1990s and banks sought ways to reduce the costs of doing business, they increasingly turned to trust accounts as a means of increasing banking activity without the associated costs of regulation. By the end of 1997, trust accounts accounted for close to 40 percent of total commercial bank assets. The result was an undercapitalized banking sector that was incapable of coping with the corporate collapses of the late 1990s. The potential systemic risks and fiscal implications of this regulatory evasion were underscored by the Korean government's decision in 1998 to extend the deposit guarantee issued in 1997 to include trust accounts.

### Merchant Banks

NBFIs (excluding trust accounts) accounted for approximately 30 percent of financial system assets at the end of 1997 and consisted of three main types of institutions: investment institutions, savings institutions, and insurance companies. Investment institutions, including merchant banks, investment trust companies, and securities companies, were the largest segment in terms of assets. In large part, the investment institutions were owned by chaebol groups (conglomerates); for example, most of the 30 merchant banks in operation in 1997 were owned by chaebols. Of these merchant banks, 24 were first established in the 1970s as short-term finance companies and were converted into merchant banks during the period from 1994 to 1996. Although, in principle, merchant banks were supervised by the MOFE, in practice, supervision was minimal; there were no rules governing asset classifications, capital, or provisioning. Standard practices, such as consolidated accounting and market value accounting, were also notably absent. During the 1990s, these institutions attracted an increasing share of funds through their offers of cash management accounts, commercial paper, and other instruments. On the asset side, they invested mainly in short-term commercial paper and commercial notes. Increasingly, however, they used their competitive advantage in

*Continued*

17

---

**Box 1.1 (Continued). The Financial Sector in Korea Before the 1997 Crisis**

accessing funds to channel resources to the chaebol groups and to intermediate chaebol notes and other paper. In this way, they relied on essentially deposit-type funding to obviate the need for the chaebols to raise capital. Not only did this increase the leverage of the corporate sector, but it also reduced both transparency and the market discipline normally associated with raising funds from the public.

**Investment Trusts**

The trusts were established in the early 1970s to develop the stock and bond markets. Investment trust companies were owned predominantly by securities companies. Securities companies were mostly owned by chaebols and acted as underwriters, dealers for their own accounts, and brokers. They mostly raised funds that were funneled to the chaebol. The Korean investment trusts diverged materially from four cardinal principles governing collective investment vehicles: transparency, mark-to-market valuation, liquidity, and absence of conflicts of interest. Investments were valued at cost and moved from fund to fund in order to smooth returns. Many investments were in illiquid corporate bonds, which could not be readily sold. Finally, custodians were not genuinely independent and did not exercise supervision, and managers had unresolved conflicts of interest with their customers. The laws and regulations were credible, but the regulatory body was slow to identify and punish abuses. In July 1997 a run on investment trusts forced the Korean government to bail them out.

---

- In this way, they encourage investment and savings and improve the efficiency of investment and savings.
- Through the provision of contingent promises, they foster a risk management culture by encouraging those who are least able to bear risk to sell those risks to those better able to manage them.

Thus NBFIs complement banks by providing services that are not well suited to banks; they fill the gaps in financial services that otherwise occur in bank-based financial systems. Equally important, NBFIs provide competition for banks in the provision of financial services. NBFIs unbundle the services provided by banks and provide the components on a competitive basis. They specialize in particular sectors and target particular groups. They overcome legal and tax impediments, and they enjoy informational advantages arising from specialization.

In addition to complementing banks, NBFIs can add to economic strength to the extent that they enhance the resilience of the financial system to economic shocks.

Alan Greenspan put forward this argument at the Financial Markets Conference of the Federal Reserve Bank of Atlanta (Greenspan 1999a). In that speech, Greenspan noted that the existence of backup financial institutions, including NBFIs, help economies to recover more quickly from financial shocks to one or another part of the financial system. In his words, "Multiple alternatives to transform an economy's savings into capital investment act as backup facilities should the primary form of intermediation fail."

A well-developed and properly regulated NBFI sector is thus an important component of a broad, balanced, efficient financial system that spreads risks and provides a sound base for economic growth and prosperity. However, in developing countries that lack a coherent policy framework and effective regulations, nonbank financial institutions, such as insurance, leasing and finance companies, and collective investment vehicles, can exacerbate the fragility of the financial system. The fragility is often the result of a conscious effort to arbitrage and circumvent banking regulations. The experience of Korea illustrates the pitfalls of an improperly regulated NBFI sector (see box 1.1 and table 1.3).

**Table 1.3. Structure of the Korean Financial System, June 1997**

| Financial institution | Percentage of total assets |
|---|---|
| **Commercial banks** | 53.4 |
| Nationwide commercial banks[a] | 22.4 |
| Trust accounts of commercial banks[b] | 21.1 |
| Regional commercial banks | 4.3 |
| Foreign bank branches | 2.2 |
| **Specialized and development banks** | 16.5 |
| Specialized banks | 9.2 |
| Development institutions | 8.1 |
| **Nonbank financial institutions** | 30.1 |
| Investment institutions | 13.5 |
| Merchant banks | 4.9 |
| Savings institutions | 12.0 |
| Life insurance institutions | 7.1 |
| **Total financial system** | 100.0 |

a. Includes the Korea Housing Bank, which became a commercial bank in August 1997.
b. Trust account business is carried out by the commercial banks but is classified as nonbank financial intermediation.
*Source:* Balino and Ubide (1999).

# Chapter 2

# The Principles of Regulation

*The regulatory framework for financial institutions has four main components:*

- *Regulatory objectives (the reasons why these institutions require regulation and what the community expects regulation to achieve)*
- *Regulatory structure (the structure of agencies that carry the delegated regulatory responsibilities of the community)*
- *Regulatory backing (the political, legal, and financial backing to enable regulators to carry out their duties effectively)*
- *Regulatory implementation (the instruments, tools, and techniques that regulatory agencies use to achieve their objectives).*

*This chapter explores the role of the regulatory framework through a systematic review of these four components.*

## Regulatory Objectives

Regulations are fundamentally rules of behavior. Every country establishes a wide range of behavioral rules as a means of reconciling the conflicting rights and interests of its citizens. Many of these rules are designed to govern how individuals interact socially. For example, most countries establish rules intended to discourage antisocial behavior such as theft, assault, and murder. They support these rules with a system of courts and enforcement agencies that monitor the observance of the rules and pursue those who violate them. Whenever human nature is involved, such rules are not only desirable but also necessary. Without rules, human behavior degenerates into anarchy. Human nature is such that it needs rules—indeed, human nature demands the order that rules confer.

Financial regulations are rules that govern commercial behavior in the financial system. In the case of social issues, rules are needed to reconcile the conflicting interests of members of the social system. In the same way, commercial rules are needed to reconcile the conflicting interests of participants in the commercial system. The financial sector, however, is often singled out as "special" and subjected to a level and form of regulation that goes well beyond that applied to other sectors of the commercial system. The reason for this lies in the fundamental importance of finance to the efficient working of the economy.

Where there are no rules governing behavior in financial markets, or where the rules are not enforced, business tends to lack confidence and trust, contracts become short term and unreliable, corruption becomes endemic, and the economic system ceases to function efficiently. Financial regulation attempts to establish a legal and ethical framework within which commerce can flourish to the mutual benefit of all involved. Viewed in this way, regulation is fundamentally about the promotion of economic efficiency. According to Merton (1990: 1): "The core function of the financial system is to facilitate the allocation and deployment of economic resources, both spatially and across time, in an uncertain environment."

This very general appreciation of why financial regulation matters, however, offers little guidance as to exactly what should be regulated or what precise form that regulation should take. Providing some structure and substance to this overall objective requires deeper consideration.

## Conventional Wisdom

The pragmatic wisdom on this subject recognizes that, while theory may identify economic efficiency as the overriding objective of financial regulation, in practice regulators usually attempt to achieve multiple objectives, of which financial efficiency is just one. For example, Herring and Santomero (1999) identify four broad rationales for financial regulation:

**Table 2.1. Regulatory Measures and Objectives**

| Regulatory measures | Systemic risk | Consumer protection | Efficiency enhancement | Social objectives |
|---|---|---|---|---|
| Antitrust/competition policy | | ✔ | ✔ | ✔ |
| Disclosure standards | ✔ | ✔ | ✔ | |
| Conduct of business rules | | ✔ | ✔ | ✔ |
| Conflict of interest rules | | ✔ | ✔ | |
| Capital adequacy standards | ✔ | ✔ | | |
| Fit and proper entry tests | ✔ | ✔ | ✔ | |
| Liquidity requirements | ✔ | ✔ | | |
| Reporting requirements | | | | ✔ |
| Restrictions on services | ✔ | | | ✔ |
| Asset restrictions | ✔ | | | ✔ |
| Deposit insurance | ✔ | ✔ | | |
| Reserve requirements | ✔ | ✔ | | |
| Customer suitability requirements | | ✔ | | |
| Interest rate ceilings | | | | |
|     Deposits | ✔ | | | ✔ |
|     Loans | | ✔ | | |
| Investment requirements | | | | ✔ |
| Geographic restrictions | | | | ✔ |

*Source:* Herring and Santomero (1999).

- Safeguarding the system against systemic risk
- Protecting consumers against opportunistic behavior by suppliers of financial services
- Enhancing the efficiency of the financial system
- Achieving a range of social objectives (such as increasing homeownership or channeling resources to particular sectors of the economy or population).

**2**

Against these four objectives, Herring and Santomero list a range of measures or tools that regulators use in their efforts to meet their objectives.[1] Their analysis is summarized in table 2.1.

Although this schema may fit comfortably with the way in which many regulators think about their objectives and methods, it is not particularly helpful in identifying the underlying principles of regulation or in serving as a guide to what and how to regulate. The problem with this schema is that almost every regulatory measure identified by Herring and Santomero affects more than one objective and may be applied by multiple regulators. Indeed, the schema provides little help in thinking about how the measures might be allocated among different regulators or how the different regulators should try to balance their impact on different objectives.

## An Alternative Framework

An alternative framework (used, for example, in Financial System Inquiry 1997) returns to the basic economic goal of regulation as its guiding principle; namely, that financial regulation should enhance the efficiency of the financial system. Starting with efficiency as the guiding principle begs the question, Why is regulation needed at all? If the financial system can function efficiently on its own, there should be no need for regulatory interference.

A large body of literature argues that financial markets (and indeed other markets) function most efficiently without regulatory interference. This literature does not necessarily assume that markets work perfectly. The reality is that all markets fail, and they fail for a variety of reasons. The issue involved is one of relative costs.

This line of argument reminds us that the case for regulatory intervention must rest on market failure and the impact of that failure on economic efficiency. The decision to intervene to alter the natural functioning of a market should be justified on the grounds that the cost of market failure is greater than any costs imposed by regulation (either direct resource costs or losses of efficiency). It also reminds us that regulators should employ the measures that best address the resolution of the market failures involved. Finally, it reminds us that the case for regulation should never be regarded as permanently given—there should be a continual process of reevaluating the costs and benefits of regulation.

---

1. This is adapted, in turn, from an earlier framework proposed by Herring and Litan (1995).

In broad terms, financial markets fail to produce efficient, competitive outcomes for one or more of the following reasons:

- Anticompetitive behavior
- Market misconduct
- Information asymmetry
- Systemic instability.

*Anticompetitive Behavior*

According to the U.S. Attorney General's National Committee to Study the Antitrust Laws (1955: 245–46), effective competition is a state in which

> no one seller, and no group of sellers acting in concert, has the power to choose its level of profits by giving less and charging more. Where there is workable competition, rival sellers, whether existing competitors or new potential entrants into the field, would keep this power in check by offering or threatening to offer effective inducements.

Governments generally foster competition in the financial sector because of the benefits this sector brings to the economy overall. These benefits include improved access to capital for business, cheaper credit and housing loans to consumers, a better match between the financing needs of deficit and surplus units, cheaper transactions, and a greater ability to manage risks.

Market forces are the main determinant of competition. The role of competition regulation is to ensure that these forces operate effectively and are not circumvented by market participants. The following key measures are used in competition policy:[2]

- Rules designed to deal with the structure of industries (merger or antitrust laws)
- Rules designed to prevent anticompetitive behavior (such as collusion)
- Rules designed to ensure that markets remain contestable (by ensuring that there is relatively free entry and exit).

---

2. The way in which these measures (and the other regulatory measures identified in this section) are used in implementing regulatory policy is dealt with in more detail in the section on regulatory implementation.

## Market Misconduct

Financial markets cannot operate efficiently and effectively unless participants act with integrity and unless there is adequate information on which to base informed judgments. Because of this fundamental need, all markets face potential problems associated with the conduct (or misconduct) of their participants.

The two areas of misconduct that are most common in financial markets are unfair or fraudulent conduct by market participants and inadequate disclosure of information on which to base investment decisions. Regulation to address these sources of market failure is usually referred to as market integrity regulation. This form of regulation seeks to protect market participants from fraud or unfair market practices. By protecting markets in this way, market integrity regulation seeks to promote confidence in the efficiency and fairness of markets.

Market integrity regulation typically focuses on the following:

- Disclosure of information
- Conduct of business rules (such as prohibiting insider trading, market manipulation, false and misleading advertising, and nondisclosure of commissions)
- Entry restrictions through licensing
- Governance and fiduciary responsibilities (including, but not limited to, removing conflicts of interest)
- Some conditions of minimal financial strength (capital requirements where the nature of the financial promises involved warrants them).

## Asymmetric Information

The third source of market failure—information asymmetry—arises where products or services are sufficiently complex that disclosure, by itself, is insufficient to enable consumers to make informed choices. This arises where buyers and sellers of particular products or services will never be equally well informed, regardless of how much information is disclosed.

The issue involves the complexity of the product and the institution offering it. This problem is common in areas such as drugs and aviation and is particularly relevant in the area of financial services. The regulatory response in these cases is to interpose a regulatory body between the supplier of the service and the consumer, to establish a set of behavioral rules for the supplier, and to ensure that the promises being made by the supplier have an acceptably high probability of being met.

The form of regulation involved in counteracting asymmetric information problems in financial markets is usually referred to as prudential regulation. The range of financial institutions and activities covered by prudential regulation is a matter of judgment. Typically, deposit taking and insurance are included under prudential regulation, although, in some countries, the prudential net is extended to include pension schemes, securities dealers, and other financial institutions.

Prudential regulation overcomes the asymmetric information market failure in part by substituting the judgment of a regulator for that of the regulated financial institutions and their customers. To the extent that the regulator absorbs risks that otherwise would be borne by financial institutions and their customers, it faces a "moral hazard" problem, whereby the perceived shifting of risk from the regulated financial institutions to the regulator may induce the institutions to take greater risks than they otherwise would.

The incentive problems associated with moral hazard explain the particular approaches that prudential regulators normally adopt to the various aspects of prudential regulation (see box 2.1). It also means that the potential cost of prudential regulation in terms of economic efficiency can be very high if the conflicting incentives are not handled carefully. Consequently, there is an onus on governments both to limit the spread of the prudential umbrella to those parts of the financial system that genuinely warrant this form of regulation and to ensure that the regulator adopts regulatory measures that correct the market failure at minimal cost.

The primary distinction between the methods used by prudential regulators and those used by competition and market integrity regulators is that the former are largely preventative (that is, they primarily seek to avoid promises being broken), while the latter are largely responsive (that is, they primarily involve prosecution of those who break their promises or who disobey the rules).

Prudential, or preventative, regulation involves the imposition of prescriptive rules or standards governing the prudential behavior of financial institutions making certain types of promises. These rules may be directed at specific areas of concern or directed more generally toward minimizing

**2**

---

### Box 2.1. Evolution of Supervisory Approaches: What Is Risk-Based Supervision?

Historically, supervisory examinations focused primarily on compliance; that is, on finding contraventions of the rules and regulations, regardless of their materiality. To assess the financial condition of regulated institutions, examiners relied extensively on transactions testing, such as reconciling data, counting cash and securities, and undertaking other detailed checking. It is now recognized that transactions testing alone is not sufficient to assess the soundness of financial institutions. Indeed, in many cases it has done little more than duplicate the external audit process. Moreover, it is very resource intensive (and therefore expensive) and often ineffective.

The risk-based approach is less well defined. Under its broadest interpretations, it relates to both policy and implementation. Under its narrower interpretations, it relates to the methodology adopted increasingly to guide on-site inspections. The following describes the main elements that might be expected under the broader definition.

At the policy level,

- *Capital adequacy.* A key element is that regulatory capital requirements should be linked directly to the risks undertaken by the institution. The seeds of this approach were sown in the 1988 Basle Capital Accord, and risk-based capital requirements are increasingly replacing the traditional solvency-based measures of capital.
- *Risk policies and procedures.* Explicit emphasis is placed on the responsibility of boards and management to manage risk. Institutions must have documented and board-approved policies and procedures that identify, measure, monitor, and manage risk exposures.

At the implementation level,

- *Allocating resources to on-site and off-site monitoring and examination.* The risk-based approach prioritizes supervisory activities according to perceived risks. Ideally, the regulator ranks all regulated institutions according to an agreed index of risk and devotes personnel to both off-site monitoring and on-site inspections

according to the rankings. Risk indexes vary greatly but typically take account of both the probability that any given institution will encounter financial difficulty and the systemic implications of such an event. Thus a large, well-run bank is likely to require more analysts and more frequent examinations than a small, poorly run non-life insurance company. However, under the risk-based approach, supervision will intensify for either institution as the measured probability of failure increases.

- *Conducting on-site examinations.* Preventive rather than remedial, the risk-based approach calls for examination techniques that emphasize evaluating the adequacy of the institution's own internal risk-management processes.
- *Assessing the commitment to risk management.* The risk-based approach evaluates the active participation of board members and senior management in developing the risk management framework, including policies and procedures. The policies and procedures should be endorsed and understood at the highest levels, and any changes should require board approval. The framework should include regular reporting to the board and management on risk levels and on the relevance of the risk framework itself and the board's recognition of its responsibility to keep shareholders and other stakeholders informed about the company's risk profile, to manage those risks, and to be involved generally in risk management.
- *Assessing risk management policies, procedures, and limits.* Sound policies, procedures, and exposure limits designed to control risk are the foundation of risk management. Risk-based inspections assess not only the adequacy and consistency of these policies and procedures but also their relevance to each institution's particular circumstances.
- *Assessing risk monitoring and management information systems.* An effective risk management framework must include systematic measurement and monitoring of risks. These func-

*Continued*

---

2

**Box 2.1 (Continued). Evolution of Supervisory Approaches: What Is Risk-Based Supervision?**

tions must be supported by effective and reliable management information systems. Risk-based inspections involve assessing the adequacy of these systems.

- *Assessing internal controls.* Best-practice risk management policies and procedures are of little use unless they are embraced and rigorously applied by all levels of staff. The adequacy of a financial institution's internal controls and audit procedures is an important element of its risk management framework. Risk-based examinations focus on the relevance of these controls to the institution as well as the extent to which they ensure that the institution's risk management policies and procedures are applied in practice.

To illustrate the change in focus from compliance-based to risk-based examinations, consider the way in which each approach deals with large exposure limits on bank lending. The compliance-based approach checks the institution's compliance with the laws and regulations regarding legal or internal lending limits. In contrast, the risk-based approach examines management's attitude to risk and the ade-

quacy of its internal controls. For example, the risk-based examination reviews the effectiveness of the internal processes, including the internal audit, loan review, and compliance functions. If the examination determines that the internal processes are weak, transactions testing might follow.

As with banking, the risk-based approach to insurance examination focuses on processes rather than on compliance. For example, examinations assess the company's processes and systems relating to product design and pricing, underwriting management, claims liability management, reinsurance management, security management, credit risk management, foreign exchange risk management, capital management, and internal controls.

The implementation of effective risk management systems is becoming increasingly complex and technically demanding. The challenge is no less demanding for regulators, which need to recruit technically sophisticated staff and management. While these skills remain in short supply, regulators will be stretched. The challenge is for industry and regulators to establish a common base of knowledge in areas that offer systemic as well as individual benefits.

the risk that these institutions may be unable to honor the financial promises that they have made.

The tools adopted by prudential regulators have altered significantly over the past decade or two. In particular, there have been both a general shift away from direct controls on balance sheet structures and price controls and a move toward more risk-based measures such as capital requirements. Most modern prudential regulators use the following measures:

- Entry requirements
- Capital requirements
- Balance sheet restrictions (including, but not limited to, reserve requirements)
- Restrictions on associations among financial institutions
- Liquidity requirements
- Accountability requirements

- Customer support schemes (such as deposit insurance and industry guarantee funds).

The measures used by prudential regulators are typically stronger and more intrusive than the equivalent measures applied by market integrity regulators.

*Systemic Instability*

The fourth main source of market failure is systemic instability. Parts of the financial system operate efficiently only to the extent that market participants have confidence in their ability to perform the roles for which they were designed.

The more sophisticated is the economy, the greater is its dependence on financial promises, and the greater is its vulnerability to failure of the financial system to deliver against its promises. The importance of finance and the potential for financial failure to lead to systemic instability introduce an "overarching externality" that warrants regulatory attention.

Systemic instability arises where failure of one institution to honor its promises leads to a general panic, as individuals fear that similar promises made by other institutions also may be dishonored. A crisis occurs when contagion of this type leads to the distress or failure of otherwise sound institutions.

It can be difficult to determine exactly where systemic risks arise or what the full set of causes might be. Contagion risk is generally regarded as highest among deposit-taking institutions because of the inherent conflict involved in their promise to transform illiquid assets into liquid liabilities. Such a commitment can be met under most circumstances, provided sufficient liquid reserves are available, either on balance sheets or through credit lines. However, when a sufficiently large proportion of depositors simultaneously demand convertibility, the promise cannot be honored without outside assistance. Since all deposit takers suffer from the same potential weakness, a crisis of confidence in one institution can spread quickly to others.

Perhaps the greatest vulnerability to systemic crisis is in the payments system. The integrity of the payments system, in which obligations are settled between financial institutions, lies at the very core of the stability of modern financial systems. The failure of institutions involved in the payments system can disrupt debt settlements and commercial transactions, thereby disrupting the economy more generally.

Although the potential for systemic instability usually is associated with payments services and deposit taking, equally disruptive consequences also can flow from other types of market disturbances such as stock price collapses and even the failure of a single large institution, where that institution is involved in a complex network of transactions, including derivative commitments. Ultimately, systemic risk is of greatest concern where there is the greatest potential for damage to the real economy.

The primary defense against systemic instability is the maintenance of a sustainable macroeconomic environment, with reasonable price stability in both product and asset markets. This responsibility falls directly to government in its formulation of monetary and fiscal policy. Having a prudentially sound system of financial institutions also supports systemic stability. Thus policies designed to combat market failure arising from asymmetric information automatically support policies designed to combat market failure arising from systemic instability.

Beyond these general macroeconomic and prudential measures, the additional regulatory tools most appropriate for resolving this type of market failure are the lender-of-last-resort facility and direct regulation of the payments system.

The lender-of-last-resort facility provides an external source of liquid funding to the financial system in the event of a systemic crisis. In many cases, the simple fact that such a facility is available is sufficient to reduce the probability of contagion.

Regulation of the payments system is integral to managing systemic risk. Payments and settlements systems in most countries encompass settlements among banks, settlements of securities, and settlements of foreign exchange. The risks in these markets are exceptionally high, and settlement integrity is of paramount importance. In many cases, exposures are carried for several days and cross international borders. Numerous techniques are available for minimizing settlement risk. These include delivery versus payments systems, real-time gross settlement systems, and netting. Regulation of the payments system requires the regulator to understand the full range of technical issues involved and to regulate in such a way that the most expeditious techniques are used. It also requires that the inherent risks are both understood and managed as efficiently as possible.

**2**

## Features of the Alternative Framework

The first thing to note about this alternative approach to regulation is that it cuts across the objectives of the conventional approach. For example, in the conventional approach, consumer protection is identified as a separate objective. As shown in table 2.1, however, consumer protection is met partly by competition policy, partly by market conduct policy, and partly by prudential regulation. Under the alternative approach, consumer protection is a natural consequence of addressing the various sources of market failure that work to the disadvantage of consumers. Similarly, market efficiency is a consequence of correcting market failure.

The second feature is that the alternative framework minimizes the overlap between regulatory objectives and measures. By approaching the question of what to regulate by first establishing whether or not there is a need to regulate, specific regulatory measures are identified much more clearly with the goal of correcting specific sources of market failure. The relationship between regulatory measures and objectives under this alternative framework is illustrated in table 2.2.

Although table 2.2 implies that there is minimal overlap between the techniques and tools used to resolve the different forms of financial market failure, some degree of overlap is inevitable. The most obvious overlap is between prudential regulation and systemic stability regulation. While prudential regulation is aimed primarily at correcting information asymmetry, it is highly complementary to correcting systemic instability. The fact that the two objectives are complementary does not imply that the regulatory measures need to be duplicated in their application. Provided the measures listed as appropriate for correcting information asymmetry are applied for that purpose, they will automatically support systemic stability.

The final feature of this alternative schema is that many of the regulatory measures covered under the conventional approach are classified as redundant under the alternative approach (they are included in the table but are not shown as contributing to the regulatory objectives). This classification recognizes that many of the measures listed in table 2.1 either were discarded by regulators during the 1980s and 1990s or do not contribute effectively to resolving the market failures that justify financial regulation.

**Table 2.2. Regulatory Measures and Objectives: Alternative Framework**

| Regulatory measures | Anticompetitive behavior | Market misconduct | Asymmetric information | Systemic instability |
|---|:---:|:---:|:---:|:---:|
| **Competition regulation** | | | | |
| Market structure policy | ✔ | | | |
| Anticollusion rules | ✔ | | | |
| Contestability rules | ✔ | | | |
| **Market conduct regulation** | | | | |
| Disclosure standards | | ✔ | | |
| Conduct of business rules | | ✔ | | |
| Governance/fiduciary responsibilities | | ✔ | | |
| **Prudential regulation** | | | | |
| Entry requirements | | ✔ | ✔ | ✔ |
| Capital requirements | | ✔ | ✔ | ✔ |
| Balance sheet restrictions | | | ✔ | ✔ |
| Associations among institutions | | | ✔ | ✔ |
| Liquidity requirements | | | ✔ | ✔ |
| Accountability requirements | | | ✔ | ✔ |
| Insurance/support schemes | | | ✔ | ✔ |
| **Systemic stability regulation** | | | | |
| Lender of last resort | | | | ✔ |
| Payments system oversight | | | | ✔ |
| **Redundant regulations** | | | | |
| Customer suitability requirements | | | | |
| Interest rate ceilings | | | | |
| Deposits | | | | |
| Loans | | | | |
| Investment requirements | | | | |
| Geographic restrictions | | | | |

*Note:* Blank cells indicate measures that either were discarded by regulators in the 1980s and 1990s or do not contribute effectively to resolving the market failures that justify financial regulation.

**2**

## Using Regulation to Achieve Social Objectives

The only conventional objective that is not captured in the alternative framework is that of achieving social objectives. Although there is a case for using regulation for social purposes, international experience with this has been less than encouraging.

Budget-constrained governments have often looked to the financial sector (in particular to banks) as a source of off-budget funds for meeting social initiatives. Governments often have favored the housing sector in two ways: (a) by granting privileged licenses for institutions that finance housing, tax concessions for institutions lending for housing, and regulated interest rate maxima for housing loans or (b) by underwriting risks in markets that channel funds to housing. Many governments also have subsidized finance to specific sectors such as exports, agriculture, or the low-income sector. Finally, many countries have imposed reporting requirements on financial institutions in an effort to combat money laundering and organized crime.

Historically, many of these efforts have worked counter to the intention of the policy. For example, interest rate ceilings on lending to particular sectors have more often than not reduced the volume of lending to those sectors. Politically connected or motivated lending policies can have a negative impact on both the efficiency and the safety of the financial system (see Santomero and Herring 1999).

The general consensus on regulation for social purposes is that it should either be eschewed or funded as a specific community service obligation on budget. Full funding removes not only the potential distortion but also much of the incentive to pursue social objectives in this way (which is to remove them from the budget).

## Drawing the Regulatory Boundaries

This alternative framework provides a basis for assessing when regulation is needed and the form that such regulation should take. The task of deciding exactly which financial activities warrant all or some of these forms of regulation nevertheless remains a difficult one. The issue is where to draw the boundaries between those activities and institutions that warrant competition regulation, those that warrant market integrity regulation, those that warrant prudential regulation (for asymmetric information failure), and those that warrant regulation for systemic stability purposes.

With one notable exception, drawing these boundaries is relatively straightforward. First, the boundaries of regulation for systemic stability are relatively well defined. Since the central bank conducts monetary policy and is usually the only regulatory agency with the capacity to write checks on itself, it is the natural agency to undertake systemic regulation. The extension of lender of last resort is a matter of judgment for the central bank, but it is often restricted to large banks, although smaller banks and other deposit takers may be included. Regulation of the payments system for stability purposes similarly would be extended to those institutions involved in the various levels of the payments system.

Second, all markets in the economy require competition regulation. In this respect, financial markets and institutions require no additional regulation for competitive purposes over and above that applied to other markets. Indeed, a case can be mounted for slightly lighter competition regulation of financial institutions on the grounds that, where information asymmetry is involved, some restrictions on entry are required for prudential purposes.

Third, all markets in the economy require some form of market integrity regulation. The case for this form of regulation in the financial sector is somewhat stronger than it is for most other markets. The importance of information for the price formation process and the scope for exploitation of information suggest the need for a higher level of market integrity regulation for financial markets and institutions than elsewhere in the economy. While all sectors of the financial system require market integrity regulation, there unquestionably will be some variations in the intensity and form of this regulation for different parts of the industry. For example, stock markets and unit trusts are likely to be regulated more intensively for market integrity purposes than the market for small business finance.

It is important to recognize two points:

- Both competition regulation and market integrity regulation apply to all sectors and institutions in the financial system.
- For many financial institutions and products, these two forms of regulation will be sufficient to remove most, if not all, of the market failure involved.

The "special" group in this framework is the group of institutions that warrant prudential regulation to correct information asymmetries. The basis for drawing this final boundary rests with the nature of the particular financial promises being made by any given financial institution.

Not all financial promises are equally intense. Financial promises can be distinguished according to the following characteristics:

- The inherent difficulty of honoring the promise
- The difficulty faced by the consumer in assessing the creditworthiness of the promisor
- The adversity caused by promissory breach.

Each of these characteristics involves risk. The more difficult the promise is to keep, the greater is the risk to the consumer and the greater is the impact of information asymmetry. Some financial promises, such as common equity claims, are relatively easy to honor in that they contain very general and flexible obligations. Other financial promises, such as demand deposits (a promise to pay a fixed nominal amount at the total discretion of the promisee), are very onerous.

The more complex is the institution making the promise, the more difficult it is for the promisee to assess its creditworthiness, and therefore the greater is the risk. Some structures, such as trusts, are relatively transparent, while others, such as financial conglomerates, are extremely complex.

Finally, the greater are the consequences of promissory failure, the greater is the risk, not only to the individual but also to the community. The consequences of the failure of a major insurance company to honor its insurance claims, for example, would likely generate much greater adversity within the community than the failure of a nonfinance company to meet its equity obligations.

Although drawing the boundaries around institutions warranting prudential regulation is a matter for judgment, a useful guiding principle is that institutions making financial promises warrant prudential regulation only where their promises are judged to have a sufficiently high intensity in all three characteristics outlined above. Only in these cases will the potential cost of the market failure dominate the potential efficiency costs of prudential regulation. This same principle is usually applied to regulation in other situations characterized by asymmetric information failure, such as air safety, drugs, and medical services.

Most countries have included banking within the net of prudential regulation. Many also have included both types of insurance. Some have added to this set of core institutions various combinations of other nonbank deposit takers, pension funds, and securities dealers. No simple formula exists for defining the best boundaries for prudential regulation. Indeed, the ideal boundaries are likely to differ between different countries and financial structures and may change for a given country as its financial system evolves. What is important is that these boundaries are assessed periodically for their relevance and efficiency against the objectives of regulation.

## Regulatory Structure

In principle, there are two fundamentally different models of regulatory structure—one based on institutions and the other based on regulatory functions. The former involves the establishment of separate agencies to regulate different institutional groups, while the latter involves the establishment of separate agencies to regulate different sources of market failure. Although the distinction between institutional and functional regulation exists in principle, the reality is that most countries have structures that combine elements of both.

The traditional approach to regulation has been institutional, assigning separate agencies to each of the prudentially regulated institutional groups, such as banks, insurance companies, securities dealers, and, in some cases, pension funds. In the purest form of this model, the institutional regulator is responsible not only for regulating the prudential behavior of the institutions in its group but also for regulating their market conduct and competitive behavior (and, where relevant, their impact on systemic stability). In most cases, single-function regulators responsible for market conduct, competition regulation, or both exist alongside these multifunction institutional regulators.

This traditional model has come under pressure, especially in recent years, from a range of factors, such as technological innovation, internationalization, and consumer expectations. The two key drivers of change have been the growing importance of financial conglomerates and regulatory arbitrage.

Financial conglomeration has raised the obvious question of whether or not the regulatory structure should mirror more closely the evolving struc-

**2**

### Box 2.2. Conglomerate Structures and Regulation

One of the driving forces behind regulatory reforms in recent years has been the convergence among financial products offered by banks and NBFIs. In part, this convergence has resulted from competition as financial institutions have encroached increasingly on each other's territory, and, in part, it has resulted from the blurring of boundaries between financial products as technological innovations have reshaped the design and delivery of products.

As these boundaries have blurred, the financial industry has evolved in two main directions: (a) boutique providers specializing in niche markets and (b) conglomerates providing a virtual supermarket of financial products. The international trend toward the amalgamation of regulatory agencies across industry groups has been partly an attempt to match the regulatory structure to the evolving structure of the industry. Even countries that traditionally forced a strong separation among providers of different types of financial services have begun to accommodate financial supermarkets.

How best to regulate financial conglomerates is still a relatively new challenge for many regulators and one that will see a range of responses in coming years. A second challenge in this environment—one that has a somewhat longer history—is whether or not to limit the permissible forms of conglomeration. The structural forms of conglomeration found throughout the world range from the universal banking model, through various forms of parent and subsidiary arrangements, to the nonoperating holding company model. Each of these has different regulatory implications.

The universal banking model, popular in continental Europe, typically permits securities dealing, investment banking, and some other nonbanking activities to take place on the balance sheet of a bank. The one financial activity that is never permitted on a bank balance sheet is insurance, although countries that allow universal banking usually allow insurance products to be sold through subsidiaries of banks. Universal banking is often seen as a more efficient model of fund raising for the conglomerate group, in terms of both the cost of funds and the access to liquidity. It also facilitates group risk management and provides access to a wider range of risk diversification than the narrower bank models. The regulatory challenges, however, are substantial, especially where nonbanking activities change the nature of the bank's risk profile or where the bank carries large exposures to unregulated subsidiaries. To complicate matters further, the appropriate measurement of bank capital becomes debatable when the bank can raise lower-tier capital and invest in subsidiaries.

The nonoperating holding company structure, pioneered in the United States and growing in popularity elsewhere, provides a much cleaner separation of the members of a financial conglomerate group. In recognition of the increasing pressure for financial conglomeration in the industry, the United States passed the Gramm-Leach-Bliley Act in 1999 to remove long-standing statutory limitations on activities permitted in banking groups. The act requires financial groups that wish to engage in both banking and nonbanking activities to organize specified activities in separate subsidiaries of a nonoperating holding company. In particular, investment banking activities and insurance underwriting can be carried out only in subsidiaries of the holding company. Some lower-risk activities, such as underwriting municipal securities and insurance agency business, are permitted in subsidiaries of either the holding company or the bank—subject to certain prudential restrictions. In this way, the banking activities are at least partially quarantined from the risks arising from other financial activities.

A particular regulatory advantage of this model is that the profits and losses of the various business lines accrue directly to the holding company and not to the banking unit. Correspondingly, the liabilities of the nonbanking units have no direct claim over the banking unit. Unlike the universal banking model, the nonoperating holding company restricts the benefits of deposit insurance and any associated implicit or explicit subsidies from the taxpayer to the banking operation.

There is nonetheless a potential loophole for conglomerate groups organized in this way to circumvent the segregation of risks by having the bank take on large intergroup exposures to its nonbank affiliates. In recognition of this potential, the Federal Reserve

*Continued*

---

**Box 2.2 (Continued). Conglomerate Structures and Regulation**

Board has formulated restrictions under section 23A of the Federal Reserve Act to govern certain transactions that expose banks to risk from nonbank affiliates. Section 23A is designed to prevent the misuse of a bank's resources through "non-arm's length" transactions with its affiliates. Covered transactions include extensions of credit and asset purchases. The regulation places quantitative limits (exposure as a percentage of capital) and, in some cases, collateral requirements on covered transactions between banks and their affiliates.

---

ture of the industries that it purports to regulate. Regulatory arbitrage also has become a major source of concern among emerging market regulators as profit-driven institutions have sought to exploit regulatory differences among regulators of similar financial products.

## Financial Conglomerates

In some countries, separation of certain financial services by institution is enshrined in legislation. More commonly, however, the extent to which institutions combine different financial services and products on one balance sheet, or in separate balance sheets within the one financial group, is left to the market. In recent decades, there has been a growing trend toward financial conglomeration. This trend has been recognized as a natural response to the potential economies of scale and scope in finance that arise from the ability of financial institutions to leverage their loyal base of retail customers in one area by cross-selling to other financial service and product areas.

The most common conglomerate structure is that in which banks establish insurance, securities dealers, and other nonbank financial institutions as subsidiaries (see box 2.2). Less popular, but still relatively common, are structures in which insurance or securities dealers form the parent company, with other financial service providers as subsidiaries. In some countries, the provision of banking, securities dealing, and other noninsurance financial services is carried out on the same balance sheet. The only financial service not commonly combined with others on the same balance sheet is insurance, although insurance activities frequently are carried out within a conglomerate structure, but in a separate subsidiary. The final conglomerate form is the nonoperating holding company structure, in which different financial services and products are offered by subsidiaries of a common, nonoperating holding company.

## Regulatory Arbitrage

It is a fundamental requirement for efficient regulation that the regulatory burden imposed on any institution should be related to the type and extent of market failures involved rather than to the institutional label that the company carries; that is, the system should, to the greatest extent possible, exhibit regulatory neutrality.

Under the institutional regulatory structure, potential non-neutralities arise, because institutions subject to different regulators can make the same promises. For example, under the institutional model, bank and nonbank deposit-takers (such as building societies, credit unions, and, in some countries, even finance companies and investment trusts) usually have different regulators, despite the fact that they make essentially the same financial promises. The potential for conflict is exacerbated in some countries by the presence of both state and federal regulators. This potential is highlighted in the United States, which has 50 separate regulators for insurance and two different federal as well as multiple state regulators for banking. Even the most assiduous efforts at coordination are unlikely to prevent differences of application across such a diverse set of regulators, each subject to its own legislative processes and resource constraints.

Where a financial institution is able to choose among different regulators, either by altering its corporate form, its regulatory jurisdiction, or simply its institutional label, there is an incentive to arbitrage among the potential regulators so as to minimize the regulatory burden. This problem is exacerbated in conglomerate situations where a heavily regulated parent is able to reduce its regulatory burden by shifting business into an unregulated subsidiary. Regulatory arbitrage of this type was common in a number of Asian countries and contributed to the depth of the financial crisis in the late 1990s.

The crux of the problem is that, in the traditional structure, the jurisdictions of the regulators are defined by the institutional groups to which they are attached. Thus, for example, a banking regulator is usually restricted to regulating banks, rather than to regulating banking-type products. This leaves an arbitrage opportunity for new institutions to offer banking-type products under a different banner, thereby remaining outside the jurisdiction of the main regulator. Where the new, unregulated institutions incur greater risk by avoiding or minimizing regulation, the stability of the whole financial system may be put at risk. Resolving this conflict requires either an amalgamation of regulators to a level where regulatory gaps are minimal or a redefinition of the jurisdictional boundaries by financial promises rather than by institutional group. Thus, for example, any institution offering deposit promises could be defined as a bank for regulatory purposes. Similarly, any institution making an insurance-type promise could be defined as an insurance company for regulatory purposes.

Not only does the institutional structure face potential non-neutralities between competing prudential regulators, but it also faces a fundamental source of non-neutrality between the prudential and other functional regulators. For example, a prudential regulator is unlikely to take the same approach as a market conduct regulator in regulating the market behavior and disclosure of a bank or insurance company. Further, the prudential regulator is less likely to have the expertise or to allocate as many of its scarce resources to issues of market conduct than is a specialized market conduct regulator. Similarly, because of its natural interest in industry stability and soundness, a prudential regulator is more inclined to impose high entry barriers and is less concerned with industry concentration than is a specialized competition regulator. Consequently, countries in which these responsibilities are delegated to prudential regulators for certain industry groups often face complaints about regulatory non-neutrality.

The situation is complicated further by the fact that few prudential regulators receive full delegation of market conduct and competition issues. For example, where the institutions in the industry being prudentially regulated take a corporate form, their disclosure requirements for raising equity funds are likely to be governed by the regulator responsible for market conduct. Similarly, some countries subject mergers of prudentially regulated institutions to the scrutiny of one or more outside processes.

Responses to the challenges of conglomerates and regulatory arbitrage have taken three main forms: the lead regulator model, the integrated institutional regulator model, and the functional regulator model. Although these models are conceptually distinct, the inevitable reality is that some countries have built structures that combine features of two or even all three models.

**2**

## The Lead Regulator Model

One of the biggest challenges to the traditional institutional model posed by financial conglomeration is the potential for individual regulators to fail to come to grips with the risks embodied in the overall group.

Among the countries that have maintained a largely institutionally based regulatory structure, many have adopted a lead regulator approach, whereby one of the institutional regulators takes responsibility for the group as a whole, as well as for coordinating among the regulators involved—thereby becoming the de facto conglomerate regulator. While a single regulator takes the lead in this way, regulation of the individual subsidiary institutions is delegated to the relevant institutional regulators.

For this model to operate successfully, there must be a high level of cooperation among the regulators involved and both a legislative capacity and a willingness to share information. It also is important for the lead regulator to have the legal powers necessary to take action against the group in the event of a problem.

Although the lead regulator model addresses the problem of conglomerates (although few see it as an adequate solution to the problem), it fails to address the problem of regulatory arbitrage.

## The Integrated Regulator Model

The term "integrated regulator" has been used to cover a wide range of regulatory structures. At the minimal end of the spectrum, the term has been applied to regulators (such as the Office of the Superintendent of Financial Institutions in Canada) that combine regulation of both banking and insurance. At the other end of the spectrum, the term includes "super regulators" (such as the Monetary Authority of Singapore) that combine all prudential regulation, market conduct regulation, and systemic stability regulation under one roof.

As noted in Taylor and Fleming (1999), many of the countries that have opted for some form of integrated regulation have cited the need to regulate financial conglomerates more effectively and the desire to extract regulatory efficiencies as the main forces driving integration. Although not cited as often as a motivation for regulatory integration, this model offers a much sounder base than the institutional model for minimizing regulatory arbitrage. Since a single regulator has jurisdiction over a much wider range of

**Table 2.3. Regulatory Structures Around the World, Mid-1999**

| Regulatory structure | Number of countries |
|---|---|
| Separate institutional agencies | 35 |
| Combined securities and insurance | 3 |
| Combined banking and securities | 9 |
| Combined banking and insurance | 13 |
| Single agency | |
|     Central bank | 3 |
|     Other | 10 |

*Source:* Courtis (1999).

institutions, it has the power to ensure that all regulated institutions observe the same impositions with respect to similar financial promises. However, since institutions (albeit a much wider range of institutions) still define the integrated regulators, there still may be the potential for unregulated institutions to compete at the fringes, without bearing the full cost of regulation. This framework requires supporting legislation that clearly defines regulated institutions by the products and services they provide.

According to Taylor and Fleming, by mid-1999, 13 countries had adopted integration of at least banking and insurance regulation; of these, all but two have added either securities regulation and some or all of market integrity regulation to the basic integrated regulator. The number of integrated regulators, however, appears set to increase markedly over the coming few years, with a significant number of countries either in the process of restructuring along these lines or considering such a move. Table 2.3 shows an approximate classification of regulatory structures around the world as of mid-1999.

The rationale for integrated regulation, at least as applied to prudential regulation, is relatively straightforward. By aligning the regulatory structure with the conglomerate structure of industry, the regulator should, in principle, be better able to regulate the conglomerate group as a whole. Further, by assembling all prudential regulators under one roof, the regulatory agency should be able to extract efficiencies in the use of scarce regulatory resources. By offering a broader career path, within a larger and presumably more prestigious organization, it also should be able to attract better-quality staff. Finally, its broader scope also should minimize gaps and overlaps, thereby minimizing regulatory arbitrage.

The main drawback of integrated regulation is the potential for consumers to assume incorrectly that all financial services and products regulated by the same regulator are subject to the same degree of public support. This potential misperception thus may heighten the moral hazard problem faced by prudential regulators.

Although the theoretical case for integration is attractive, full integration of regulatory methodology, which is necessary for true regulatory neutrality, is still to be achieved. In some countries, the move to full integration has been hampered by internal structures that have maintained institutional groupings. In others, it has been hampered by legislative differences among institutional groups. These limitations notwithstanding, experience with integrated regulation to date appears to have been positive, with most countries reporting satisfaction with their efforts to build regulatory capacity and to extract efficiencies.

The case for integration across different regulatory functions, such as prudential and market integrity, is less compelling than that for integration within regulatory functions. Although it increases the potential for regulatory efficiencies, the super regulator variation of this model needs to reconcile the different cultures and methods inherent in addressing the different forms of market failure. Not only does the super regulator version of integrated regulation raise the potential for conflict between the objectives of the different regulatory functions, but it also exacerbates the moral hazard problem by extending even further the regulatory net covered by the prudential regulator.

## The Functional Regulator Model

The third response has been to structure regulators in strict accordance with the four sources of market failure: one for competition, one for market conduct, one for asymmetric information, and one for systemic stability. The distinguishing feature of this model is that each regulator regulates a single function, regardless of the institutions involved. Thus, for example, the competition regulator is responsible for competition issues for banks, insurance companies, and securities dealers, as well as for all other sectors in the economy.

## Box 2.3. Functional Regulation: The Australian Experience

During 1996, the Australian government commissioned a committee to review the Australian experience with financial deregulation, to assess the forces for change in the financial system over the coming decade or so, and to recommend a regulatory structure for coping with these changes (see Financial System Inquiry 1996, 1997).

The committee (known informally as the Wallis Committee) reported in March 1997 with 115 recommendations ranging from the competitive structure of the financial system to detailed legislative changes. At the time of writing, the Australian government had implemented all but a few of these recommendations. At the core of these recommendations was a proposal to realign the country's hybrid structure of institutionally based prudential regulators and more functionally based integrity and competition regulators into a consolidated group of functionally based regulators.

The primary motivation for the change was an acceptance that the financial conglomerate was quickly becoming the dominant form of financial service provider and that the forces for change in the financial system would put intolerable strain on the regulatory structure, unless it was better aligned with the underlying sources of market failure. The committee was particularly conscious of the need for regulatory agencies to focus on correcting market failure and to minimize the potential for impeding innovation and adding unnecessarily to the cost of providing financial services. The committee sought to recommend a structure that would facilitate new market entrants and new ways of providing financial services, and financial innovation generally, without sacrificing financial safety and soundness.

In July 1998, based on the committee's recommendations, the government instituted a functional regulatory structure based on four agencies:

- The Australian Competition and Consumer Commission (ACCC), which is responsible for regulating competition and protecting consumers throughout the economy
- The Australian Securities and Investments Commission, which is responsible for regulating market integrity, including consumer protection, in the financial system
- The Australian Prudential Regulation Authority, which is responsible for ensuring the prudential soundness of all deposit-taking, general, and life insurance and private pension schemes
- The Reserve Bank of Australia (RBA), which is responsible for stabilizing the system.

The committee considered a wide range of issues in arriving at its recommendations. Among the more difficult were whether or not to separate banking supervision from monetary policy, where to draw the boundaries around those institutions and financial services warranting prudential supervision, and how best to ensure interagency cooperation.

The committee recognized that there were significant synergies between banking regulation and monetary policy. Coupled with the credibility enjoyed by the RBA as a successful banking regulator, there was a strong case to retain banking supervision within the RBA. There was, however, an equally powerful argument that the growth of financial conglomerates required a more coherent approach to prudential regulation than could be provided by different agencies. While the committee considered adding regulation of insurance and other deposit takers to the responsibilities of the RBA, there would have been a danger of distracting the RBA from its primary role of monetary policy. Ultimately, the committee decided that a new agency dedicated to all forms of prudential regulation and a streamlined central bank responsible for systemic stability through its control of monetary policy and the payments system offered a more focused and flexible structure.

Drawing the boundaries around prudential regulation also was difficult. While the case for including all deposit-taking institutions and all forms of insurance within the prudential net was very strong, the case for pensions was much less so. The situation was complicated by the way in which the Australian pension system had evolved since the mid-1980s. To reduce the burden on a growing unfunded public pension

*Continued*

---

**Box 2.3 (Continued). Functional Regulation: The Australian Experience**

scheme, successive Australian governments had encouraged private provision through tax concessions and a series of compulsory pension contributions imposed on employers as an offset to wage claims. The pension owner ultimately bore the market risk of such pensions. Although this made a strong case to treat pensions like any other form of investment, the fact that the pension contributions were mandatory and the choice of fund was restricted meant that the government retained at least an implicit responsibility associated with the risk of fraud and poor management. For these reasons, the committee recommended including private pensions within the prudential responsibility of the Australian Prudential Regulation Authority.

Finally, to encourage interagency cooperation, the committee recommended establishing the new pru-

dential agency with a board that would include ex officio representatives from the Australian Securities and Investments Commission and the RBA.

The new structure has been in operation since July 1998 and has functioned effectively and efficiently to date. In line with the expectations of the Wallis Committee, streamlining the old regulatory structure lowered the cost of regulation significantly and facilitated new entrants to the field, without reducing safety or soundness. Indeed, the case could be made that safety and soundness improved as a result of harmonization of prudential standards not only within institutional groups but also among groups. In 1999 the Australian Prudential Regulation Authority helped to form an international group of integrated regulators and is generally regarded as being at the frontier of integrated regulatory policy.

---

The strength of this approach is that it brings together under one roof all regulators specializing in the same form of regulation, thereby offering efficiencies, and fosters regulatory neutrality, without creating conflicts among the regulatory objectives within each agency. Defining regulators by function also offers them ample scope to minimize regulatory arbitrage, provided they are willing to harmonize standards fully across all industry groups that fall within their jurisdiction.

To date, Australia appears to be the only country to adopt this model in its purest form, although several of the super regulators have effectively replicated this type of model by establishing functional regulation within their internal structures (see box 2.3).

Although the functional model is attractive in that it aligns regulatory agencies with market failures, it is not entirely free of regulatory conflicts. Indeed, eliminating regulatory overlaps and conflicts completely is virtually impossible. Some conflicts arise automatically among the objectives of competition regulation, market conduct regulation, and prudential regulation. Most institutionally based structures attempt to resolve these conflicts by granting prudential regulators jurisdiction over competition and market conduct for the institutions involved. This eliminates the conflict for the institutions but does so at the cost of lack of uniformity in the application of the other forms of regulation. For example, a prudential regulator may be tempted to pursue breaches of disclosure requirements less vigorously for banks than would a dedicated market conduct regulator, because of the potential for public punitive action to weaken the prudential standing of the bank in question.

The functional regulatory structure attempts to resolve the conflict by dividing each industry's regulation among the various regulators, with each regulating the component of the institution's behavior that falls within its jurisdiction. Although this also eliminates the conflict, it does so by subjecting each industry to multiple regulators and creating potential conflicts between the regulators. For example, a banking regulator seeking an expeditious merger between two large banks to avoid a capital deficiency may find its plans blocked by the competition regulator.

The super regulator version of integrated regulation seeks to resolve the regulatory conflict by having one regulatory agency cover most or all areas of regulation. Again, this resolves the conflict, but at the possible cost of internal conflicts of style, as the agency attempts to reconcile fundamentally different regulatory approaches (proactive approaches and reactive approaches). There is also the possibility that interagency conflicts under the alternative structures simply become interdepartmental conflicts within a super regulator.

## Selecting the Appropriate Regulatory Structure

There is no ideal regulatory structure that fits all financial systems. The ideal structure is a matter of judgment and needs to take into account the stage of financial development, the legislative environment, and the range of regulatory skills available.

Where the financial system is largely bank based, the case for integrated regulation is less likely to be pressing. First, a bank-dominated system is unlikely to face a major problem of institutional blurring. In such a system, there may also be benefits from maintaining a closer link between prudential regulation of banks and systemic stability regulation. With the exception of Singapore (which has the advantage of a relatively small, centralized financial system), countries that have adopted integrated regulation have established this within a new agency, independent from the central bank. Although this separation is helpful for maintaining the regulatory focus of the agency and ensuring that it takes a broad perspective across all regulated institutions (not just banks), it does so at the cost of separating prudential oversight of banks from the systemic responsibilities of the central bank. In a bank-dominated financial system, the benefits of keeping banking regulation within the central bank may outweigh the benefits of integrated regulation.

Where the government's objective is to foster a strong and competitive nonbank sector, the case for integrated regulation and its associated benefits of regulatory neutrality and scale efficiencies are likely to be stronger.

## Regulatory Backing

Regulatory effectiveness refers to how well and how cost-effectively the regulator of a particular intermediary group or financial product meets its objective of counteracting market failure.

The cost aspect is critical and is often overlooked. It is easy for a regulator to think of regulatory effectiveness simply as eliminating market failure (for example, ensuring that insurance companies meet their promises under all possible circumstances). True regulatory effectiveness, however, requires that the cost of eliminating the market failure is not greater than the cost of the market failure itself.

Effectiveness ultimately comes down to two issues: the backing or support available to the regulator (the effectiveness of the political, legal, and financial backing in enabling a regulator to carry out its duties) and regulatory implementation (the effectiveness of the tools and techniques employed by the regulator). This section deals with regulatory backing, while the next deals with the issue of implementation.

The critical support issues that affect a regulator's capacity to function effectively include political support, appropriate legislative backing, adequate funding, appropriate skills, and appropriate review processes. These backing requirements constitute a set of preconditions for effective regulation.

## Political Support

It is fundamentally important that the government and the regulator share the same philosophy with respect to the particular form of regulation involved. This means sharing a common view about the roles and objectives of regulation. It also means keeping open the channels of communication so that the government is aware of issues facing the regulator as well as an evolution in the regulator's approach and in the regulated industries. Finally, it means having clear lines of responsibility and accountability between the regulator and the government. The ideal combination of responsibility and accountability is one in which the regulator is demonstrably independent in its actions, but fully accountable to the government for the outcomes of those actions.

It is critical that the government stands willing to support the regulator in the event that legislative changes are needed, either to correct legislative deficiencies in the regulator's powers or to adjust the legislation to cope with evolution in the financial system.

The regulatory structure established by the government is another important factor influencing the regulator's effectiveness. In particular, many regulatory structures have multiple regulators with potentially conflicting areas of jurisdiction. Regulatory duplication not only is costly but also can create uncertainty and inconsistency.

At a broader level, a supportive government also will ensure that the regulator has functional links with other nonregulatory bodies whose policies and decisions influence the effectiveness of the regulator. Of relevance here are industry and government bodies concerned with matters such as accounting standards and bankruptcy laws.

## Legislative Backing

Possibly the most fundamental backing that any regulator needs is the legal power to carry out its functions effectively. This gives the regulator not only the power to function but also the ability to protect the government's own exposure.

The powers required by a regulator to meet its objectives may vary considerably according to the nature of the market failure involved. For example, the legislative backing for a regulator whose primary focus is market integrity typically includes the power to undertake the following:

- Regulate disclosure for securities and retail investment products
- Regulate market conduct to promote orderly and efficient price discovery, trading, and securities settlement
- Determine the licensing and oversight conditions of financial institutions and organized exchanges

2

- Regulate investment advice and market participants
- Regulate the establishment and compliance of collective investment schemes
- Regulate the conduct of dealings with consumers and the prevention of fraud
- Take injunctive action against the operations of suspected fraud
- Seize and dispose of assets acquired by fraud
- Levy fines on inappropriate behavior
- Approve and oversee industry codes of conduct
- Delegate accreditation and disciplinary functions to self-regulatory bodies where appropriate
- Set benchmarks for the performance of self-regulatory bodies.

The activities of market integrity regulators inevitably involve the prosecution of those who break the rules. Legislative backing therefore must provide the market integrity regulator with sufficient powers of enforcement. This includes the establishment of sufficient clarity of intent in the legislation as well as sufficiently strong sanctions.

These requirements are far from simple to implement and require strong support from the courts. For example, most market integrity regulators are empowered to prosecute insider trading in stock markets. Yet, in practice, insider trading is extremely difficult to establish in most courts of law. The greater is the clarity of the law, the more stringent are the penalties, and the more extensive are the powers of the regulator to access information and pursue potential miscreants, the more effective is the regulator's role in preventing such abuses.

The legislative backing for a regulator whose primary focus is competition regulation typically includes the following powers:

- Establish rules dealing with the competitive structure of industries
- Prevent mergers of financial institutions
- Force divestiture where industry concentration becomes uncompetitive
- Prohibit collusion on the price or nature of promises made by financial institutions.

Prudential regulators are fundamentally different from market integrity and competition regulators. Although the regulatory approach of the latter may include some proactive elements, such as licensing or approval of markets and mergers, the primary approach is reactive—prosecuting market participants who break the rules established by the regulator. The reactive nature of these regulators is a natural consequence of the objective of efficiency—the cost of policing these rules ex ante to prevent transgressions is typically so high as to dwarf the costs of the market failure. This is not the case for prudential regulators.

With prudential regulation, the cost of market failure due to asymmetric information (and the possible systemic risks involved) usually is judged to be so high that the government interposes a regulator between the promisor and the promisee to remove, or at least greatly reduce, the need for the promisee to make judgments about risk. This creates an implicit risk transfer from the individual to the government, since creditors of a failed institution that has been prudentially regulated have a natural incentive to look to the government for restitution. Many governments have attempted to make this liability explicit (and to limit it in the process) by instituting public insurance or guarantee schemes for creditors of prudentially regulated institutions.

Because of this implicit liability to the government, prudential regulation tends to be more proactive or preventative than reactive. To prevent promissory failure in sectors where there is either information asymmetry or potential systemic instability requires the regulator to have the power to respond quickly and flexibly to changing circumstances. This includes the power to merge distressed institutions before their capital has been completely eroded.

Effective powers of enforcement for a prudential regulator typically include the following:

- To inspect
- To request information
- To direct (for example, to cease certain activities)
- To remove directors and auditors
- To suspend operations
- To appoint an administrator
- To transfer engagements.

The preventative nature of prudential regulation has raised a debate about the ideal legislative backing. Whereas a market integrity or competition regulator needs all its powers and rules to be clearly defined in legislation, a prudential regulator usually seeks to resolve problems before they become cases for legal action. This places a different set of requirements on the nature of the rules themselves in the case of prudential regulation.

Prudential regulators around the world currently operate under one of two models: either the "black letter law" model or the "guidelines" model. The former (used extensively in regulating insurance companies) puts all prudential rules into the act governing either the particular financial institution or its regulations. The latter (adopted more in banking regulation) usually involves conferring on the regulator a very broad regulatory power under the act. The regulator then implements this power by promulgating guidelines or prudential standards. In some countries, the standards have the same legal status as regulations; in others, they draw their enforceability from the regulator's ability to impose its will through a regulation, if needed.

From a regulatory standpoint, the most attractive feature of the guidelines approach over the black letter law approach is the flexibility that it affords the regulator. First, the regulator can issue or amend a guideline quickly, without the need to pass legislation through the Parliament. Second, there should be no dispute over the interpretation of a guideline. If there is any ambiguity in the wording of a guideline, the regulator can either issue an interpretative note to clarify the matter or amend the guideline. The ultimate jurisdiction for the interpretation lies with the regulator. In contrast, where the interpretation of a regulation comes into dispute, jurisdiction for the interpretation lies ultimately with the courts. Some of the world's more spectacular regulatory failures can be traced to the inability of legal draftsmen to draft legislation tightly enough for effective enforcement.

## Funding

A fundamental precondition for regulatory effectiveness is adequate funding. Without adequate financial resources, the regulator will be unable to attract staff with the requisite skills, undertake analyses or inspections in the case of prudential regulators, prosecute market misconduct in the case of fraud, or force divestiture in the case of monopoly.

There are two main models for funding regulatory agencies throughout the world. The first allocates resources to the regulator through the government's budget. The second recovers the cost of regulation from the industry by levy.

The advantage of the budgetary approach is that it imposes the cost of regulation on taxpayers, who are the ultimate beneficiaries of regulation. The drawback of the budgetary approach is that the regulators are forced to compete with social programs for funding in every budget round. The budgetary model also contains a potential conflict. In times of financial stringency, the low public profile of regulation makes it a prime target for budgetary cuts. Cutting back on regulatory resources during recession could lead to regulatory failure as the economy recovers and financial activity increases.

The advantage of the industry-funded model is that it removes the regulator's funding from the government's budgetary process, thereby ensuring a more consistent level of funding over the business cycle. Another advantage is that, since industry bears the cost directly, it plays a natural watchdog role over the cost of regulation. The drawback of the industry-funded model is that the cost of regulation falls not on the beneficiaries, but rather on the regulated industry itself. This weakness is mitigated partly by the ability of the industry to pass the cost of regulation on to its customers (which should occur provided the system is regulatory neutral).

## Skill Base

Every regulator is critically dependent on its staff for its effectiveness. An effective regulator requires a sound regulatory culture among its staff and an appropriate set of skills to deal with what often can be extremely complex issues.

An appropriate staff culture is a concept that is easy to discuss, but very difficult to achieve. The ideal culture for a regulator is one in which staff are fully aware of and committed to the regulatory philosophy of the agency and to achieving its regulatory objectives. The ideal regulatory culture is one that is driven by a commitment to outputs rather than inputs. In practice, many regulators around the world are staffed by public servants who come from a culture that does not often fit the ideal model.

In recognition of this constraint and the disincentive it creates for high-quality regulation, governments around the world are increasingly allowing regulatory agencies to break away from their centralized public service groupings. Regulators, in turn, are adopting private sector–style industrial structures that reward excellence and commitment and are attempting to refocus attention away from inputs (such as time spent on the job) and toward outputs (such as objectives achieved).

One of the great difficulties facing every regulator is that, even with this distancing from public sector terms and conditions, salary differentials between the industry and the regulator remain such that the most highly skilled staff usually work for the industry rather than the regulator. This makes it difficult for regulators to keep abreast of frontier developments in products and techniques in the industry.

## Regular Review

The issues discussed above impinge largely on the ability of the regulator to carry out its duties effectively. Adequate support in each of these areas does not guarantee that the regulator will carry out its duties efficiently. The two most important steps that can be taken toward maintaining an appropriate balance between efficiency and effectiveness are to include efficiency as an explicit objective in the regulator's charter and to mandate a process of periodic review, possibly including representatives from the regulator, the industry, and the government.

The following subsections present a set of principles against which such a review might be conducted.[3]

### Competitive Neutrality

Competitive neutrality requires that the regulatory burden applying to a particular financial promise should apply equally to all financial institutions that make promises of that type. This objective requires that there be minimal barriers to entry and exit from markets and products and that institutions not be subjected to undue restrictions on the products they offer. Where restrictions are imposed on a particular promise for prudential purposes, they should apply equally to all market participants making those promises.

---

3. These principles of efficient regulation are adapted from Financial System Inquiry (1997).

2

## Cost-Effectiveness

Cost-effectiveness is a fundamental tension facing every regulator. Regulations usually can be made completely effective by making the cost of certain actions prohibitively expensive. For example, banks could be forced to back their deposit promises 100 percent with government securities. Alternatively, firms wishing to underwrite insurance risks could be required to submit a bond to the regulator equal to the value of the securities being underwritten. Such an approach clearly would be contrary to the objective of ensuring that the financial system functions efficiently.

A cost-effective regulatory system requires the following:

- A presumption in favor of lighter regulation unless a higher level of regulation can be justified in cost-benefit terms
- An allocation of regulatory functions among regulatory agencies that minimizes overlaps, duplications, and conflicts
- A clear distinction between the objectives of financial regulation and broader social objectives
- The allocation of regulatory costs to those who enjoy the benefits.

## Transparency

Transparency of regulation requires that all guarantees be made explicit and that all purchasers and providers of financial products and services be made fully aware of their rights and responsibilities. In other words, it is important that all parties involved understand the nature and extent of financial promises.

## Flexibility

One of the most pervasive influences over the continuing evolution of the financial system is technology. Technological innovations have the potential to reshape financial services and delivery mechanisms in a very short space of time. These developments and the impact they can have on regulated industries and products mean that regulatory flexibility is critical. The regulatory framework and the powers of individual regulators must be flexible enough to cope with changing institutional and product structures as they occur, without losing their effectiveness.

*Accountability*

Regulatory agencies should operate independently of sectoral interests. Each regulatory agency should be accountable to its stakeholders.

## Regulatory Implementation

Regulatory effectiveness depends on both the backing available to the regulator and the methods or tools used by the regulator to implement its regulatory powers and responsibilities. This section reviews the main tools available to regulators.

Each tool is considered separately for how it might be applied to varying intensities of financial promises (in terms of their three characteristics: inherent difficulty of honoring the promise, difficulty faced by the consumer in assessing the creditworthiness of the promisor, and the adversity caused by promissory breach). The section breaks these tools into four main categories: preconditions for entry into the market (licensing, ownership restrictions, and capital requirements), ongoing conditions for continued participation in the industry (market structure requirements, market conduct rules, disclosure, governance and fiduciary duties, balance sheet restrictions, associations among financial institutions, liquidity requirements, and accountability), surveillance methods (complaints mechanisms, off-site monitoring, and inspections), and enforcement practices (prosecution, problem resolution, and support schemes). The section finishes with some comments on the delegation of responsibilities and incentives.

## Preconditions for Entry

As a general principle, freedom of entry is the basic foundation of competition policy. Many financial regulators, however, impose some restrictions on entry as part of either a market integrity regime or a prudential regime.

*Licensing*

The most basic form of entry restriction is licensing. Where there is potential for financial institutions to take advantage of consumers through false or misleading promises or through manipulation of the institution's activities, licensing provides a minimum level of assurance to consumers of the institution's services. Among other safeguards, a license provides a traceable record of the firm's location, owners, and management. It also imposes an implicit sanction, in terms of delicensing, for those institutions that misbehave. The focus of licensing on consumer protection has led many countries to exempt institutions from the need to hold a license where they do not make financial promises to the public at large.[4]

The licensing regime can be made more restrictive as the intensity of the promises made by the institutions involved increases through the following:

- Requiring professional qualifications or accreditation of staff and management
- Requiring a detailed business plan
- Requiring enforceable undertakings by directors with respect to certain actions or situations
- Requiring the license holder to submit to various forms of ongoing regulation
- Imposing "fit and proper" tests on directors, management, or staff
- Imposing ownership restrictions, including limiting or prohibiting the issue of licenses to certain groups
- Imposing minimum size restrictions.

Professional qualifications are commonly required for complex areas, such as securities dealers, and also where the institution deals with unsophisticated consumers, for example in the case of retail investment advisers or insurance agents.

Fit and proper persons tests can be applied at the board and senior management level to limit the entry of individuals of questionable integrity into the world of financial service provision. Among regulators of securities dealers and collective investments, it is common to refuse licenses where the

---

4.  The definition of "public dealing" can vary greatly, from situations excluding only totally private institutions (where ownership is not offered to the public at all) to situations excluding offerings that are restricted to below a certain number of subscribers.

applicants have a criminal record involving crimes such as fraud. Prudential regulators also apply fit and proper tests to specialized staff to ensure that the institution has the necessary base of skills to manage the risks to which it is exposed.

## Ownership Restrictions

Ownership restrictions are a form of entry requirement and often are imposed as a means of counteracting (however modestly) the anticompetitive effects of the other elements of entry restrictions, particularly in the case of high-intensity promises. Many countries, for example, restrict the issue of banking licenses to institutions that do not hold other financial service licenses. Others prohibit the issue of banking licenses to nonfinancial corporations, and others prohibit the issue of licenses to foreign entities.

A second form of ownership restriction involves concentration limits. It is common among prudential regulators, although it is by no means limited to prudential regulators, to limit the ownership of a financial institution by a single investor, or group of related parties of investors, to a maximum percentage. This is designed to prevent control of the institution from falling into the hands of a small group and then being used to benefit that group rather than to perform the general financial functions for which it was licensed.

For the same reason, and to ensure that conflicts of interest do not arise between the financial institution and its customers, some regulators limit or prohibit direct shareholdings by commercial enterprises in certain financial institutions.

## Capital Requirements

Capital requirements typically take one of two forms: minimum size requirements and variable capital adequacy requirements. The two serve quite different purposes and typically are employed to address different market failures.

Market conduct regulators typically employ minimum size restrictions as a blunt instrument to ensure that there is some substance behind the promises made by financial institutions. For example, where the risk of fraud or market abuse is judged to be particularly high, a market integrity regulator may choose to impose a minimum capital requirement as part of its licensing regime. The capital serves as a deterrent to fraud by putting a high cost on the loss of the license.

Minimum size restrictions should be applied sparingly because they can inhibit the start-up of new intermediaries, thereby acting as a barrier to competition.

The imposition of a variable capital adequacy requirement usually serves a different purpose. Capital adequacy requirements are intended to absorb unexpected losses incurred by financial institutions. Consequently, they usually are scaled to be consistent with the size of the institution's balance sheet and with the level of risk undertaken by the institution. In the case of many financial promises, the discipline of the market and the self-interests of investors are sufficient to ensure that the financial institution is adequately capitalized. However, rational investors will never capitalize an institution to the point where its probability of failure is zero. Where intense promises are involved, the regulator may need to impose a variable capital adequacy requirement to reduce the probability of failure to an acceptable level, in view of the nature of the promises involved.

Capital adequacy has been used widely in banking and other deposit-taking regulation since the introduction of the Basle Concordat in 1975. Most insurance regulators implement the same principle by imposing minimum solvency requirements on life and general insurance companies. Some securities regulators also impose capital adequacy requirements consistent with the risks that are incurred by those with exposures to them, although this is less common.

In the case of prudential regulators, capital adequacy requirements establish a trigger level of solvency that provides the regulator with some breathing space in which to resolve a situation of distress before the institution involved becomes unable to honor its promises.

Like minimum size restrictions, capital adequacy requirements should be applied sparingly because they can inhibit the start-up of new intermediaries. They are applied most commonly in areas where the intensity of the financial promise is extremely high and where prudential regulation is involved, for example, in deposit taking and insurance.

## Ongoing Regulatory Requirements

In addition to preconditions for participation in many areas of the financial system, most regulators also impose an array of ongoing requirements. Typically, these include continuous observance of license conditions, including any ownership and capital requirements. Additional ongoing regulatory tools include market structure requirements, anticollusion rules, market contestability rules, disclosure, market conduct rules, governance and fiduciary duties, balance sheet restrictions, associations among financial institutions, liquidity requirements, and accountability requirements.

*Market Structure Requirements*

The structure of an industry is important, because it can influence the way in which firms behave in the market. Regulations to deal with industry structure are primarily the preserve of competition regulation and include controlling mergers, forcing divestiture to break up existing institutions, and granting exemptions from these measures for prudential purposes.

Mergers can be procompetitive, anticompetitive, or neutral. Thus, in regulating mergers, judgments have to be made based on the facts in each case. What is important is the outcome for competition and efficiency.

It is important to recognize that entry and market structure policies are not the only ways in which governments influence competition. To the extent that market integrity and prudential regulation lead to exemptions and impositions that weaken the foundations of free entry and a competitive market structure, these regulations can themselves create competitive imbalances.

Many government policies not related to regulation also have unintended side effects on competitiveness, particularly in the financial sector. In many cases, government legislation or lack of legislation can hinder the development of a competitive financial system. For example, technology has been a major driver of change in the global financial system. Not only has technology shifted the boundaries of traditional financial products and markets, but it also has changed the delivery mechanisms in many cases. If legislation does not respond to these changing circumstances, it can impede the adoption of new technologies and create competitive disadvantages within the industry as well as internationally. In other cases, the absence of an appropriate legislative framework can give a competitive advantage to institutions that operate outside the regulations, but in direct competition with regulated institutions.

Taxes are another source of competitive interference. In many countries, tax rules introduced to foster a particular sector or product can confer unintended competitive advantages on related industries. The following aspects of the tax system typically influence competition in the financial sector:

- Capital gains tax
- Dividend imputation
- Interest withholding tax
- Tax concessions for particular products or sectors
- Offshore banking unit provisions
- Variations between state and federal tax regimes.

## Anticollusion Rules

Anticompetitive behavior—price fixing, predatory pricing, or collusion among buyers or sellers to set the price or other competitive aspects of a service or product—is a form of market misconduct, although its regulation typically falls within the jurisdiction of competition regulation rather than market integrity regulation.

Anticompetitive behavior usually is addressed by the establishment and policing of trade practice laws that are motivated by the need to protect consumers from exploitative pricing by institutions with excessive market power. They also are motivated by the desire to harness market forces to ensure the efficient allocation of financial resources among competing investment projects, including preventing the underprovision of services essential to economic growth and welfare.

## Contestability Rules

In general, markets remain competitive provided they are contestable. This requires primarily that there are no significant barriers to entry and exit. In some cases, barriers are inherent to the industry (for example, where a substantial capital outlay is needed to meet minimum scale economies), and in others they are imposed artificially (for example, where the existing members of an industry form unofficial "clubs" through industry accreditation or common access to infrastructure). In principle, even a market that is highly concentrated can be competitive if alternative providers are able to enter the market at minimal cost. In general, competition regulators seek to dismantle artificial barriers to entry and also to ensure that industry exits are not impeded by artificial constraints.

In the finance sector, there is a basic conflict between the objectives of competition regulators, who prefer full and open entry, and the objectives of market integrity and prudential regulators, who need to balance the desire for competition with the need for fairness and safety. The lighter forms of entry restriction, including basic licensing and licensing with conduct restrictions, create only minor tensions with the competition objective. However, the more intrusive restrictions, including minimum capital requirements and ownership restrictions, can create significant tensions, particularly where they result in very high market concentration and franchise values to the license holders.

## Disclosure

In the same way that freedom of entry is the foundation of competition regulation, disclosure of information is the foundation of market integrity regulation. The underlying market failure in many financial promises can be resolved simply be ensuring that all parties to the promise are fully informed about all issues that are relevant to understanding the nature of the promise, pricing the promise, and assessing the probability of its being honored.

The price formation process is a major focus of market integrity regulators. Financial market prices can be extremely sensitive to information, which raises the potential for the misuse of information. The role of information, however, extends well beyond market abuse. When parties to a transaction have inadequate information on which to base their decisions, there may be a loss in efficiency to the extent that the parties price the cost of uncertainty into their transactions.

Regulation of disclosure is central to consumer protection in financial markets, because it provides the basis on which to make informed choices. However, the important factors are the quality and usefulness of information, not its quantity. Excessive or complex information can be counterproductive: it not only confuses consumers but also may discourage them from using the disclosure documents. Complex disclosure also can be costly to the issuer.

Regulation of disclosure usually takes some or all of the following forms:

- General disclosure, including ongoing disclosure of material information, disclosure of fees and commissions, and disclosure of specific information for investment products
- Rules governing the release of accounting data disclosing the general financial health of institutions
- Prospectus provisions governing the information required for capital raisings
- Special reporting to regulatory bodies.

General disclosure of material information is relevant to the efficient operation of organized markets such as stock exchanges. Disclosure of fees and commissions is helpful in protecting the rights of consumers when purchasing financial services such as investment advice or insurance.

Rules governing the release of accounting data (for example, rules governing the extent of information required, its frequency, and its timeliness) vary greatly across different countries and depend heavily for their effectiveness on the quality of the underlying accounting standards.

Rules governing the issuing of prospectuses for capital raisings are important for building investor confidence in the market. Most regulators trade off the value of additional information against the cost that can be incurred in assembling and verifying prospectus material.

There is a distinction between the information that is required by regulators of financial institutions and the information that is required for general disclosure. In many cases, the regulator has specific information needs that are not necessarily relevant to the public. Where institutions are prone to systemic instability and where a prudential regulator is involved, there is a case for exempting the institutions from the rigors of public reporting in return for the high level of disclosure demanded by the regulator.[5]

---

5. This case is not universally accepted, and some countries have imposed general disclosure requirements on all prudentially regulated institutions.

**2**

*Market Conduct Rules*

In addition to regulating disclosure of information, market integrity regulation also seeks to ensure that:

- Markets are sound, orderly, and transparent.
- Users of financial markets are treated fairly.
- Markets are free from misleading, manipulative, or abusive conduct.

Regulatory tools to meet these objectives include placing prohibitions on and prosecuting those who engage in insider trading, market manipulation, false and misleading advertising, and fraud.

As the financial promises involved become more intense (for example, in the case of securities dealing, deposit taking, and insurance), the regulator involved may impose more demanding conduct requirements to reduce the probability of misconduct.

*Governance and Fiduciary Duties*

Financial institutions operate with a high level of trust from the community. Indeed, without that trust, these institutions would not contribute much at all to the overall efficiency of the financial system. The level of corporate governance imposed on the corporate sector at large is generally of a lower level than is consistent with the degree of trust involved in intermediation.

Governance provisions attempt to regulate the internal structures, controls, and procedures of financial institutions in an effort to ensure prudence, underpin trust, minimize conflicts of interest, and avoid consumer exploitation. They are particularly important where the institution plays a fiduciary role in which it acts for the investor or client in a position of trust.

The following regulatory tools are used to encourage good governance:

- Independent auditors
- Appointment of a minimum percentage or number of directors who are independent of management
- Appointment of an independent custodian, with clear hypothecation and segregation of customer/client assets
- Independent valuation of assets

- Limits on pricing and fees that can be charged for certain services
- Rules to limit other conflicts of interest, including limits on related-party transactions.

Although these tools are applied most commonly in regulating securities dealers, pension funds, and collective investments, general governance rules are being applied increasingly in deposit taking and insurance.

*Balance Sheet Restrictions*

Balance sheet restrictions interfere with the natural workings of the market in a major way. As such, they are used mainly where high-intensity promises are involved to quarantine risks by limiting the types of assets and liabilities that can be combined on one balance sheet and by limiting the net exposure of the total balance sheet.

Regulators use the following balance sheet restrictions:

- Limits on asset/liability mismatches
- Prohibitions on particular classes of assets or liabilities
- Restrictions on the type of assets held
- Mandated maximum or minimum holdings of particular assets.

Risks arising from a maturity mismatch between assets and liabilities are a particular concern of life insurance regulators. Regulators often seek to limit mismatch risk by imposing restrictions on the maturity structure of insurance balance sheets.

Prohibitions also commonly are used to separate the risks in different types of financial intermediation. For example, many countries prohibit deposit-takers from investing in equity-type promises or limit the extent of such investments to shareholders' funds.

Asset restrictions by type or by credit rating are common among regulators of insurance companies and securities dealers. Asset restrictions rarely are placed on collective investments, although regulators usually attempt to ensure that investments by these vehicles are consistent with their disclosure statements and trust deeds.

Regulators of deposit-taking institutions usually impose large exposure limits by borrower and by sector to ensure that these institutions gain the benefits of diversification and do not expose their capital unduly to single sources of risk. Less common at the beginning of the twenty-first century are restrictions forcing these institutions to invest or lend minimum proportions of their assets in particular industries or to certain sectors of the community. Although a number of countries still impose reserve requirements on banks, these have been made largely redundant by capital adequacy requirements.

*Associations among Financial Institutions*

In similar fashion to balance sheet restrictions, regulations that limit associations among financial institutions interfere with the natural workings of the market. Again, they are relevant mainly in the case of high-intensity promises as a way of quarantining exposures. Many countries attempt to segregate the following:

- Deposit taking from insurance
- Deposit taking from securities dealing
- Securities dealing from securities brokering
- Various combinations of these and other segregations.

Some countries allow these various financial activities to take place through subsidiaries. Others allow different activities to be conducted in subsidiaries of a nonoperating holding company, provided adequate firewalls are in place. Firewalls include limitations on the use of common brand names, requirements for independent directors among the various subsidiaries, and limitations on intercompany exposures.

*Liquidity Requirements*

Liquidity requirements are designed to ensure that a regulated institution has the funds available to meet any undertakings it has made concerning the liquidity of its promises. Promises that do not involve such undertakings do not need this form of regulation.

Liquidity restrictions are commonly used by regulators of deposit takers and by open-end mutual funds where the fund undertakes to repurchase units at market value.

Minimum holdings of highly liquid assets are a sound first line of defense against the inability of these institutions to meet their promise to convert illiquid assets into liquid liabilities. Some prudential regulators also require institutions to have liquidity policies and to operate liquidity management systems.

*Accountability Requirements*

Accountability requirements usually take the form of restrictions on the valuation of assets and liabilities. In most countries, applicable corporate accounting rules provide considerable scope for institutions to choose among alternative methods of valuing both assets and liabilities. Where the institution involved makes particularly onerous promises, such as are involved with deposit taking and insurance, and where solvency is fundamental to the ability of the institution to meet its promises, the regulator may choose to restrict the scope of valuation methodologies available to the institution. Such restrictions are commonly applied by prudential regulators in the areas of loan-loss provisioning in banking and the measurement of outstanding claims in insurance.

## Surveillance

In addition to establishing rules of behavior, regulators need to monitor industry's compliance with the rules. There are three basic methods for monitoring compliance. In order of increasing intrusiveness and resource intensity, these are consumer complaints mechanisms, off-site monitoring, and on-site inspections.

*Complaints Mechanisms*

The least intrusive and least costly approach to surveillance is reliance on direct complaints by consumers. This approach is most appropriate where more intrusive forms of surveillance are prohibitively expensive. In many cases, this approach is sufficient to identify regulatory breaches. Most competition and market conduct regulators, for example, rely heavily on consumer complaints tribunals as a means of uncovering lack of compliance. Where the social costs of regulatory breaches are higher, regulators usually are forced to consider more resource-intensive approaches.

2

*Off-site Monitoring*

Off-site monitoring involves statistical and other reviews of data provided by the regulated institutions. Market integrity regulators often use it to assess compliance with disclosure requirements. For example, many market integrity regulators require companies to submit proposed prospectuses for regulatory review as part of the process of raising funds from the public. Prudential regulators use it more extensively to preempt regulatory violations. The general objective of off-site analysis is to detect deterioration in an institution's financial position by comparing its current position to its historical experience and to that of its peer group.

Some prudential regulators use statistical techniques, including linear regression, logit and probit analysis, discriminant analysis, and even artificial neural networks to detect the probability of financial distress.

*Inspections*

On-site inspections are a time- and resource-intensive way of testing an institution's compliance with regulations. These are mostly the preserve of prudential regulators. Although they are used by some market integrity regulators, the resource cost involved, the wide range of institutions typically included under their purview, and the lower intensity of the promises involved make it difficult for market integrity regulators to justify extensive use of inspections. In particular, the intrusiveness of inspections can be contentious unless prudential issues are involved.

Inspection methodologies range from the U.S. approach, in which large teams of inspectors spend long periods of time sifting through a comprehensive review of most areas of regulatory compliance, through to the more risk-based British approach, in which small teams spend relatively short periods of time reviewing specific issues identified by off-site analysis.

On-site inspections can be particularly helpful in identifying areas in which reported information is inadequate or misleading. They also are helpful in testing the extent to which financial institutions implement the governance and conduct principles laid down by the regulator.

## Enforcement

Techniques available to regulators to resolve problems with regulated institutions range from prosecution of those who fail to observe the regulations through to preemptive action to change behavior or force mergers and industry exits. In the case of prudential regulation, the enforcement process is designed to be more preemptive, so as to protect the government's implicit or explicit obligations. The extent of these obligations often is defined through explicit industry support schemes.

### Prosecution

The threat of prosecution is the main enforcement tool used by most competition and market conduct regulators. Where the financial promises involved are not especially onerous, the regulator need play no special role in resolving problems, leaving that to the interested parties and the courts. Provided the laws governing property rights and liquidation are adequate, many institutional difficulties can be appropriately resolved in this way.

Self-regulatory bodies can play a useful role in dispute resolution among financial institutions through arbitration. Arbitration is a contractual, nonjudicial method for resolving disputes. It can be a fair and low-cost way of enhancing investor confidence in a market.

However, when the normal processes of the market are inadequate, the regulator has a clear responsibility to act. These circumstances include situations where there is an unfair imbalance between the financial resources of the offender and the offended party—for example, in the case of consumer exploitation by a large firm.

Where the problems involve market misconduct, the regulator may be required to intervene to injunct the firm involved, to revoke a license, to seize assets, or to levy fines and disgorge ill-gotten gains.

Where the problems involve anticompetitive behavior, the regulator may be required to prosecute the offender (for example, in the case of collusion), to stop a proposed merger, or to force the breakup of a firm with undue market power.

**2**

*Preemptive Problem Resolution*

Where the financial promises are more onerous, as is common in the case of prudential regulation, the role of the regulator in resolving problems becomes more demanding.

Provided the regulator has been monitoring its regulated institutions closely, regulatory breaches should be able to be rectified before the financial institution becomes unable to honor its promises. In practice, this process can be complicated by the infrequency and inaccuracy of reported data. This reliance on reported information reinforces the incentive for regulators to impose accountability restrictions.

The most demanding level of problem resolution is where the regulator takes control of the troubled institution. It may do this by installing an administrator or by forcing windup operations. This is most common in the case of prudential regulation, where the regulator has a responsibility to intervene when capital adequacy or statutory solvency falls below the critical level.

*Support Schemes*

Support schemes such as deposit insurance and statutory guarantee funds for insurance or securities firms are employed by many regulators to back up the promises made by regulated institutions in the event that other preventative measures fail. There are many variations on such support schemes:

- Fully funded guarantees
- Partial guarantees (limited by size of exposure)
- Unfunded schemes (which rely on an industry levy after a problem occurs)
- Variable premium schemes (in which the institutions pay premiums consistent with their assessed risks)
- Private insurance schemes.

Although these schemes give the regulator a degree of comfort in the event of institutional failure, they also have the potential to create incentive problems through moral hazard. Where the scheme is fully or partially funded, it also can introduce another layer of regulation if the industry insurance vehicle seeks to protect its own exposure through a degree of regulatory oversight.

## Delegation of Responsibilities

Self-regulatory organizations exist in many parts of the financial system, either as formal member-owned institutions or as industry associations. Self-regulatory bodies such as exchange members and clearinghouses carry out most of the day-to-day operation and oversight of organized markets, such as stock markets and derivatives markets.

The existence of some self-regulatory bodies is both inevitable and positive. In the case of organized markets, it is not possible for them to operate without a set of operating rules and a body to enforce them. Many of these rules will be matters of internal interest among the members and will be of no interest to the regulator. It is in the interests of the members to establish and enforce rules that ensure a fair and open market.

The interests and incentives of these organizations are closely aligned with those of official regulators. Consequently, some countries have left regulation of these markets entirely to these bodies, others have permitted their official regulators to delegate some of their responsibilities to them, and others have adopted a co-regulatory approach.

The extent to which regulatory oversight can be delegated to self-regulatory bodies depends on the balance of market forces among the members. The potential for particular members to exercise undue market influence means that, in practice, self-regulation tends to work best when there are both low industry concentration and strong official oversight. The scope for delegation is reduced as the intensity of promises increases, for two reasons: first, the responsibility of the regulator increases and is therefore more difficult to delegate, and, second, entry restrictions imposed by market conduct or prudential regulators often mean that these industries are more concentrated than others. Self-regulatory bodies and industry associations can play a useful role in market conduct by formulating codes of conduct for their members.

## Incentives

Aligning, to the greatest extent possible, the incentive structures of the various stakeholders in a regulated industry enhances the effectiveness of regulation (this section draws on Claessens and Klingebiel 1999). Equity holders in financial institutions have both the ability and the incentive to monitor the actions of their institutions. The potential to lose their investment provides a basic incentive to encourage prudent behavior. In practice, however, this incentive is no greater than that facing other industries, and in one important respect it may be weaker.

In other industries, the outside market imposes a discipline on owners and managers by constantly assessing and reassessing the risks involved with either buying into the company as an owner or doing business with it as a customer or trade creditor. In the case of large listed financial institutions, this discipline is still present. In smaller institutions and unlisted institutions, the presence of a regulator (especially a prudential regulator) can weaken the incentive for market participants to expend the resources needed to monitor the institution accurately. This incentive is weakened considerably if the exposure of market participants and customers is covered totally, or even in part, by deposit insurance or an industry guarantee scheme.

In general, the other aspects of regulation (prudential regulation in particular) operate to more than replace the discipline lost from the market. Indeed, failure to replace the weakened market discipline would result in a failure rate higher than the average for the economy—an outcome that would be inconsistent with the objectives of regulation.

Although most regulations attempt to create incentives compatible with reduced risk taking and honest behavior, incentive compatibility cannot be taken for granted. History is full of examples where inappropriate regulation has created perverse incentives that have contributed to the failure of institutions.

Incentives are important not only for the regulated industries but also for the regulator. Incentives for the regulator to monitor efficiently and to take appropriate actions based on that monitoring are compatible with the interests of the community on whose behalf the regulator is acting. The need for such incentives arises from the potential for regulators to become "captives" of the industries they regulate and the natural incentive for regulators to forbear in cases of distress.[6]

One way to promote better regulation is to offer regulators better incentive payments. Another is to tie the regulator's hands in the event of a problem. The measure "prompt corrective action and structured early intervention" has now been legislated in the United States and a growing number of other countries for banking regulators. It calls for the following:

---

6. It is easier for a regulator to forbear and hope that the problem goes away than to close an institution down and face the immediate disgrace of having failed in its monitoring.

- Higher capital
- Structured, prespecified, publicly announced responses by regulators, triggered automatically by performance criteria (such as a fall in capital adequacy below a specified level)
- Mandatory resolution of a capital-deficient bank once it reaches a set capital ratio trigger
- Market value accounting and reporting of capital.

This approach is not universally popular among regulators because it removes discretion and mechanizes the regulator's role. Equally important, regulators see this type of incentive measure as reflecting a loss of confidence by the government in the regulator's ability to meet its objectives.

2

# Chapter 3

# Insurance (Risk-Pooling) Companies

3

*This chapter discusses the global insurance market and factors affecting the growth of insurance in different countries. The chapter explores the variety of ways in which insurance companies contribute to economic growth: by promoting financial stability among households and firms, mobilizing savings, relieving pressure on government budgets, fostering trade and commerce, and assisting the community in mitigating risk. It then focuses on the application of the regulatory framework to insurance companies and examines the regulatory tools and techniques required.*

The regulatory framework outlined in chapter 2 introduces a number of guiding principles that can be applied in constructing a regulatory system for nonbank financial institutions (NBFIs). This and the following three chapters review the main groupings of NBFIs and how the framework can be applied to them. In doing so, they expand on the brief outlines of the industry groups introduced in chapter 1 and the ways in which they contribute to economic growth. This chapter draws heavily on Skipper (2000).

## The Market for Insurance

Insurance markets vary widely in size and structure around the world. By the standards of other financial institutions, insurance is a genuinely interna-

**Table 3.1. Penetration of Life and Non-Life Insurance in Select Countries**
(premiums as a percentage of gross domestic product)

| Country | Total | Non-life | Life |
|---|---|---|---|
| Switzerland | 12.84 | 4.78 | 8.06 |
| Japan | 11.17 | 2.3 | 8.87 |
| United Kingdom | 13.35 | 3.05 | 10.3 |
| OECD | 6.48 | 2.64 | 3.85 |
| Argentina | 2.3 | 1.5 | 0.81 |
| Brazil | 2.01 | 1.66 | 0.35 |
| Chile | 3.78 | 1.13 | 2.65 |
| Mexico | 1.68 | 0.86 | 0.82 |
| China | 1.63 | 0.61 | 1.02 |
| India | 1.93 | 0.53 | 1.39 |
| Indonesia | 1.42 | 0.75 | 0.66 |
| Korea, Republic of | 11.28 | 2.89 | 8.39 |
| Malaysia | 3.88 | 1.72 | 2.16 |
| Philippines | 1.37 | 0.61 | 0.76 |
| Thailand | 2.27 | 0.97 | 1.3 |
| Czech Republic | 3.4 | 2.32 | 1.08 |
| Greece | 2.07 | 0.93 | 1.14 |
| Hungary | 2.6 | 1.55 | 1.05 |
| Poland | 2.94 | 1.97 | 0.96 |
| Turkey | 1.26 | 1.03 | 0.23 |
| Egypt | 0.65 | 0.46 | 0.18 |
| Israel | 6.14 | 3.25 | 2.89 |
| Morocco | 2.78 | 2.01 | 0.77 |
| Nigeria | 0.95 | 0.88 | 0.07 |
| South Africa | 16.54 | 2.62 | 13.92 |

*Source:* Swiss Re (2000: table IX, p. 33).

tional market, with a large number of global players with subsidiaries and branches in many countries.

The most common measure of the size of insurance markets is gross written premiums. Globally, gross written premiums totaled more than $2.1 trillion in 1997. Growth of premiums has averaged around 5 percent annually over the past decade. Premium growth in emerging markets has been particularly strong and above the world average.

Life insurance accounts for almost 60 percent of world premiums, with the balance of just over 40 percent due to non-life premiums. This global average hides considerable regional diversity, with Asia showing the highest proportion of life premiums at more than 75 percent, reflecting the high propensity of Asians to save through life insurance.

The U.S. and Japanese insurance markets, with almost $700 billion and $500 billion, respectively, of gross premiums written in 1997, account for almost half of the world's insurance market.[1] Among the emerging markets, Korea has the largest insurance market, with a little over $100 billion of gross premiums written in 1997. This figure is dominated by life insurance and reflects favorable tax treatment and the high propensity of Koreans to save through life insurance companies.

Insurance penetration measures the ratio of yearly premiums written to gross domestic product (GDP). This measure of the relative importance of insurance is shown in table 3.1 for select emerging markets. Table 3.1 shows that, with the exception of Korea, South Africa, and Israel, insurance penetration among the emerging markets is well below the average for countries in the Organisation for Economic Co-operation and Development (OECD). As a reference point, the table includes penetration figures for Switzerland, Japan, and the United Kingdom, which, as of 1999, had the highest penetration ratios among the developed financial systems; their ratios of 12.8, 11.2, and 13.4 percent, respectively, compare with an OECD average of 6.5 percent.

## Factors Affecting the Growth of Insurance

National insurance markets have evolved to meet each country's particular environment. The major characteristics of those environments that influ-

---

1. As noted by Skipper (2000), the Japanese figures are understated due to the failure to include premiums written by Kampo (in affiliation with the Japanese Post Office) and Zenkyoren (agricultural cooperative insurers).

**3**

ence the penetration of insurance are economic factors, demographic factors, social factors, and political factors.

## Economic Factors

Given that life insurance plays a major role in household savings, it is not surprising that the demand for life insurance is strongest in countries with high savings rates and high per capita income. Indeed, studies of the insurance industry consistently find that the income elasticity of insurance is greater than unity (that is, insurance premiums grow more quickly than national income).

Apart from income, economic factors such as inflation and market depth also affect the penetration of insurance. Increases in inflation usually are associated with increases in general uncertainty within the community. In times of high inflation and economic volatility, consumers tend to seek out shorter-term, more liquid investments. Since life insurance usually is perceived as a long-term, fixed commitment, high inflation usually is associated with a reduction in demand for insurance. This effect is exacerbated further by the perception that inflation erodes the value of nominally fixed life insurance policies.

Market depth also can influence the demand for insurance. In markets such as Korea where there are both a high propensity to save and a limited set of alternative savings vehicles, life insurance penetration can be surprisingly high.

## Demographic Factors

Changes in demographics appear to affect insurance consumption. It is widely recognized that the world's population is aging as a consequence of decreasing fertility rates and increasing longevity. Increasing life expectancy generally translates into an increase in demand for savings-based life insurance products and annuity income streams.

Another demographic factor that has influenced the demand for insurance is education. Casual empiricism suggests that a more educated population is better able to understand the need for insurance, both life and non-life.

Another demographic factor that appears to have influenced the demand for insurance is household structure. Western societies are dominated by nuclear families, consisting of husband, wife, and dependent children. In more agrarian societies and in those of many emerging markets, the dominant family structure is the extended family, in which grandparents and sometimes other relatives live and work together. To the extent that extended families provide shelter and comfort for the elderly, they reduce the need for retirement savings and thereby the demand for life insurance.

Finally, urbanization and industrialization lead to specialization within the workforce. Specialization increases vulnerability to changes in tastes, changes in technology, and changes in economic circumstances. This increase in vulnerability to the adverse consequences of lost income, health, and property tends to increase the demand for insurance.

## Social Factors

Cultural factors can play an important role in determining the level of insurance penetration. In many countries, especially in Asia, life insurance products are purchased primarily as savings instruments. Thus countries with a high propensity to save tend to have a higher insurance penetration. In some cultures, social standards have influenced insurance penetration. For example, in Korea, it is considered impolite to refuse an offer from close friends or relatives. Since insurance is usually sold on a person-to-person basis, many policies are sold in Korea, only to lapse shortly thereafter.

In other cultures, social standards work against the growth of insurance. For example, in many Muslim countries, especially in Asia, traditional insurance is considered to be inconsistent with religious beliefs. In some countries, the products are adjusted to better meet these beliefs.

## Political Factors

The most obvious way in which governments influence the growth of insurance is through tax policy. Countries, such as Korea and South Africa, that give substantial tax concessions to life insurance tend to have better-developed insurance markets. The role of tax concessions and other incentives as a means of promoting the growth of financial institutions is addressed further in chapter 7.

Governments also can influence the growth of insurance in a variety of other ways. Of these, the most fundamental is direct government provision of insurance. As noted in chapter 1, governments have long been providers of social insurance. In many countries, governments also have become actively involved in the provision of market insurance. The motives for public provision of market insurance vary from country to country, including

- Nationalism
- Public ownership of economic resources (as is the case in command economies)
- An intention to extend social insurance by providing affordable insurance across a wide range of events
- Infant industry situations.

The issue of public involvement in the provision of financial services is taken up further in chapter 7.

Political stability also can influence the demand for insurance. Since life insurance involves long time horizons, political and economic stability is conducive to a strong insurance industry. Unstable political environments depress the demand for insurance (especially from local insurance companies) because individuals tend to lose confidence in the ability of insurers to meet their promises.

Governments also determine the competitive environment in which the industry works. Possibly the single most important competitive issue facing governments in the area of insurance is whether to allow foreign competition into the domestic market. Some view foreign competition as a positive factor for growth and efficiency, to the extent that it is a source of both capital and expertise for local markets and a means of diversifying risk as broadly as possible. Alternatively, some view it as a negative factor for growth to the extent that financially strong foreign insurers are able to "cherry pick" the best risks, thereby weakening and even impeding the growth of the local industry. The case for foreign competition is taken up further in chapter 7.

Governments also can have an indirect influence over the growth of the insurance industry through their provision of alternative sources of long-term savings. A generous public pension scheme can be a disincentive to the growth of the contractual savings component of life insurance. On the converse side, it has been argued that one of the reasons that the German life insurance industry has grown as strongly as it has is the widely held perception that the public pension scheme will be unable to meet its promises.

Finally, the regulatory system that the government institutes can be a critical factor in developing a safe, but competitive, industry.

## The Contribution of Insurance to Economic Growth

It is argued in chapter 1 that financial development generally is synergistic with economic development. This section considers in greater detail the ways in which insurance contributes to this process.

At the most basic level, insurance promotes financial stability among households and firms. The essence of insurance is that the insured, who is financially least able to withstand the vicissitudes of fortune, transfers those risks to an entity better able to withstand risks because of its size and ability to pool risks. In this way, insurance enables risk to be managed efficiently within the community. Without insurance, individuals and families would face a greater prospect of becoming financially destitute in the face of adverse outcomes from particular events. Without insurance, the rate of business failure would be greater, with consequent losses to other businesses, employees, and tax revenues. The stability provided by insurance encourages individuals and firms to specialize, to create wealth, and to absorb only those risks that they can reasonably withstand.

A second important way in which insurance supports economic growth is through its capacity to mobilize savings. Studies have show that, on average, countries that save more tend to grow quicker. Life insurers are an effective conduit for mobilizing savings from the household sector and channeling them to the corporate sector. In the process, insurers provide divisibility, store of value, and risk-pooling services. The long-term nature of life insurance liabilities is conducive to capital formation. The fact that life insurers are typically large and specialized in project, information, and investment analysis is also conducive to efficient capital formation.

A third way in which a strong insurance industry can assist economic growth is by relieving pressure on the government's budget. This occurs to the extent that private insurance reduces the reliance on government social security programs. Life insurance, in particular, is a potential substitute for public pensions. Studies have confirmed that greater private expenditure on life insurance is associated with a reduction in government expenditure on social insurance programs. This issue is addressed further in the section on contractual savings institutions.

A fourth way in which insurance complements economic growth is through its impact on trade and commerce. Insurance underpins much of the world's trade, commerce, and entrepreneurial activity. Many goods are transported great distances between the buyer and seller. Insurance to

**3**

cover the potential for damage during transit acts to facilitate such exchanges. Insurance is also a precondition for engaging in certain activities. Loans secured by equipment and property usually are only extended subject to adequate insurance of the collateral items. Similarly, venture capitalists often require insurance of the lives of key personnel before they will undertake risky investments that rely heavily on the ideas or inventions of those individuals.

Finally, insurance companies can assist the community in mitigating risk. Insurers have an incentive to minimize risks to which they are exposed. Their scale and exposures mean that they are well positioned to analyze loss-causing events and to promote risk mitigation activities. These include programs such as fire prevention education, occupational health and safety education, industrial loss prevention, theft awareness programs, and incentives for insured parties to reduce risk through safety precautions. Society as a whole can benefit from these risk mitigation programs and activities.

## Regulating Insurance Companies

The regulatory framework developed in chapter 2 can be used to assess the regulatory style and intensity for insurance companies.

### The Appropriate Form of Regulation

Like all financial institutions, insurance companies warrant regulation for market failure associated with competition and market integrity. Life insurance companies, in particular, are often very large international companies with considerable market power in dealing with retail customers. The scope for miss-selling insurance products has been an issue for market conduct regulators in both emerging and developed financial systems.

Beyond these basic regulatory needs, there is a strong case that insurance companies also face market failure associated with asymmetric information due to the complexity of insurers and insurance products.

Identifying an asymmetric information problem is a necessary, but not a sufficient, condition for justifying prudential regulation. The case for prudential regulation requires that the insurer's promises rank highly on all three of the following conditions:

- They are onerous for the insurer to honor.
- It is difficult for the insured to assess the likelihood that the insurer will meet its promises.
- The failure of an insurer to honor its promises will occasion significant hardship for retail customers or for society more generally.

There can be little argument that the insurance promise is onerous for the insurer to honor. A life insurance policy, for example, is a promise to pay a defined benefit in the event of the death of the insured. Although the insurance company may be able to make sound estimates of the probability of death of any individual or group of individuals, it cannot control the event of death. Similarly, a general insurer is exposed to making defined payments based on uncertain events over which the insurer has no control. The tight specification of the triggering events and the fact that the insurer is unable to influence the occurrence of the events make insurance promises among the most onerous of financial promises.

Insurance promises are extremely difficult to assess. The size and complexity of insurance companies, both life and non-life, is such that the average retail customer cannot reasonably be expected to assess the risks involved or the ability of the insurer to honor its promises. Insurers (both life and non-life) base their pricing on statistical probabilities of the occurrence of particular events. Any number of events can change these probabilities significantly over time, in favor of either the insured or the insurer (for example, flood, disease, medical breakthroughs, and so on). The difficulty of assessing insurance promises is increased further in the case of long-tailed risks (such as occur, for example, in life insurance and some liability insurance). In these cases, the insured may be required to pay premiums for many years before a claim is made, thus creating a significant timing mismatch between the cash flows of the two parties.

Finally, failure of an insurer to meet its promises can cause significant hardship. In the case of general insurance, it can be argued that insurance promises are special in that, by their very nature, they transfer risk from those in the community least able to assess it or to bear the consequences of adverse outcomes to those who are professionally and financially able to

3

do so. In the case of life insurance, policies often are motivated by a desire to insure those, such as spouses and children, who may be left financially devastated by the death of the main income earner. It is significant that the insured party pays for all of these risk transfers.

The fact that insurance promises rank highly on all three of the criteria for prudential regulation explains why most countries include them within the prudential net. However, the case for prudential regulation of insurance arises from the risk-pooling function that it performs, not from its role as a contractual savings institution. Although the contractual savings role is important, the nature of the promises involved is much weaker than that of those involved in risk pooling. This point is taken up further in the section on contractual savings institutions.

Although it is generally agreed that insurance is characterized by market failures in the areas of competition, market conduct, and asymmetric information, few would argue that insurance companies provide a systemic threat. It certainly is true that the failure of an insurance company could cause some disruption to markets if it were sufficiently large. This prospect, however, is probably no worse than that which would occur in the event of the failure of a very large manufacturer. Although the impact on individual policyholders could be devastating, the impact should be confined largely to those affected directly. Insurers are not characterized by the highly liquid liabilities that confront deposit takers. Even though insurers may rely on new premiums to generate profits, the loss of new premiums in the event of market concerns is unlikely to cause the failure of an otherwise sound insurer. Nor is it likely to cause the failure of other sound insurers through association. The normal course of closure for a distressed insurer is either through merging with another company or through winding its book down over a defined period of time, commensurate with the life of the policies involved.

As is the case in other areas where prudential regulation is warranted, the objective of insurance regulation should not be to remove risk completely—insurance is, after all, fundamentally about managing risk—or to shift risk inadvertently from the insurer to the government. Most prudential regulators work under the principle that the primary responsibility for prudence rests with the boards and management of the companies involved. The role of the regulator is to work with the industry to promote sound business practices and to protect consumers of insurance products from undue risk.

## Regulatory Tools and Techniques

Insurance regulators worldwide have traditionally relied on six main regulatory tools:

- Entry requirements
- Solvency (capital requirements)
- Balance sheet restrictions
- Restrictions on associations with other financial institutions
- Accountability requirements
- Governance requirements.

In broad terms, this set of tools is consistent with the framework of chapter 2. The extent to which insurance regulators around the world focus on market conduct issues, such as disclosure and selling practices, depends primarily on whether the regulator has delegated responsibility for market conduct regulation as part of its prudential responsibilities or whether those responsibilities lie with a separate market conduct regulator.

International cooperation among insurance regulators was advanced greatly by the formation, in 1994, of the International Association of Insurance Supervisors (IAIS). Since its formation, the IAIS has issued a number of documents aimed at standardizing the international approach to insurance regulation and to enhancing international cooperation. These papers include the following:

- Insurance Core Principles
- Insurance Supervisory Principles
- Guidance on Insurance Regulation and Supervision for Emerging Market Economies
- Insurance Concordat
- Model Memorandum of Understanding
- Supervisory Standard on Licensing
- Supervisory Standard on On-site Inspections
- Supervisory Standard on Derivatives.

Of these, the key document is the first, which updated and replaced the second. The core principles, which follow in broad style the core principles of the international banking regulators, reflect an attempt to harmonize regulatory approaches and methods around the world. Although the principles are couched in very general terms at this early stage, they provide some useful guidance as to internationally accepted best practice.

### Organization of an Insurance Regulator

The IAIS principles require that the regulator be organized so as to be effective. This means that it should be independent and accountable, have adequate powers and skilled staff, and be transparent in its operations.

### Licensing (Entry Requirements) and Changes of Control

The IAIS principles on entry requirements include the following:

- All companies wishing to underwrite insurance in the domestic market should be licensed to do so.
- In granting a license, the regulator should assess the suitability of the owners, directors, and senior management and the soundness of the business plan, including its capital plan and projected solvency margins.
- The regulator should review any changes in the control of an insurance company and should establish clear requirements for changes of control.
- In permitting access to its domestic market, a regulator may choose to rely on supervisory work carried out by a regulator in another jurisdiction, provided the two regulatory jurisdictions are broadly equivalent.

The regulator should review changes of ownership and control and establish clear criteria that must be met when changes occur.

Implicit in these conditions (and made explicit elsewhere in the IAIS principles) is the requirement that the regulator have the legal power to issue a license and to withdraw a license once issued.

### Corporate Governance and Internal Controls

The size and complexity of insurance companies have led many regulators to impose standards on the corporate governance and internal controls of insurers. The IAIS principles suggest that regulators should set requirements with respect to the following:

- The roles and responsibilities of the board of directors
- The internal controls that boards of directors and management approve and apply internally (these should be open to review by the regulator)
- Prudential oversight of the insurer's operations by the board of directors
- Distinction between standards for companies incorporated locally and branches of companies incorporated in other jurisdictions.

In some jurisdictions, regulatory standards of corporate governance extend well beyond these basic requirements to deal with matters such as internal policies and procedures manuals, processes for the adoption of governance policies, requirements for the separation of duties, and so on.

*Prudential Standards (Solvency)*

Insurance companies, by the nature of their business, are exposed to risk. It is a widely agreed principle that capital in a financial institution should be available to meet unexpected losses.[2] This kind of capital is a necessary buffer to absorb discrepancies between anticipated and actual expenses and profits. Solvency is a measure of capital in that it measures the difference between the assets and liabilities of an insurer. The difference between solvency and accounting capital arises from certain restrictions that the regulator may put on the inclusion or exclusion of certain assets.[3] The two concepts are, however, essentially comparable.

The IAIS guidance on solvency is quite vague. It requires only that the minimum levels of capital should be clearly defined and should reflect the size, complexity, and business risks of the insurer. In practice, most insurance regulators impose a fixed minimum level of capital for licensing and some form of adjustable capital requirement according to the scale of the insurer's operations. These requirements vary greatly across jurisdictions.

---

2. This concept of the role of capital in a financial institution is quite distinct from the role of capital in a nonfinance company. In the latter, capital is viewed largely as a source of funding for business operations (see Matten 2000: vii).

3. For example, the regulator may exclude assets held in the form of investments in related companies or loans to the board or senior management or to parties related to them.

---

### Box 3.1. Solvency versus Risk-Based Capital Adequacy

Internationally, a distinction has been drawn between what can be loosely termed the European Union solvency approach and the North American risk-based approach to insurance regulation. The essential difference is that the solvency approach bases the institution's regulatory capital requirement on one or a combination of liability measures, while the risk-based approach uses a broader measure based on both asset and liability measures or, in its more sophisticated forms, on modeled measures of the company's risk profile. In practice, there are many variants of the two approaches, as well as hybrid regimes, with the result that the differences are often poorly understood.

Underlying both approaches is the implicit philosophy that expected losses due to claims are a normal cost of the insurance business and should be covered by adequate provisions. Risk relates to unexpected losses arising from divergences between expected and actual outcomes. Failure occurs when a divergence exceeds the institution's capacity to absorb it. The role of capital is to provide a buffer against unexpected losses. At issue is nothing more than how best to measure the minimum capital needed to reduce the risk of failure to an acceptable level. Although the two philosophies are identical, the differences in measurement methodology are nonetheless significant.

The solvency approach typically applies a "multiplier" to one or more of the following liability measures: net written premiums, net notional claims incurred, net policy liabilities (reserves in the case of life insurance and claims in the case of non-life insurance), and total sum at risk (total sum insured minus provisions). Multiples usually are different for life and non-life and vary according to the class of insurance (increasing for longer-tailed risks). The multiples may

be applied on a stand-alone basis or in combination. For example, the European Union directive imposes on non-life companies a solvency margin that is the greater of an amount calculated on net written premiums and an amount calculated on the basis of claims. The solvency calculation usually is supported by rules governing the valuation of liabilities and by rules restricting the eligibility of certain assets for inclusion in the measurement of capital.

The risk-based approach casts a wider net. It recognizes risk as arising not only from uncertainty in the valuation of liabilities (insurance risk) but also from uncertainty in the valuation of assets. The latter arises from fluctuations in asset values due to fluctuations in market prices and also due to changes in credit standing (including from default). In its less complex variants, the risk-based approach extends the solvency approach by simply adding capital requirements based on measures of asset risk (usually based on rules drawn from banking regulation). In its more complex variants, it also seeks to increase the range of risk grades on the liability side. In its most sophisticated form, this approach relies on internal models of unexpected risk built by the insurance companies themselves.

In practice, the regulator's choice between the two approaches comes down to the question of relevance. Although the risk-based approach is conceptually superior, its usefulness is critically dependent on the quality of the models used, the reliability of the data, and the presence of sufficient skilled staff in both the insurance company and the regulator. In contrast, although the solvency approach is relatively unsophisticated and may fail to detect problems in certain cases, it is relatively simple to understand and to apply.

---

The scalable requirement usually is related to premium income or outstanding claims liabilities. In this respect, insurance regulation is less advanced than banking regulation, where there is a more rigorous attempt to link capital requirements to the risks actually undertaken by the company in question.

Several countries, including the United States, Canada, Norway, and Australia have attempted to put in place a more comprehensive risk-based capital requirement (see box 3.1).

The measure of solvency relies heavily on the measurement of assets and liabilities. The IAIS principles recommend that standards be set with respect to both the assets and liabilities of insurers. In respect of liabilities, the guidelines suggest that the regulator should specify clearly what is to be included as a liability of the company. These include claims incurred but not yet paid, claims incurred but not yet reported, amounts owed to others, amounts in dispute, premiums received in advance, technical provisions set by actuaries, and the amount of credit to be allowed for amounts recoverable under reinsurance arrangements.

In respect of assets, the guidelines suggest that the regulator should set requirements that address diversification requirements, limits that may be imposed on assets held in certain classes (such as property), the safekeeping of assets, matching requirements for assets and liabilities (especially where long-tailed risks are involved), and the liquidity of assets.

The measure of solvency is affected not only by the range of assets and liabilities included but also by their method of valuation. Indeed, the measurement of liabilities associated with claims activity is possibly the single most important risk to an insurer's solvency. Liabilities arise with respect to outstanding claims (claims against existing policies that have yet to be filed) and future claims (claims against existing policies that have yet to occur, as of the time of valuation). Variations in the measurement of these liabilities can have a material impact on the measurement of the insurer's solvency.

The IAIS principles suggest that regulators should set standards for the valuation of these liabilities and for the resulting technical provisions. This is usually done in conjunction with the relevant accounting standards body for the country. Although most countries set such standards, practices vary according to whether or not the regulator allows discounting to take account of the time value of money in assessing future liabilities and the extent to which a prudential or conservative margin is added to the assessed liability to allow for measurement uncertainty.

In addition to setting valuation standards for liabilities, the IAIS principles require regulators to set standards, where appropriate, for the valuation of assets. Again, practices vary according to the allowance for discounting and also according to whether or not the regulator imposes full mark-to-market valuation.

*Other Principles*

In total there are 17 core principles. Beyond the key areas of licensing, governance, and solvency, the principles cover a wide range of secondary issues:

- The use of derivatives and other off-balance-sheet financial instruments (restrictions on their use, disclosure requirements, and establishment of internal controls)
- Reinsurance (review of provisions plus rules on the extent to which reinsurance can be included in valuing assets and liabilities)
- Market conduct (requirement to ensure that insurance companies act at all times with honesty, skill, care, fairness, and prudence)
- Financial reporting (establishment of the frequency and accounting requirements of reporting to the regulator)
- On-site inspections (the right to inspect and to receive information)
- Sanctions (the power to levy sanctions on companies that do not meet the prudential standards and to direct a company to cease practices that are unsafe)
- Cross-border operations (assurance that no insurance company that operates across international borders is able to escape proper regulation and that there is effective consultation between international regulators—this principle is expanded in a separate recommendation on coordination and cooperation)
- Confidentiality (subject to professional constraints of secrecy in respect of information obtained in the course of their regulatory activities).

Although the issue of associations is not addressed explicitly in the IAIS principles, it is common practice among insurance regulators around the world to restrict the business that can be done on an insurer's balance sheet to insurance-type business. The IAIS accepts that insurers may have a legitimate need to engage in derivatives and other off-balance-sheet business. Correspondingly, it suggests that regulators set requirements with respect to these activities, including restrictions on their use, disclosure as to the extent of off-balance-sheet positions, and internal controls to measure and monitor these positions. Beyond this type of business, regulators usually require activities other than insurance to be carried out either in subsidiaries or in separate companies under a nonoperating holding company structure.

## Specific IAIS Guidelines for Emerging Markets

The specific guidelines prepared by the IAIS for emerging market economies reflect its recognition of the unique challenges facing insurance industries in emerging markets. While recognizing the uniqueness of emerging market economies, the IAIS also recognizes that there is a wide range of experiences within this group and that implementation of its principles needs to be adapted to each situation.

The guidelines note that instability in the insurance industries of emerging markets has been due largely to a combination of unstable macroeconomic environments and lax management within the companies, many of which are state owned. In general, regulatory oversight has been equally lax and much in need of overhaul.

The IAIS offers the following guidance:

- Create the essential legal infrastructure for effective market functioning (in particular, there is a need in many countries to strengthen not only the insurance regulations but also the underlying accounting principles, commercial codes, and corporate laws)
- Create an insurance supervisory authority with adequate powers to license, apply prudential standards, and impose sanctions, skills, and funding (the regulator should be independent of the political authorities and the industry as well as accountable in the use of its powers and resources)
- Encourage self-regulatory mechanisms such as industry codes of conduct and professional accreditation bodies
- Promote market discipline through disclosure, competition, and good internal governance
- Separate insurance companies from other commercial and financial activities, insurance from reinsurance, and also life from non-life insurance activities (these are stronger restrictions than are usually permitted in developed markets)
- Control licensing of insurance companies, as well as their ongoing right to operate, through strict minimum capital requirements (undercapitalization is a common problem in emerging markets)

- Include on-site examination in ongoing supervision and legislate measurement and monitoring rules for the valuation of assets and liabilities
- Since emerging markets often suffer from limited investment opportunities and inadequate disclosure, pay particular attention to companies' procedures for assessing and managing risks and set standards with respect to diversification, asset valuation matching, and so on
- Monitor reinsurance closely and avoid inhibiting domestic access to foreign high-quality reinsurers (reinsurance is an important means of assessing foreign capital support but also has been abused in emerging markets as a means of transferring cash abroad)
- In the early stages of market development, have the regulator approve both premium rates and insurance products (this practice would need to be monitored closely with a view to returning at least premium determination to the market as soon as the market becomes sufficiently mature)

### Surveillance

The IAIS principles make it clear that sound prudential supervision of insurers requires both off-site monitoring and on-site inspection. With respect to off-site monitoring, the guidelines suggest that a process should be established for the following:

- Setting the scope and frequency of reporting by insurance companies
- Setting the accounting requirements for these reports
- Ensuring that external audits are of an acceptable standard.

With respect to on-site monitoring, the principles suggest that regulators should undertake the following:

- Carry out regular inspections to review the company's business and inspect the books, records, and accounts
- Have the power to request and receive any information that it believes is necessary from companies licensed in its jurisdiction.

# Chapter 4

# Contractual Savings Institutions

4

*Contractual savings institutions are the primary means for mobilizing savings and allocating resources to productive uses in most economies and therefore are critical to the process of capital formation. Nonbank contractual savings institutions can be divided into three main groups: life insurers, mutual funds (or investment companies), and pension funds. Chapter 3 deals with life insurance companies. This chapter deals with mutual funds and pension funds.*

## The Market for Contractual Savings

The nonbank, noninsurance contractual savings industry involves collective investments, whereby funds from a number of entities and investors are pooled and managed by a professional investment manager on their behalf. The defining characteristic of this industry is that investors themselves bear the risk of loss associated with movements in market prices and default of borrowers. That is, the professional manager acts in a fiduciary role, managing the investments in return for a fee, rather than taking a principal position in the transaction.

Collective investments can be distinguished by the nature of the investments they make or by the nature of the funds being invested. The generic collective investment vehicle is a mutual fund, in which the funds invested have no specified purpose, and therefore no special constraints on either the form or management of the funds are involved beyond those specified under general trust law. Subject only to the terms of the deed or prospectus of their trust, mutual funds invest in a wide range of risk assets from cash to derivative products.

The role of "trust" in these vehicles is fundamental. Originally, a trust involved a relationship of trust between the settlor of the trust and the trustee for the benefit of third parties who, for whatever reason, were incapable of controlling their own investments. The trustee, accepting that responsibility, was bound by the terms of the trust deed to act in the interests of the third parties. Historically, trustees acted primarily for deceased estates. In most countries, any company can act as a corporate or private trustee (for example, to manage a family trust), while public trustees require a license.

Over time, the traditional basis for trusts has been overtaken by their role in collective investments and also their role in investing funds for private clients. Trust banks in many countries, for example, invest deposited funds of wealthy individuals into high-yielding assets. Trustee companies (or simply trust companies) in many other countries oversee the compliance of fiduciary responsibilities in publicly offered collective investments.

The relationship between the trustee and the investment manager is not always clear. In some countries, trustee companies act purely in an oversight role, with independent fund managers taking responsibility for investment decisions. In others, the roles of investment manager and trustee are combined into a single responsible entity. In some countries, where trustee companies have been separated from the management of collective investments, they still retain the right to manage trust funds deposited directly with them (for example, from deceased estates), and some also are allowed to pool trust funds and offer participation to the public through a prospectus.

As a result of these different models, there is a wide range of experiences with the growth of the trusts themselves (the quantum of funds under management), investment managers (banks, investment banks, specialized nonbank fund managers), and trustee companies. Where trusteeship and investment management are separated by law, the trustee sector tends to be relatively small. Where this separation is not imposed, trustee companies are sometimes the dominant form of investment manager for collective investments.

Despite the conceptual distinction among mutual funds, trustee companies, and pension funds, according to the nature of the funds being invested, it is often difficult in practice to distinguish the groups. In many countries, the same institutions offer both mutual funds and pension funds. In others, pension funds often act as the point of pooling, but then they invest the pension contributions into a range of mutual funds. Similarly, where a trustee company prefers not to support a large investment staff, it can invest the pooled resources from estates into existing mutual funds. Trustee companies also often act as trustees for mutual funds (where a trust structure governs operation of the mutual fund).

In absolute terms, contractual savings institutions are most prominent in the United States, where their growth over the past few decades has been quite spectacular (see table 4.1). According to Kumar (1997: 1) and the OECD (2000: 20–24)[1], contractual savings assets in the United States grew from $118 billion in 1960 to a staggering $6.6 trillion in 1990 and since then the figure increased to $15.4 trillion in 1997. Of the institutional groups comprising this sector, pension funds experienced the most spectacular asset growth in absolute terms, growing from $58 billion in 1960 to $2.5 trillion in 1990 and to $6.1 trillion in 1997. Assets of mutual funds (including both open-end and closed-end funds) increased between 1960 and 1997 from $17 billion to $4.2 trillion. Although life insurance assets grew significantly, from $43 billion to $3.4 trillion over the same period, their share of total institutional assets declined from around 36 to 22 percent.

Growth of the contractual savings sector, particularly in the past decade, was equally impressive in other developed financial systems. In emerging markets, while the growth was much more subdued in absolute terms, some of the increases were spectacular in percentage terms, given the almost nonexistent bases in many countries a decade ago.

1. Kumar (1997: 1) figures for 1960 and OECD (2000: 20–24) figures for all other years.

**Table 4.1. Financial Assets of Institutional Investors in Select Countries, 1990 and 1997** (in billions of US dollars)

| Country | Total institutional investors | | Insurance companies | | Pension funds | | Investment companies | | Other institutional investors | |
|---|---|---|---|---|---|---|---|---|---|---|
| | 1990 | 1997 | 1990 | 1997 | 1990 | 1997 | 1990 | 1997 | 1990 | 1997 |
| Australia | 145.6 | 384.3 | 72.9 | 138.3 | 50.3 | 183.1 | 18.8 | 50.4 | 3.7 | 12.6 |
| Austria | 38.8 | 93.6 | 24.5 | 45.2 | — | 3.4 | 14.3 | 44.9 | — | — |
| Belgium | 87.0 | 180.6 | 55.5 | 80.4 | 3.9 | 11.6 | 25.6 | 82.2 | 2.1 | 6.4 |
| Canada | 332.7 | 616.8 | 137.7 | 179.7 | 164.6 | 263.0 | 30.4 | 174.1 | — | — |
| Czech Republic | — | 8.4 | — | 3.3 | — | 0.6 | — | 1.3 | — | 3.3 |
| Denmark | 74.2 | 124.5 | 51.1 | 81.1 | 19.5 | 30.4 | 3.7 | 13.1 | — | — |
| Finland | 44.7 | 72.7 | 8.7 | 16.7 | — | — | 0.1 | 3.1 | 35.9 | 52.9 |
| France | 655.7 | 1,329.2 | 262.6 | 764.7 | — | — | 393.1 | 564.5 | — | — |
| Germany | 599.0 | 1,201.9 | 400.3 | 666.1 | 51.5 | 60.6 | 147.2 | 475.2 | — | — |
| Hungary | — | 3.2 | — | 1.7 | — | 0.3 | — | 1.2 | — | — |
| Iceland | 2.8 | 6.3 | 0.3 | 0.7 | 2.3 | 4.9 | 0.3 | 0.7 | — | — |
| Italy | 146.6 | 607.3 | 66.2 | 150.4 | 38.5 | 34.4 | 41.9 | 209.3 | — | 213.3 |
| Japan | 2,427.9 | 3,205.1 | 1,074.3 | 1,594.5 | — | 611.7 | 390.0 | 665.3 | 963.5 | 333.7 |
| Korea | 121.8 | 164.5 | 47.8 | 70.2 | 7.9 | 7.9 | 66.1 | 86.3 | — | — |
| Luxembourg | 94.1 | 442.1 | — | 13.9 | — | — | 94.1 | 428.1 | — | — |
| Mexico | 23.1 | 19.2 | 2.7 | 5.9 | — | 0.8 | 20.4 | 12.6 | — | — |
| Netherlands | 378.3 | 666.8 | 116.5 | 221.3 | 229.7 | 368.2 | 32.1 | 69.0 | — | 8.3 |
| Norway | 41.5 | 69.9 | 33.8 | 46.5 | 5.1 | 10.1 | 2.6 | 13.4 | — | — |
| Poland | — | 3.5 | — | 3.0 | — | — | — | 0.5 | — | — |
| Portugal | 6.2 | 54.2 | 1.9 | 21.8 | 1.1 | 10.5 | 3.0 | 21.4 | 0.2 | 0.5 |
| Spain | 64.5 | 290.7 | 48.7 | 111.5 | 14.4 | 10.0 | 15.9 | 179.2 | — | — |
| Sweden | 196.8 | 316.7 | 79.5 | 149.5 | 3.8 | 6.0 | 38.8 | 76.7 | 74.7 | 84.5 |
| Switzerland | 271.7 | 236.8 | 115.5 | 183.6 | 137.7 | — | 18.6 | 53.2 | — | — |
| Turkey | 0.9 | 2.3 | 0.4 | 1.2 | — | — | 0.5 | 1.0 | — | — |
| United Kingdom | 1,116.8 | 2,624.4 | 454.4 | 1,213.5 | 536.6 | 1,066.6 | 125.8 | 344.3 | — | — |
| United States | 6,630.0 | 15,432.6 | 1,884.9 | 3,355.5 | 2,533.1 | 6,059.2 | 1,154.6 | 4,187.5 | 1,215.4 | 2,184.1 |

— Not available

Source: OECD (2000: 20–24).

**Figure 4.1. Financial Assets of Contractual Savings Institutions, 1998**

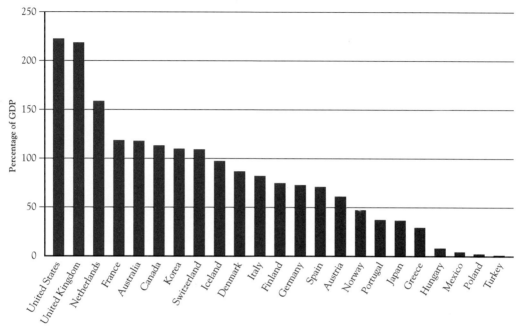

*Source:* OECD (2000: table S.6, p. 26).

The growth of mutual funds has been closely associated with the development of securitization, whereby liquidity and divisibility are added to otherwise illiquid and large-scale assets. This process is described more fully in chapter 6 in respect of mortgages. Mutual fund growth has also been boosted by the growth of pension funds since, in addition to investing directly in capital market instruments, pension funds in many countries invest their assets back into the mutual fund industry as a convenient way of building a diversified portfolio of assets.

Total assets of contractual savings institutions, including both pension funds and mutual funds, are shown relative to gross domestic product (GDP) for a range of countries in figure 4.1.

## A Note on Pension Fund Growth

The relationship between the assets and liabilities of pension funds is complicated by the presence of public schemes, as well as by the range of pension fund characteristics. National pension schemes are differentiated by the following:

- The extent to which provision is provided publicly
- The extent to which private contributions are mandatory
- The extent to which the pension liabilities are funded by investments
- Whether the pensions are defined benefit or defined contribution
- Who retains responsibility for the management of the fund.

Pension provision in most countries is a combination of public provision, publicly mandated private retirement savings, and voluntary private retirement savings.

Public provision has a long history. Indeed, until recently, providing for the retired generation was widely regarded as a responsibility of governments. However, the aging of populations worldwide and the attendant explosion of public pension liabilities have forced some rethinking of the mix of provision between public and private.

The explosion of public pension liabilities has been exacerbated by the tendency for public provision to be defined benefit in nature and largely unfunded. Defined benefit schemes link pension entitlements to a combination of wages during employment and term of service. In contrast, defined contribution schemes link pension entitlements to the amount contributed and to the return on the scheme's investments over the term of the contributions. In the case of defined contributions, workers assume the performance risk of the fund unless its performance is guaranteed directly by government or through a guarantee fund. In the case of defined benefits, the employer (or an insurance company, where the fund is offered as a life policy or a fixed annuity) assumes the performance risk of the fund, while the worker assumes the solvency risk of the employer (or insurance company) to the extent that the fund proves inadequate. Defined benefit schemes are linked more directly to replacement of earnings during retirement, while defined contribution schemes are more like general investments.

In principle, either of these entitlement structures can be funded or unfunded. In funded schemes, the liabilities are fully backed by investments. In unfunded (pay-as-you-go) schemes, resources are transferred directly from the currently working generations to the retired generation through the government's budgetary process. In practice, most public pension schemes throughout the world are described more correctly as partly funded rather than as unfunded. For the purposes of this discussion, unfunded and partly funded schemes share the same characteristics, and both are referred to as unfunded. Since, by definition, unfunded schemes do not (fully) support the pension liabilities with actual investments, they are only appropriate for defined benefit structures, where

**Figure 4.2. Implicit Public Pension Debt in OECD Countries, 1994**

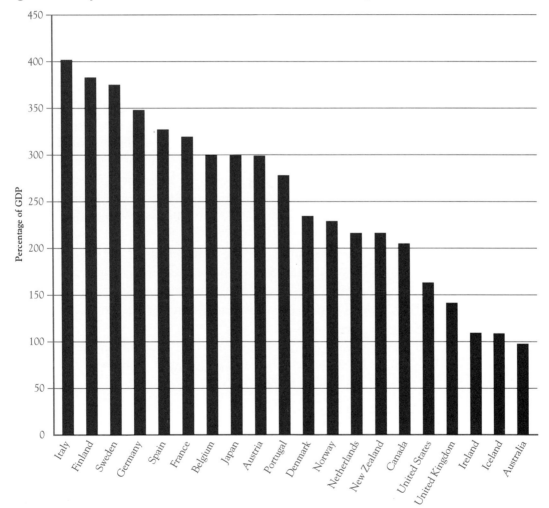

*Source:* OECD (1996: table 2.2, p. 36).

defined benefits include the possibility of a single universal rate of pension.[2] Although many governments have identified particular taxes with pension contributions, few have actually allocated those funds to investments, preferring instead to fund pension entitlements largely from current revenue. Thus public pension schemes generally have tended to be defined benefit and unfunded.[3]

The extent of the implicit unfunded liability of these schemes relative to GDP is shown in figure 4.2 for the Organisation for Economic Co-operation and Development (OECD) countries. The liabilities are calculated by estimating the net present value of pension expenditure. Among the countries with the largest implicit liabilities, the pension debt is typically several times larger than the level of government debt on issue.

Where countries have elected to shift some of the burden of pension provision to the private sector, most have mandated retirement savings in one way or another. Among mandated pension schemes, the industry is further divided according to where responsibility for the management of the assets resides. Employer-based or industry-based schemes reflect the origins of many private pension schemes as employer-sponsored benefits designed to attract and retain staff. The management of these funds typically resides with either the employer or an investment committee composed of representatives of both the employees and the employer (or union, where the scheme is the result of organized bargaining between employers and unions).

In some countries, the government has retained management of the assets of mandatory pension funds. The best examples of publicly managed, fully funded pension schemes are in Asian countries such as Singapore and Malaysia, where national provident funds are among the most important institutional investors in the country.

Pension coverage throughout the world is significant and growing. Palacios and Pallarés-Miralles (2000) estimate that some 800 million

---

2. Unfunded schemes are difficult to conceptualize for defined contribution schemes since the payoff from defined contributions is supposed to depend on the fund's performance. However, as Vittas (1998) notes, several countries, including Sweden, recently have introduced public, unfunded defined contribution schemes based on notional accounts and notional rates of return.

3. According to Iglesias and Palacios (2000), fully funded defined benefit plans run by national governments simply do not exist in practice.

workers (about 30 percent of the total workforce) are covered by either a publicly provided or a publicly mandated pension scheme. Coverage is related largely to per capita income, with countries having higher per capita income generally providing a high rate of coverage. Of this coverage, about half is in the form of public, unfunded, or partly funded defined benefit schemes. About another third is in the form of publicly managed, funded defined benefit schemes. The balance consists mostly of

**Figure 4.3. Private Pension Assets in OECD Countries, 1998**

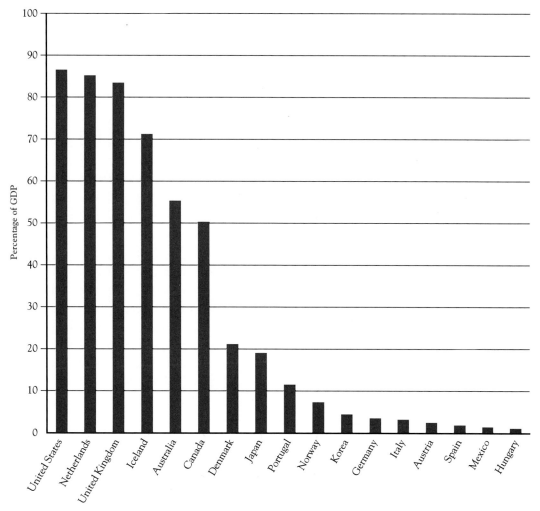

*Source:* OECD (2000: table S.8, p. 28).

defined contribution schemes, managed either publicly or privately, and various combinations of defined benefit and defined contribution schemes. Iglesias and Palacios (2000) estimate that the total stock of pension assets of all types has grown to the point where it is now as much as 50 percent of world GDP. Figure 4.3 shows the assets of private pension funds (mandated and voluntary) relative to GDP for a range of OECD countries.

In recent decades, several distinct trends have emerged in pension fund provision around the world:

- A trend toward pension reform that has included an increase in pension provision, especially among emerging market countries
- An increase in funding levels of public pension schemes
- A shift away from defined benefit schemes in favor of defined contribution schemes
- A shift toward privatizing the management of centralized public schemes
- A trend toward giving individuals greater choice and control over the management of their pension assets, either through self-managed funds or through individual choice of public-offer pension trusts, encouraged by the growth of voluntary private pension assets and the advantages to individuals of consolidating their investments from different employers and different schemes.

As a result of these reforms and the growing trend toward private pension provision, the pension literature has begun to define national pension systems by their particular combination of three pillars. In this framework, the first pillar refers to a government-funded public pension scheme that is directed toward alleviating poverty in old age for those members of society who, for whatever reason, retire with insufficient assets. The second pillar refers to workers' mandatory contributions to pension funds, which transform these contributions into retirement incomes. The third pillar refers to voluntary savings for retirement over and above the savings mandated by the second pillar.

## Factors Affecting the Growth of Contractual Savings Institutions

In general, the factors listed in chapter 3 as influencing the growth of life insurance companies are equally relevant to other contractual savings institutions. As is the case with life insurance, the dominant factors influencing the growth of these institutions are income and wealth. To an extent, this argument is circular. On the one hand, low income and low wealth lead to low savings, and low savings means that there is little need for contractual savings institutions. On the other hand, the absence of a well-developed group of contractual savings institutions itself may inhibit the rate of savings by reducing the diversity of investment opportunities. It is nonetheless a fact that the poorest countries generate very little private sector savings and therefore have little need for institutions whose main role is to broaden the range of savings instruments. As these countries begin to grow, savings often increase sharply, but they often are retained in bank deposits and other highly liquid forms. In many cases, banks are the only institutions available in rural and semirural areas, and the limited demand for a fuller range of investment instruments does not justify the development of more specialized contractual savings institutions and products.

The question for emerging markets is at what point of growth of income and wealth should the emergence of specialized contractual savings institutions be expected and even encouraged.

In addition to the general factors common to life insurance, other factors such as the provision of publicly funded social security and regulatory considerations can influence the emergence and growth of contractual savings institutions.

### Government Provision of Social Security

The nature and extent of public involvement in pension provision can have significant implications for the extent to which pension assets are accumulated and the extent to which those assets contribute to economic growth and development.

Publicly provided social security is essentially socialized savings. For many individuals, especially those with lower levels of income, the existence of a public pension scheme obviates the need for any further private retirement savings. The existence of a public scheme therefore can be a sub-

**4**

stantial impediment to private pension savings. This impediment can be accentuated where the public scheme imposes qualifying conditions. In a growing number of countries, for example, public pensions are regarded as a safety net rather than as an entitlement, playing as much a distributional role as a savings role. To qualify for a public pension, individuals are subjected to a means test based on income or wealth. Under these circumstances, the implicit tax associated with the means test greatly reduces the incentive for lower-income earners to save privately for retirement.

The extent to which public social security obligations crowd out the accumulation of private pensions in OECD countries is evident in figure 4.4. The figure shows private pension assets and implicit public pension liabilities in a range of countries, both as ratios to GDP. In general, the greater is the public liability, the smaller are the private pension assets.

Since public provision of retirement incomes crowds out private provision, the nature of the public scheme is of central importance in determining the impact of pension growth on asset accumulation. Where the public scheme is unfunded, the scheme is likely to replace private savings with current-period government transfers. Not only does this reduce the need for a contractual savings sector, but it also reduces the demand for investment assets, thereby reducing the availability of resources for development of domestic debt and equity markets.

One way of resolving this problem has been for governments to fund part of their public pension obligations. In some cases, governments have privatized the investment function (for example, by contracting it out to a range of private sector fund managers). To the extent that this leads to an efficient allocation of resources in capital markets, private management of a partly funded public pension scheme can provide a significant boost to national savings and economic efficiency.

Some governments, however, have not privatized the investment function, notwithstanding their commitment to full funding, and have taken on the investment management role of contractual savings institutions themselves. Apart from the likely absence of appropriate incentives for efficient management of the resources involved, there is a temptation for government-run pension funds to invest the community's resources back into the government's own debt instruments (indeed, in many countries they are required to do so by regulation).

Mandating private pension investment is another way of resolving the disincentive to accumulate assets that arises from an existing unfunded pub-

**Figure 4.4. Public Pension Debt and Private Pension Assets as a Percentage of GDP in OECD Countries, 1994**

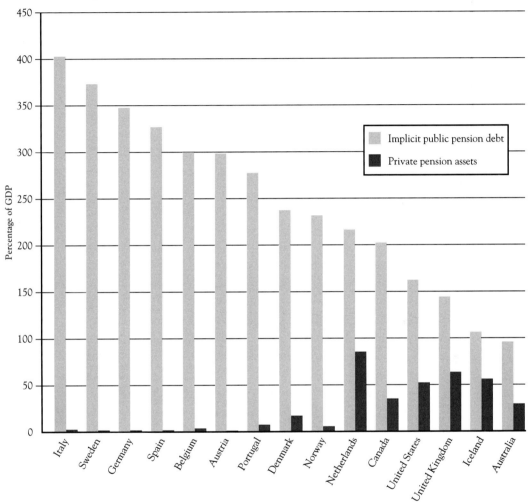

*Source:* OECD (1996: table 2.2, p. 36; 2000: table 5.8, p. 28).

lic scheme. The case for mandatory pension savings is usually based on the argument that individuals suffer a form of myopia when it comes to retirement. To many workers, retirement is too far away to concern them during their most productive earning years; in economic terms, their intertemporal rate of time preference is argued to be too high for them to make rational judgments about retirement savings. Whatever the merits of this case, the natural impediment of an existing public pension scheme may well be sufficient to inhibit substantial accumulation of private pension assets without a public mandate. In practice, there is little difference between a mandatory private pension scheme and a public, fully funded scheme that has been contracted out to the private sector for management.

## Taxation Incentives

Many countries provide tax advantages to savings conducted through life insurance companies or through approved pension funds. The desirability of this incentive is a matter for each country to assess in the context of its long-term objectives and current budgetary constraints. The case for tax incentives usually rests on whether or not there is a need to stimulate national savings; in emerging market situations, this will usually be a strong case. One situation in which tax incentives can be justified readily on equity grounds is where a mandatory private pension scheme is introduced explicitly as a means of phasing out an unfunded public pension scheme. In this case, the current generation is required to fund not only its own retirement income but also that of the existing generation of retirees.

Tax laws also can influence the structure of the contractual savings sector. For example, in many countries, trusts are taxed in the hands of the recipients after distribution, while companies are taxed prior to distribution. Unless the ultimate recipients of the income have the right to offset taxes paid by companies through an imputation system, tax rules such as these create an incentive to structure contractual savings vehicles as trusts rather than as companies.

## Regulation

The contractual savings industry relies critically on a high level of trust. Since savings are often tied up for long periods of time, it is fundamental that individual investors have confidence that their savings are secure. Confidence in the security of these institutions is greatly enhanced by sound regulatory foundations. Scandals, such as that which occurred in the Philippines in the early 1970s, can lead to both a loss of confidence by investors as well as an unwillingness by regulators to issue new licenses.

Repressive regulation can inhibit the development of contractual savings institutions, especially where it imposes balance sheet restrictions that constrain risk management and earnings capacity. Balance sheet restrictions, often imposed in the name of safety, can be particularly repressive in terms of inhibiting the growth of these institutions. For example, pension funds and insurance companies in many continental European countries historically have been restricted by regulation to invest predominantly in debt-type promises. Similarly, until the 1980s, Australian insurance companies were a captive market for government bonds. In some developing countries where investment restrictions are less debt-oriented, the scope for wider investment is still constrained by regulations limiting investment in foreign assets for balance-of-payments reasons.

Among the emerging markets, Korea, India, Thailand, and Malaysia encouraged the development of mutual funds by providing a supportive, largely deregulated regulatory framework. However, problems with the integrity of the industry emerged during the Asian crisis in 1997 and 1998, occasioning a rethinking of the foundations of the approach to regulation.

## The Contribution of Contractual Savings Institutions to Economic Growth

Contractual savings institutions contribute to economic growth and development through their impact on savings and resource allocation, their addition to the depth and liquidity of capital markets, and the social benefits of providing security in old age.

### Impact on Savings and Resource Allocation

Contractual savings institutions help nations to mobilize savings by providing a greater and more attractive range of investment opportunities. By adding divisibility to large-scale assets, they enable investors to create better-diversified portfolios. In the ordinary course of investing, individuals are unable to purchase ownership rights in large-scale assets such as commercial real estate and many foreign assets. It also is difficult for small-scale investors to acquire well-diversified portfolios of equities or to hedge risks with derivative products. By pooling the resources of many small investors, mutual funds are able to offer each participant a better-diversified portfolio and a more-efficient use of risk management tools than would otherwise be possible.

By adding liquidity to their holdings, through either a buy-back facility or through stock market listing of the funds' shares, mutual funds also offer investors a much greater level of flexibility in managing their affairs. The net effect of these divisibility and liquidity services should be to stimulate total savings as well as to do a better job of matching investor preferences with the range of investment possibilities. By extending the availability of different investments both geographically and across income groups, contractual savings institutions help not only to mobilize savings but also to ensure their efficient allocation to the most productive uses.

The impact of pension reform on national savings and economic growth can be quite dramatic. The impact is likely to be greatest where the reforms replace an overburdened, unfunded public pension scheme with a funded mandatory private pension scheme.

Growth effects from any source are notoriously difficult to measure. The available evidence from studies of pension schemes nonetheless suggests that they are positive and possibly substantial. In simulation studies for Australia, Bateman and Piggott (1998) find that the introduction of mandatory private pensions would increase national savings 70 percent and GDP 1.5 percent. In a similar study for Mexico, Ayala (1996) finds that GDP should increase between 0.4 and 2.1 percent. In Switzerland and Chile, where reforms have been in place long enough to assess the impact empirically, the national savings rate rose from 6.0 to 8.5 percent of GDP and from 16.7 to 26.6 percent of GDP, respectively, since the introduction of pension reform (James 1997).

## Depth and Liquidity in Capital Markets

By providing access to wholesale capital markets for small investors, contractual savings institutions increase the demand for capital market products such as debt and equities. The most obvious impact of this increase in demand is on liquidity and turnover in these markets. In addition, the introduction of new investors through mutual funds and pension funds should help to lower the cost of capital to firms, potentially stimulating capital formation. The inherent long-term focus of pension fund investments is consistent with the development of long-term capital markets, which otherwise might not be adequately supported by banks and other investment vehicles with a relatively short-term focus.

In examining the relationship between contractual savings and capital market depth in OECD countries, Catalan, Impavido, and Musalem (2000) find a strong positive correlation between contractual savings assets as a percentage of GDP and both market capitalization and the value of stocks traded. Their findings support the proposition that contractual savings help to stimulate capital market liquidity and activity.

James (1997) offers further support for the impact of pension growth on financial market deepening by noting that, in Chile, financial markets have become more liquid as pension funds have diversified their portfolios, both the number of traded shares and their turnover have increased, the variety of financial instruments traded has increased, and asset pricing has improved. Holzmann (1996) estimates that the financial market deepening induced by Chile's pension reforms increased total factor productivity 1 percent a year (half of the total increase).

Vittas (1996) argues that pension funds go even further in contributing to growth and development. He argues that pension funds are a positive force for innovation, for corporate governance, and for privatization. As pension funds grow in size and importance, they create demand for new instruments and for broader markets. Vittas cites the role that pension fund growth played in the development of securitization and financial derivatives in the United States. He also attributes the emergence of block trading and the worldwide reform of stock brokering commissions at least partly to pressure from pension funds. Their role in corporate governance arises from the size of their collective voice. The role in privatization also derives from their size and consequent capacity to absorb large-scale assets.

A concern for some countries is whether or not to allow mutual funds and pension funds access to offshore investments. Although there can be little argument with the proposition that extending the range of investment opportunities is in the interests of the investing public, where the exchange rate is fixed, foreign investment by contractual savings institutions can place heavy demands on scarce foreign exchange reserves. This pressure may be mitigated to the extent that foreign capital is allowed access to domestic capital markets. The key judgment involved is not so much whether, but rather when and under what conditions, to open domestic markets to foreign investment and to allow domestic funds to invest abroad.

### Indirect Effects

In addition to their direct impact on economic growth and development, mutual funds and pension funds make an indirect contribution to economic welfare to the extent that they provide alternatives to the banking system as a vehicle for national savings, contribute to security in retirement, and relieve pressure on government budgets.

Since mutual funds and pension funds invest directly into debt and equity instruments, they provide an alternative to the banking system for savings. The benefits to individual savers have already been outlined. In addition, the country can benefit from the development of alternative sources of financial intermediation between the suppliers and users of financial resources. The expansion of intermediation alternatives stimulates competition and efficiency, and the reduction in reliance on banks makes the financial system as a whole less vulnerable to banking crises and therefore more resilient in responding to external shocks.

The greater is the security that individuals feel about the future, the more they are willing to undertake normal business risks in the present and the more they are likely to contribute to the overall economic welfare of the community.

Private pensions also relieve pressure on governments by removing the reliance on public pensions. Not only does this reduce the government's implicit pension liability, but it also relieves pressure on taxes, which might otherwise inhibit capital formation and growth.

## The Appropriate Form of Regulation

Mutual funds fall relatively clearly into the category of institutions that warrant no more than regulation for market integrity and competition. The case for pension funds is more complex, especially where the funds are publicly mandated, but privately managed. Consideration of the issues therefore starts with mutual funds.

## Regulating Mutual Funds

In terms of the criteria introduced in chapter 2, the activities of mutual funds do not carry any automatic systemic risks. The one possible exception to this proposition, as with any category of institutions, is where an individual fund (or group of funds) reaches a size of operation or degree of interrelatedness with other financial institutions at which its failure could have systemic consequences.

Such was the case with Long-Term Capital Management (LTCM) in the United States in the late 1990s. By virtue of its credibility in the market, LTCM was able to leverage a relatively small base of capital into an exposure of such proportion that its failure not only would have endangered several financial institutions, but also could have substantially disrupted the operation of world derivatives markets. In the event, the U.S. Federal Reserve Bank played a role in brokering a solution to the problem, although it stopped short of committing public funding as part of that solution. In the aftermath of the LTCM crisis, discussion has focused on tighter regulation of those financial institutions that extend credit to such funds and stronger disclosure requirements for the funds; there has been very little support for the suggestion that such funds should be prudentially regulated as a way of reducing systemic risk.

Similarly, there is no case for regulating mutual funds on the grounds of asymmetric information failure. Mutual funds do not make particularly onerous promises to the public. In most cases, the "promise" of the fund is to manage the investor's resources to the best of the manager's ability, within the parameters established by the investment prospectus. Investors in a mutual fund take principal positions and bear risk in the same way that equity investors do. To protect investors in mutual funds to a higher level than that of other equity investors would create a regulatory inequality that would have no basis of justification. The primary protection available to investors in mutual funds should lie in licensing, disclosure, and good governance, all of which fall under market integrity regulation and are discussed in greater detail below.

## Regulating Pension Funds

It is difficult to analyze the appropriate form of regulation for pension funds independently of the nature and level of government involvement in pension provision. Where pensions are entirely voluntary, there is, at best, only a weak case for regulating them much beyond the level of regulation applied to mutual funds. That case rests largely on the tax concessions that usually apply to voluntary pension funds and the need for any government to protect its tax exposure from abuse. Even so, the form of regulation warranted by tax considerations is more consistent with market conduct regulation than with prudential regulation. As the level of government involvement increases, the case strengthens for some form of prudential regulation.

At the other end of the spectrum, pensions that are entirely publicly provided through an unfunded or partly funded scheme are difficult to regulate, given that the risk faced by the "investors" is largely political risk. Indeed, that risk crystallized when many governments recognized their inability to meet their unfunded pension obligations, and this recognition led to the emergence of publicly mandated private pension schemes in an effort to replace publicly funded schemes.

The case for prudential regulation arises most clearly where the government mandates pension fund contributions, and, for this reason, this section is primarily concerned with the regulation of mandatory funds. By removing the freedom of the individual to choose his or her own level of retirement savings, the government takes on a degree of responsibility. It is important, however, to identify the limits of that responsibility. Those limits are determined, in turn, by the nature of the government and private sector promises involved.

It is useful to start with the least onerous pension promises and consider how the approach to regulation may need to be strengthened as the implicit promises are made more onerous.

*Defined Contribution Schemes Managed by Competitive Private Sector Funds*

Defined contribution pension schemes involve a fiduciary promise. In the absence of any specific regulatory impositions, the manager of the assets promises, in return for a management fee, to act honestly and fairly in investing them. The market and default risks on the investment in this case are borne entirely by the owner of the pension investment.

Provided the investor has freedom of choice in selecting an asset manager and provided the market for asset managers is competitive, the regulatory requirements for this type of fund are arguably not much greater than those for general mutual funds.

The primary regulatory tools for managing this type of fiduciary relationship are licensing requirements, disclosure standards, governance standards, and minimum capital requirements. There are a number of aspects within these regulations in which pension regulation may need to be stronger than the equivalent rules for mutual funds. The nature of these regulations and the specific features relevant to pension regulation are taken up further below.

It is difficult to justify the imposition of more interventionist regulations in the case of competitively provided defined contribution pensions where there is freedom of choice.

*Defined Contribution Schemes Managed by Uncompetitive Private Sector Funds*

Not all countries have seen fit to allow competition among pension managers. Indeed the case for unfettered competition is still under debate. Practices range from countries such as Australia, where there are several thousand industry and public offer pension funds,[4] to countries such as Bolivia, where the government has restricted the management of mandatory pension funds to just two agencies.

Uncompetitive supply can arise either because the government restricts the number of licenses available to pension managers (the Latin American model) or because it empowers the employer (or a union) to determine where the worker's pension will be invested (the model adopted by a number of OECD countries, including Australia and Switzerland).

In Australia, where prudential regulation of pensions is relatively light, entry is open to any firm that passes the entry criteria of the regulator. Although there can be little objection to the principle involved, the exceptionally large number of small providers in a such a small economy makes supervision and enforcement extremely difficult. Yet the fact that the investment decision is mostly not in the hands of the worker makes the market much less competitive than might be expected (most suppliers are effectively "captives" of the employers or unions) and makes the strength of the regulations and their enforcement even more critical.

---

4. In addition to these larger funds, there are more than 200,000 self-managed funds with fewer than five members.

There are two main areas in which a case can be made to tighten the regulations for uncompetitive supply of defined contribution pensions:

- Limits on the size of management fees
- Restrictions on portfolio composition.

The former arises from the effective monopoly power that pension suppliers have relative to pension investors when there is little or no choice. The latter arises from two possible extremes: where there are too few suppliers, they have potential market power in the market for investments, and where there are many small "captive" suppliers, there is a risk that they will be unable or unwilling to provide the investors with adequate diversification benefits.

The issue is that when legislation imposes limits on investor choice, either by mandating which fund an investor must use or by restricting the number of funds from which the investor can choose, the government is implicitly strengthening its promise to protect the interests of pension investors. This promise, in turn, can require stronger regulatory intervention to protect the government's exposure to its promises.

*Defined Contribution Schemes with a Government Guaranteed Minimum Return*

It is common among a wide range of countries to impose minimum return requirements (and in some cases, a maximum as well) on private suppliers of mandatory pension plans. The rationale for such profitability rules is to reduce the risk to individual pension investors that their funds will underperform the industry average. Such a restriction is only justifiable where pension contributions are mandatory and where choice of either fund manager or type of fund is limited by law. In effect, the guarantee reflects the moral obligation imposed on government to ensure an adequate pension income in a system where the individual has no control over his or her investment.

In some cases, the minimum is specified in absolute terms; for example, Switzerland imposes a minimum nominal rate of return of 4 percent, while Singapore sets it at 2.5 percent.[5] In others, it is specified relative to a benchmark; for example, Chile and Argentina define a profitability band set as the lesser of 2 percentage points or a fixed fraction above and below the average

---

5. The figures reported in this section are taken from Srinivas and Yermo (1999).

annual return of the industry. These return limits are nearly always imposed in combination with some limitations on the competitiveness of supply.

A guarantee such as this increases the intensity of the government's promise to pension investors even further. Two types of regulation are appropriate to this type of promise:

- Restrictions on the portfolio composition of pension funds to ensure that there is a high probability that their performance will fall within a narrow range
- Establishment of a guarantee fund to supplement shortfalls when they occur.

The potential costs associated with these strategies are significant. Restricting the portfolio composition of pension fund managers is almost certainly inefficient. Srinivas and Yermo (1999: 29), for example, find that, where such restrictions apply in Latin America, asset allocation of different pension fund managers is very similar, with the result that "funds managers are virtually indistinguishable in terms of their asset-allocation and investment strategies." They also find that the risk-adjusted performance of pension funds in Latin America suffered as a result of investment regulation and improved dramatically when those restrictions were relaxed.

*Defined Contribution Schemes Managed by the Public Sector*

The logical limit of restricting the number of pension suppliers is to have a single government-run pension scheme, to which individuals make mandatory contributions. In a variant of this model, the government may, in turn, subcontract some of the investment management back to the private sector. The pension schemes in Singapore and Malaysia are of this general type.

In this case, the government explicitly adopts the responsibility for pension management and the interests of pensioners. The nature of regulation under this model is arguably the same as in the case of defined contributions with uncompetitive supply. Its implementation, however, is complicated by the fact that few governments are enthusiastic about establishing a regulatory agency purely for regulating the government's own activities.

The dangers in this model are many and are difficult to contain by conventional regulatory methods. First, there is always a temptation for governments when a large pool of funds comes directly under their control. At

115

a minimum, there is a temptation to direct the investment of those funds into government securities (this is common practice) to help fund the government's budget spending aspirations. A more serious concern is that the funds may be directed to fund politically attractive projects, without concern for the interests of the pension investors. Second, the internal governance of publicly managed funds is typically weaker than that of equivalent private sector funds, thereby increasing the probability of fraud and misuse of funds.

An effective pension scheme of this type would require, at a minimum, the following:

- A very strong government commitment to disclosure, of both the composition and performance of the portfolio
- A strong and publicly disclosed set of internal governance standards
- A commitment to submit to a regular audit by an independent public audit agency for compliance and efficiency
- Reporting against publicly agreed benchmarks for performance.

*Defined Benefit Schemes*

Defined benefit schemes have a much higher intensity of promise than defined contribution schemes. Where management of defined benefit pension assets is privatized or contracted out to the private sector, there is a need to impose strong regulatory standards to ensure that the promise of a specified payout can be honored. The same issue arises where lump sum pension payouts from the scheme are converted into annuities. Since an annuity may run for many years and is completely prefunded at the time of retirement, the retiree has a significant exposure to the seller of the annuity.

In both cases, there is a need for regulation to impose strict standards for the security of the pension entitlement. As with the various forms of defined contribution schemes, defined benefit schemes require high standards of licensing, disclosure, and governance. The primary regulatory tool in this case, however, is capital.

The problem of ensuring that providers of defined benefit pension schemes are able to meet their promises is usually approached by requiring periodic actuarial reviews of the funds. From the reviews, an assessment is made about the capacity of the fund to meet the promises of defined benefits to which it is committed. Where the current assets of the fund are insufficient to meet these promises, the manager is required to inject additional capital to restore its actuarial value.

## Regulatory Tools and Techniques for Collective Investments

A summary of the different types of pension schemes and the main regulatory responses to deal with the particular risks involved with each is presented in table 4.2.

### Licensing

Licensing requirements for fund managers should focus on establishing that the individuals associated with the fund manager are fit and proper persons to carry out their responsibilities to investors. This should include professional references and police record checks for criminal histories, as well as requirements for evidence of professional qualifications consistent with the types of investments being offered.

Where the fund makes particular claims, such as capital guarantees or liquidity facilities for exiting investors, the licensing conditions should require justification for these promises and evidence of how the promises

**Table 4.2. Type of Pensions Scheme and Appropriate Regulatory Responses**

| Pension scheme | Licensing, disclosure, and governance | Minimum capital requirements | Management fee restrictions | Portfolio restrictions | Guarantee fund | Actuarial review |
|---|---|---|---|---|---|---|
| Defined contribution | | | | | | |
| Competitive supply | ✔ | ✔ | | | | |
| Uncompetitive supply | ✔ | ✔ | ✔ | ✔ | | |
| Guaranteed return | ✔ | ✔ | ✔ | ✔✔ | ✔ | |
| Public management | ✔✔ | | | | | |
| Defined benefit | ✔ | ✔✔ | | | | ✔ |

*Note:* ✔✔ indicate that intensified regulation is warranted.

will be supported. Where the regulator is not satisfied that promises can be kept under reasonable circumstances, the license should be denied or modified. The license also should require the entity to acknowledge that continuation of the license to operate is dependent on meeting the regulator's standards of disclosure and governance.

The licensing requirements for pension fund managers should be broadly similar to those for the managers of mutual funds. However, given that protection of pensions from fraud and embezzlement is paramount, given that the investments involved are of a long-term nature, and given that pension contributions are usually mandatory, licensing standards should be stronger for pension funds than for mutual funds. For example, in determining whether the managers are fit and proper for the management of pension contributions, the standard may rule out involvement of anyone who has a criminal conviction or even an existing charge against their name (until that charge has been answered and the individual has been cleared of any wrongdoing). Further, the standard should require evidence of back office systems capable of meeting the complex legal and accounting requirements of pension management.

Many countries have used licensing restrictions as a way of shaping the structure of the pension industry. Minimal entry requirements encourage a diverse and competitive, but potentially less safe, industry. At the other extreme, countries in Latin America have used stringent licensing conditions to promote safety above efficiency. These more stringent conditions include licensing only a small number of firms dedicated solely to providing pension services. In some cases, existing financial institutions are excluded from license considerations. The balance between efficiency and safety is a matter of judgment and should depend at least partly on the state of financial development.

## Disclosure

Disclosure is the cornerstone of regulation of mutual funds. Investment into mutual funds should be by public prospectus, and the disclosure standards of prospectuses should be extremely high and enforceable by law. Penalties for providing misleading information in a prospectus should be onerous. Given the cost and complexity of printing and distributing prospectuses and the fact that more information is not always helpful to investors, regulators should consider the practice adopted by many countries of requiring a full prospectus to be available to the regulator and to investors on request, but insisting only on the distribution of a short-form prospectus with investment applications. The short-form prospectus should summarize all the essential features of the investment in a form that investors can readily digest.

The nature of mutual fund investments is such that performance should always be measured and reported on a mark-to-market basis. Where markets are too thin to support regular mark-to-market valuation, the disclosure standards should make the alternatives clear and unambiguous. Strong disclosure requirements are particularly important in the case of trustee companies, given that many jurisdictions have applied relatively lax disclosure standards on the basis of the historical role of trustees (in which trust was often regarded as more important than performance).

The second aspect of disclosure that is relevant to mutual funds is their fee structure. There is a wide range of disclosure practices around the world with respect to reporting fees. There is, however, little justification for anything less than full disclosure. This includes the disclosure of entry and exit fees, both in absolute terms and relative to industry averages. It also should include requirements for funds to disclose all fees paid to agents and investment advisers, as well as the nature of those fees (whether they are once-off fees or trailing fees that continue as long as the investor remains with the particular fund). Regulation of agents and advisers is also advisable to ensure that they also reveal to investors the fees paid to them by different mutual funds. Only full disclosure can expose the full range of potential conflicts of interest faced by advisers.

Where mutual funds are regarded as containing a potential systemic threat due to their size and the nature of their activities, the regulator should consider requiring more regular and detailed reporting of positions. Since these position reports would be commercially sensitive, the regulator would need to maintain them in confidence.

Disclosure standards are equally critical for mandatory pension investments. The overall return on pension investments depends on two factors: the return on the assets and the administration costs of the fund. To enable individuals to make informed choices, where choice is permitted, disclosure should include all administrative costs as well as fund performance. Both of these should be reported in absolute terms as well as relative to industry averages or external benchmarks. Some countries have adopted the same standard of disclosure as is applied to mutual funds; namely, on a full mark-

4

### Box 4.1. Mutual Funds Governance Matters!

As is the case with all corporations, the directors or trustees of a mutual fund or investment company have responsibility for overseeing the management of the fund's business affairs and are mandated to play an essential role in protecting the interests of the fund's shareholders. When established as a corporation, a mutual fund is governed by a board of directors, while a mutual fund established as a business trust is governed by a board of trustees. The duties of directors and trustees in respect of mutual funds are essentially identical. Under common law, corporate directors are expected to exercise a "duty of care and loyalty": they are required to exercise the same care that a reasonably prudent person would take with his or her own business and to have undivided loyalty to any corporation on whose board they serve. In the context of mutual funds, they are expected to exercise sound business judgment in their investments, to establish policies and procedures for the safe operation of the fund, and to perform oversight and review functions to protect the interests of shareholders.

The nature of mutual funds is such that they involve inherent conflicts of interest that, in turn, demand rigorous standards of governance as a counterbalance. Mutual funds involve large pools of liquid assets managed by external investment advisers or management companies in return for fees. The mutual fund itself typically has no employees of its own and a fragmented ownership structure composed mostly of small shareholders. This structure can lead to direct conflicts between the shareholders, whose interests are to protect and appreciate their investment, and the investment adviser, whose interest is to maximize fees.

In 1940, recognizing the unique nature of mutual funds and the inadequate protection offered under federal securities laws (mainly dealing with disclosure and antifraud provisions), the U.S. Congress enacted the Investment Company Act. The fundamental precept of the 1940 act is that independent fund directors should serve as watchdogs for the shareholders' interests. Specifically, the legislation provides that at least 40 percent of the board must consist of independent directors who

have no other business or family relationships with the fund's investment adviser, principal underwriter, officers, or employees. The independent directors are vested with special responsibilities on key matters, including initial approval and periodic renewal of investment advisory and distribution contracts. In this context, the act mandates that these contracts be renewed annually after the first two years following initial approval by a majority of the fund's independent directors. The key oversight functions of the independent directors are to evaluate the performance of the investment adviser, underwriter, custodian, and other parties that perform services for the fund and to authorize and renew their contracts in accordance with their performance. During the annual renewal process, independent directors typically request and review detailed information about the advisory and underwriting organizations and the quality of services they provide to the fund.

In recent years, there has been a growing movement to enhance the governance of mutual funds in the United States. For example, in 1999 the Investment Company Institute convened an advisory group, consisting of independent directors and leaders in the mutual fund industry, to identify best practices in fund governance (Advisory Group on Best Practices for Fund Directors, Investment Company Institute 1999). Among the 15 key recommendations in the advisory group's report was a call for independent directors to constitute a "super-majority" (at least two-thirds) on all fund boards, rather than the 40 percent prescribed at the time by law. The report also recommended that former officers or directors of a fund's investment adviser, principal underwriter, or certain affiliates not serve as independent directors of the fund; that the fund's independent directors have legal counsel; and that a fund's independent directors meet separately from management.

In addition to the governance requirements imposed on mutual funds in the United States, the funds are regulated for market conduct by the U.S. Securities and Exchange Commission (SEC). The

*Continued*

---

### Box 4.1 (Continued). Mutual Funds Governance Matters!

SEC imposes a number of additional safeguards for investors, including:

- *Disclosure.* All mutual funds must provide investors with full and complete disclosure in a written offering circular or prospectus. The prospectus mandated as part of a sale is required to describe, among other things, the fund's investment objective, its investment methods, information on how to purchase and redeem shares, information about the investment adviser, the level of risk the fund is willing to assume (including investment instruments and leverage), and fund fees and expenses. Mutual funds are required to file prospectuses with the SEC before distributing them to investors; the information included in these prospectuses must be presented clearly and simply. Mutual

funds are required to provide their shareholders with annual and semiannual reports that contain recent information on the fund's portfolio, performance, investment goals, and policies. Every mutual fund is also required to disclose its fees in a standardized fee table at the front of the prospectus.

- *Arm's-length transactions.* Custodians and public accountants also perform watchdog functions. SEC regulations require mutual funds to have independent custodians and to produce certified financial statements prepared by independent public accountants. These ensure that the investments and their performance are consistent with the mutual funds' periodic reports to shareholders and with the information in their prospectuses.

---

to-market basis. Others, most notably in Europe, have adopted the insurance industry approach of declaring a rate of return at annual intervals. The similarity between pension funds and mutual funds suggests that the former is preferable, and the international trend is clearly in this direction.

Where choice is not permitted, reporting of performance on both an absolute and relative basis remains critical. Although it does not assist pension investors in selecting between competing suppliers, it does provide a regular check on the diligence of the pension manager. Reasonable performance over time should be a condition for retaining the privileged right to manage mandatory funds in an uncompetitive environment.

## Governance

Mutual fund regulation also relies on a high level of corporate governance (see box 4.1). As noted, the role of trust is fundamental to mutual fund operation. To exercise its responsibilities fully to investors, the manager of a mutual fund should have a culture of compliance and responsibility. To encourage the development of such a culture, the regulator might consider requiring the manager to establish a compliance committee including external parties (with appropriate qualifications) with specific responsibility to report breaches of compliance to the regulator. The regulator also may impose specific requirements for the committee to ensure that information is properly disclosed to the investors and that sound policies and procedures are adopted and practiced by the manager.

Governance regulations also may include requirements covering the responsibility of fund managers to advise clients as to the appropriateness of certain investments to their particular situation. This duty of care should be supported by onerous sanctions for violation, including financial penalties and, in particularly egregious cases, loss or suspension of license.

In addition to these internal controls, regulators of mutual funds, and especially regulators of pension funds, should adopt protective governance requirements such as the compulsory use of custodial services, proper segregation of assets, and external audits. Governance rules also should aim to prevent conflicts of interest and to restrict investment into related-party assets. In the case of defined benefit funds, regular external actuarial reviews also are essential.

## Capital Requirements

Minimum capital requirements play two roles. First, they provide a minimum level of substance to those who seek to take on the onerous fiduciary responsibility of managing mutual funds or pension funds. Second, they provide a buffer of resources in the event of fraud. Many countries impose a minimum level of around 1 percent of assets under management, although some countries require capital of up to 3 percent of assets. Where a fund manager promotes a fund with guarantees (for example, a minimum return or a capital guarantee), the regulator should increase the capital requirement to add substance to the guarantee, unless the guarantee is supported by an external party such as an insurance company.

The role of capital is even more important in the case of defined benefit pension funds and annuities. The participants in a defined benefit scheme are exposed to the solvency of the sponsor in the event that the performance of the fund's investments falls short of that needed to sustain the promised benefits. The recipient of a pension annuity is totally exposed to the solvency of the provider.

In the case of a defined benefit fund, the regulator should require regular actuarial reviews of the fund's capacity to meet its programmed benefits and ensure that the sponsor tops up any deficiencies. Where the defined benefit plan is promoted by a fund manager, the regulator should require the manager to hold sufficient capital to meet any unexpected changes in the fund's value. Many countries restrict public promotion of defined benefit plans and sales of annuities to prudentially regulated financial institutions such as life insurance companies.

## Limits on Management Fees

In a competitive market for mutual funds and pension plans, where there is adequate choice, the case for restricting the level of management fees is relatively weak. Provided there is adequate disclosure of fees on a comparable basis across funds, investors should be able to make informed choices and to take responsibility for their own investment decisions.

The case for putting a cap on fees is stronger in the case of "captive" pension funds, where contributions are mandatory and the choice of fund is heavily restricted or even prohibited. In this case, the fund manager is in a position of effective monopoly, and price regulation is an acceptable regulatory response. The level of the cap should not be set so high that there are excessive returns to the monopoly. Nor should it be set so low that the fund manager is forced to cut essential administrative expenses in order to earn an acceptable return on its capital.

## Investment Guidelines and Restrictions

The essence of mutual funds is to have the manager disclose sufficient information for investors to take responsibility for their decisions. The trust deed and prospectus should clearly disclose the permissible investments that can be undertaken by the fund, the risks involved with those investments, and the strategy that the fund manager intends to adopt to manage these risks. In addition, various countries prescribe prudential norms of varying degrees of intensity, such as those which require a minimum level of diversification and which restrict the types of investments (with the objective of ensuring liquidity of open ended funds); and those which impose maximum percentages of any one issuer that may be owned (control issues).

The situation is much less clear-cut in the case of pension funds. First, pension funds are long-term investments undertaken on behalf of workers to provide them with retirement incomes. Many of these investors are relatively unsophisticated in financial matters and may not be well placed to make wise long-term investment decisions. Second, where there is freedom of choice in a mandatory contribution scheme (second pillar) plus a public pension scheme as a safety net (first pillar), there is a potential moral hazard problem. Street-wise investors may deliberately choose high-risk pension portfolios, knowing that the worst-case outcomes are effectively insured against by the state.

Regulatory responses to these problems vary in intensity. In some cases, a more restrictive approach may be justified on the grounds of safety. At the same time, the more intense and interventionist are the restrictions, the greater is the potential cost in terms of investment efficiency and the more difficult it can become for the scheme to meet its intended purpose of providing adequate retirement incomes.

At the lighter regulatory end of the scale, many countries counter these problems by relying on the "prudent person" principle to govern the decisions of the pension fund manager. This principle puts a burden of responsibility on the fund manager to invest in the way that a prudent investor would, given the circumstances of the individual on whose behalf it acts.[6] This usually is regarded as adequate where the investing population is reasonably sophisticated. The weakness of this approach is that it relies on the courts to determine the substance of the principle. Where court systems are well developed and reliable, this approach can work very effectively. Where they are not, the result can be long delays and inconsistency in the establishment of precedents.

Where there are concerns about the effectiveness of the court system or about the vulnerability or gullibility of investors—for example, in countries in the early stages of pension reform—there is a case for greater intervention into the process of investment decisionmaking.

Where further intervention is warranted, the most common approach is to impose minimum diversification regulations. These may be in the form of setting maximum holdings of individual issues of related parties or maximum holdings of investments in different sectors of the economy or in different types of investment. Many countries also rule out or at least limit the use of leverage in pension portfolios, since leverage increases risk for a given asset structure. Some limit the use of derivative products to hedging transactions.

---

6. An additional method of encouraging incentive compatibility between the interests of the asset owners and the asset managers is to require the managers to invest their capital in the fund itself.

At the more draconian end of the scale, regulatory restrictions can extend to minimum holdings of certain investment classes and prohibitions on certain types of investments. Minimum holdings have been used widely to create captive markets for government securities. Prohibitions have been used, out of (often misplaced) concerns about risk, to exclude holdings of equities and foreign investments; they also have been used to protect foreign currency reserves.

Although these restrictions usually are applied in the name of safety, they generally are contrary to the interests of the pension investor and can be costly in terms of investment efficiency. Minimum holding requirements also can encourage pension funds to hold disproportionate quantities of the investments in some markets. Not only does this lead to a control problem, but it also can destroy liquidity in those markets. From a systemic development perspective, exclusion of equity investments, which has been common in emerging market countries, also inhibits the growth of equities markets by denying them access to one of the largest and fastest-growing sources of funds in the system.

To the extent that minimum holding and prohibition restrictions increase risk and inefficiency in pension investments, they place a further moral burden on government. Although regulations of this type are difficult to justify in terms of market failure and the objectives of a pension scheme, they can play a role in the evolution from a purely public pension system to one dominated by mandated private pensions.

Regulators sometimes apply yet another type of investment restriction in an attempt to increase safety. For example, the Latin American model of pension reform restricts mandatory contributions to a single investment instrument created specifically for private pension accounts. Similarly, each provider is limited to administering only one fund (or, in some cases, two funds). The rationale behind these types of restrictions is the perception that the tasks of regulating and supervising a multiple-instrument, multiple-fund industry are too complex for regulators. Restricting pension managers to a single fund and investors to a single instrument also helps to remove the moral hazard problem created by choice, essentially by removing choice from the scheme. The main cost of these restrictions is that they not only eliminate the scope for investors to reduce risk by diversifying their pension holdings with different managers but also remove their ability to select a portfolio structure that best suits their age, career, and risk preferences. In effect, young investors starting their first job are required to hold the same portfolio composition as older workers close to retirement. These additional restrictions should not be applied without a clear understanding of their costs.

## Guarantee Funds

Guarantee funds associated with pension funds are used for two main purposes. First, they are used in some countries to compensate pension investors for losses incurred through fraud. Second, they are used to provide a guaranteed minimum rate of return on pension investments. This second form of guarantee is common in Latin America.

The first type of guarantee fund usually is activated after a fraud has occurred and usually takes the form of a levy on the industry. In view of the government's role in mandating pension contributions and in limiting choice (where it imposes such restrictions), there is a strong case for guarantee funds of this type, and they raise few, if any, issues of concern.

The second type of guarantee fund is more problematic. The only justification for guaranteeing a minimum return on pension investments arises from the fact that the government mandates the contributions without empowering the individual to control his or her investment. The most obvious solution to the problem is to introduce greater freedom of choice for the investor. Where that is impractical for some reason, it is important to establish a mechanism for delivering against the guarantee when it is needed.

Establishing a guarantee fund, however, requires yet another level of regulation to remove the moral hazard problem associated with guaranteeing a minimum return for those who underperform, effectively funded by those in the industry who do not underperform. Where the guarantee fund is an actual pool of funds to which managers contribute, there is a further issue of how these funds should be invested and how their management should be regulated.

Mutual funds and pension funds sometimes warrant regulation beyond the level consistent with the promises they make. Where these funds reach a size sufficient to influence markets or to pose a systemic threat, additional regulation may be warranted. These considerations are particularly relevant in the case of uncompetitive pension funds provision, in which a very small number of institutions may grow over time into a position of market dominance. They also are relevant where minimum holding provisions lead to market dominance in a small number of securities.

To limit the market dominance of pension funds, regulators sometimes impose maximum holdings of the shares of any given issuer or group of related issuers. To limit their negative impact on the liquidity of debt instruments, some regulators similarly impose maximum holdings on the debt issues of any given issuer or related group of issuers. These regulations, which limit the amount of any given investment that pension funds can hold, have the potential to come into direct conflict with portfolio restrictions that limit the range of investments.

**4**

## Surveillance

Given the market conduct focus of mutual funds regulation, surveillance is usually dominated by off-site analysis of data and information collected through the regulatory process. The potentially large number of funds and the wide range of their investment activities make active on-site inspections extremely expensive to support. Inspections and investigations of mutual funds usually are triggered by complaints. To a large extent, mutual fund regulators depend on external auditors, compliance committees, and disgruntled investors to find regulatory breaches beyond what can be identified through off-site analysis.

The case for inspecting pension funds is stronger, in view of the higher level of regulation that typically is applied. Where pensions are supplied competitively by a large number of providers, the viability of inspections is again questionable. Notwithstanding the cost, several regulators with large pension industries still attempt to maintain a regular program of on-site inspections. For example, despite having several thousand pension funds answering to one regulator in Australia, the regulator maintains an active on-site inspection program. Because it would take many years to visit the entire industry, the regulator is forced to prioritize inspections according to its own internal risk assessments.

On-site inspection programs are not only easier to manage but also more critical as the intensity of regulation increases and the number of pension providers decreases. As the industry becomes more concentrated, pension investors as a group become increasingly exposed to mismanagement, fraud, and failure of a small number of institutions.

## Special Issues in Pension Reform in Emerging Markets

The principles for regulating mandatory pensions in a developed financial system are relatively well defined. The main choice for a government is where on the spectrum between safety and efficiency it wishes to be placed. If the investing public is still relatively unsophisticated, the balance should fall more toward safety, with some sacrifice in efficiency. Nonetheless, provided markets are well developed and have a high level of integrity, the regulatory emphasis should still be on promoting competition and investor choice, while the regulatory approach should rely largely on licensing, disclosure, and governance. Regulatory tools such as investment restrictions and guaranteed rates of return will be largely irrelevant.

The situation is likely to be much more ambiguous for emerging market economies. Although the ideals of competition and investor choice are likely to be long-term goals, the immediate problem usually involves how best to move from a nearly bankrupt pure first-pillar system to one in which the government's long-term pension liability is manageable. To add to the complexity, the path to an open, competitive pension system usually has to contend with underdeveloped capital markets, limited foreign exchange reserves, and poor regulatory foundations.

The potential rewards from a successful transition are, of course, substantial. Successful pension reform can remove a financially debilitating liability overhang from the old first-pillar system. It can increase national savings. It can be a source of capital market development and a stimulant to growth. It can be a source of financial innovation. It can be a means of reducing the wealth imbalance within the community. With such a high payoff, it is not surprising that a number of countries have started the reform process in recent years. The question is how best to manage the transition and, in particular, how best to harness the synergies between the pension system and domestic capital markets.

During the past decade or more, Latin America has been at the forefront of pension reform. Following the success of the Chilean experiment started in 1980 (see box 4.2), Argentina, Colombia, Peru, Uruguay, and Mexico all have followed a similar pattern of reforms. Although there are some variations in detail, these reforms all share common elements:

- The second pillars all are mandatory and managed by the private sector.

---

**Box 4.2. The Chilean Model of Pension Reform**

Chile is often regarded as a model for pension reform, as much for the success of the final structure that has evolved as for the way in which government managed the process of change (this case study is based closely on Vittas 1996).

At the time of its initial pension reforms, Chile imposed very tight portfolio limits on different categories of investments, including 100 percent for state securities, 80 percent for mortgage bonds, 70 percent for bank liabilities, 60 percent for corporate bonds, and 20 percent for quotas of pension funds. All other investments were prohibited, including equities and foreign investments.

Over time, the following liberalizations were introduced:

- In 1982, the limit on bank liabilities was reduced to 40 percent.
- In 1985, the limits on state securities and corporate bonds were reduced to 50 and 40 percent, respectively.
- In 1985, pensions were permitted to invest up to 30 percent in equities of privatized state enterprises, with a maximum of 5 percent for any one issuer.
- In 1986, they were allowed to invest in the equities of companies with dispersed ownership.
- In 1989, investment was permitted in real estate companies, subject to individual and global limits.
- In 1990, investment was allowed in foreign securities, subject to a very low, but slowly increasing, limit.
- In 1990, the limit on state securities was lowered further to 45 percent, while the limits on both bank liabilities and corporate debt were increased to 50 percent.
- In 1993, investment was allowed in venture capital and infrastructure funds.
- In 1995, the limits on equities and foreign investments were raised to 37 and 9 percent, respectively.

By the mid-1990s, Chilean pension funds had developed well-diversified portfolios. As an indication of the success of the gradual relaxation of these portfolio restrictions, Srinivas and Yermo (1999) find a marked improvement in pension fund performance over the period since introduction of the reforms. After a decade of underperformance relative to a balanced portfolio benchmark, the pension funds actually outperformed all benchmarks over the five years from 1993 to 1997, by which time the relaxation of the portfolio restrictions was largely completed.

---

- The second pillars are defined contribution in nature.
- The pension fund industries are subject to very tight regulation over industry structure (limited licenses and one or two funds per provider), portfolio composition (investment restrictions and exclusions), and performance (a mixture of maximum and minimum rates of return, supported by guarantee funds).

The most restrictive regulations have been those governing portfolio composition. Using a sample of three countries—Chile, Peru, and Uruguay—Srinivas and Yermo (1999) estimate the cost of these draconian regulations to have been substantial. They find that the structural restrictions created a false impression of investor choice. During the period in which these restrictions were in place, fund portfolios were largely identical, and competition between funds was negligible. Pension portfolios sig-

nificantly underperformed market benchmarks, and, unless fund performance improves, income replacement rates of retiring workers will be substantially below what they would have been in alternative investments.[7]
Their finding that Chile's investment performance improved markedly after
the restrictions were relaxed supports their argument that draconian regulations have a high efficiency cost.

These findings, however, do not suggest that the staged approach of the
Latin American countries was necessarily inappropriate. The justification
for the initial "heavy-handed" approach relies mainly on the combination
of limited experience with fund management and underdeveloped domestic
capital markets. As Srinivas and Yermo (1999: 11) put it, "Asset allocation
limits are a way of isolating pension assets from agency and systemic risks in
capital markets. As a consequence, self-regulation of the prudent person
type may not be viable in countries where capital market infrastructure is
underdeveloped and prudential controls are not in place."

Initially, pension investments were limited to government and other
high-quality bonds. As these restrictions were relaxed to include corporate
debt and equity, they, in turn, stimulated the growth of those markets.

Although the evidence is still preliminary, and each situation inevitably
has its own unique characteristics, the following suggestions drawn from the
Latin American experience may provide some helpful guidance in
approaching key issues in the staging of reforms:

- Portfolio restrictions, including exemptions of some higher-risk asset
  classes, have a role to play in the early stages of the pension reform
  process.
- These restrictions should be relaxed progressively as capital markets grow and mature and as the regulatory system matures—a natural progression for relaxation might be from government debt, to
  bank liabilities, to corporate debt, to equities, and then to foreign
  investments.
- The absence of deep domestic capital markets should not inhibit
  pension reform—as the investment restrictions are relaxed, they will
  naturally stimulate the growth of the asset classes affected.

---

7. For example, it is estimated that, in Chile, a balanced portfolio would have outperformed
the pension fund industry, earning an average annual return of 17.4 percent over the 15
years to 1997 compared with 10.2 percent in the pension industry.

- Liquidity requires careful management—pension funds that "buy and hold" reduce liquidity, while funds that trade excessively for short-term performance can increase the cost of administering the fund.
- Foreign assets increase diversification, thereby lowering risk or increasing expected returns, especially where pension funds are very large relative to domestic markets. However, according to Vittas (1996: 3), "Unrestricted foreign investment may institutionalize capital flight and prevent domestic markets from reaping the benefits of creating pension funds with long-term financial resources." Foreign investment should be introduced progressively into pension fund assets and should be accompanied by other reforms designed to strengthen the economy generally and to reduce its vulnerability to capital flight.
- Ultimately, a soundly regulated mandatory pension system in which financially well-educated individual investors have freedom of choice among a manageable range of competitive providers and products is likely to provide the greatest benefits to all involved.

4

# Securities Markets

*This chapter examines the importance of equity and bond markets as essential components of the financial system. It reviews the remarkable growth of emerging markets over the 1990s, examining the development of the regulatory framework and trading infrastructure and identifying some of the factors motivating the growth of emerging capital markets—improved regulation, privatization of state assets, and the growth of institutional investors. It then explores the profound benefits that the development of capital markets has for economic growth and stability, including the creation of a more balanced financial structure through improved allocation of resources as well as better management of risks. Next, it reviews the underpinnings of the regulatory structure for securities markets—a regulatory approach that relies on arm's-length disclosure, self-regulation of markets and intermediaries, as well as strong corporate governance. The final section covers select policy priorities for emerging markets.*

The 1990s witnessed a dramatic period of growth in the capital markets of developing countries. There were major achievements in capital markets development: construction of regulatory standards, improvements in market infrastructure, and achievement of greater market depth and liquidity. From an almost exclusive reliance on banking systems in the 1980s, in the 1990s countries began to focus on the development of securities markets.

The growing depth and breadth of emerging markets during the 1990s are a success story. The combined market capitalization of select emerging equity markets[1] increased from $339.3 billion in 1990 to $2.2 trillion in 2000 (see figure 5.1). As a share of GDP, the average market capitalization in these countries increased from 16.7 to 45.5 percent during this period of time,

## Figure 5.1. Market Capitalization in Emerging Markets, 1990–2000

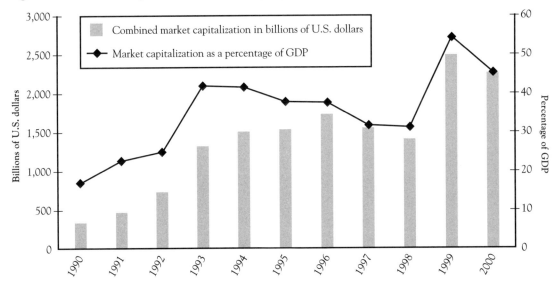

Source: Market capitalization figures for sample emerging markets are from Standard & Poor's Emerging Markets Data Base. Figures for GDP are from the World Bank's central database: Global Development Finance and World Development Indicators. Market capitalization and GDP figures begin in 1992 for China, Hungary, Poland, and South Africa; 1994 for Czech Republic; 1996 for Egypt and Morocco; and 1997 for Israel.

---

1. The sample includes 22 emerging equity markets: Argentina, Brazil, Chile, China, Czech Republic, Egypt, Greece, Hungary, India, Indonesia, Israel, Jordan, Korea, Malaysia, Mexico, Morocco, Nigeria, Philippines, Poland, South Africa, Thailand, and Turkey.

**Figure 5.2. Liquidity in Emerging Markets, 1990–2000**

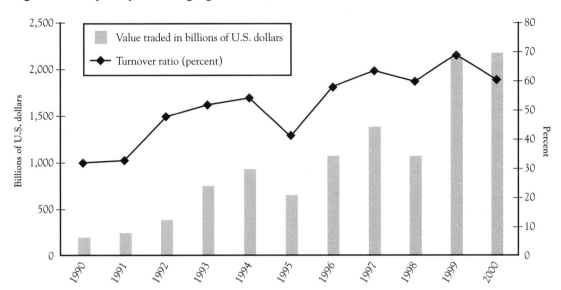

*Source:* Standard & Poor's Emerging Markets Data Base and International Finance Corporation (1999). Data on value traded begin in 1991 for China, Poland, and Hungary and in 1994 for Czech Republic. Data on turnover ratio begin in 1992 for China, Hungary, and Poland; 1995 for Czech Republic; and 1997 for Israel.

while their share of world market capitalization expanded from 3.6 percent in 1990 to almost 7.0 percent in 1999 (world market capitalization figures are from the World Bank's central database: Global Development Finance and World Development Indicators). Outstanding equity markets, such as China's, have grown in importance both relative to the domestic economy as well as relative to other equity markets worldwide.

Market liquidity, in absolute as well as relative terms (as measured by the value of shares traded annually as a percentage of market capitalization), also rose dramatically during this period (see figure 5.2). The annual value of shares traded increased from $180.4 billion to $2.2 trillion in the previously cited sample of 22 equity markets, while the unweighted average turnover ratio increased from 32 percent in 1990 to 62 percent in 2000.

Although capital markets in most emerging markets grew strongly in the 1990s, that growth was uneven across regions and countries. Several countries and regions did better than others. For example, Asian capital markets, such as Hong Kong and Malaysia, were relatively successful, while the

**Figure 5.3. Number of Listed Companies by Region, 1990 and 2000**

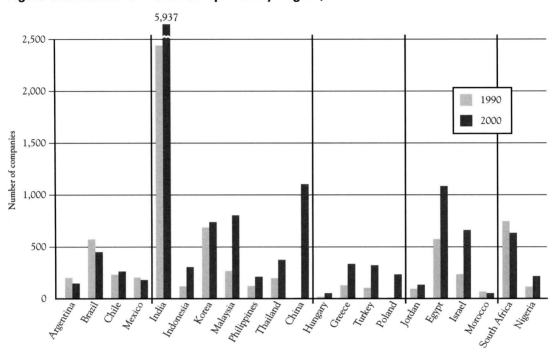

*Source:* Standard & Poor's Emerging Markets Data Base and International Finance Corporation (1999). Data begin in 1991 for China, Poland, and Hungary.

prospects for Eastern European markets—with the exception of Hungary and Poland—still are not encouraging (Claessens, Djankov, and Klingebiel 2000). The transition economies initiated their macroeconomic adjustment and structural reform programs in the early 1990s, and the lag in the development of equity markets reflects, in part, the slower pace of economic reform and growth.

Still, developing countries are benefiting from the advent of domestic capital markets. Between 1990 and 2000, the number of listed companies rose sharply in select countries (see figure 5.3). For example, in India the number of listed firms increased from 2,435 in 1990 to 5,937 in 2000, while in China it increased from 14 in 1991 to 1,086 in 2000. With the improvements in depth and liquidity, domestic firms began to mobilize significant amounts of

**Figure 5.4. Concentration of Top 10 Domestic Companies, 1998 and 2000**

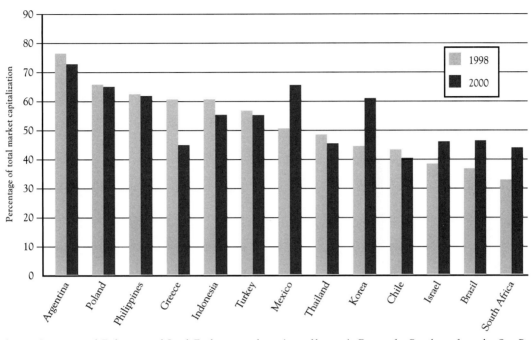

*Source:* International Federation of Stock Exchanges website (www.fibv.com). Figures for Brazil are from the São Paulo Stock Exchange.

new capital. New equity issues during 1990–2000 ranged between 1.8 and 4.8 percent of market capitalization in a select sample of countries.[2]

Notwithstanding the evident progress, emerging markets, even the more progressive ones, continue to lag significantly behind industrial-country markets in several respects. First, they are not as liquid. Second, much of the increase in market capitalization, and especially liquidity, is concentrated in a relatively small number of listed firms. For instance, the degree of market concentration is quite striking. In 2000 between 40 and 72 percent of market capitalization was concentrated in the 10 largest stocks in the previously cited sample (see figure 5.4), and this has not improved much since 1998. Trading activity is equally concentrated.

---

2. From 1990 to 2000, new equity issues as a percentage of market capitalization averaged 1.8 percent in Chile, 2.3 percent in Nigeria, 2.9 percent in Argentina, 3.8 percent in Greece, 4.1 percent in Korea, and 4.8 percent in both Jordan and Thailand (*Source:* Standard and Poor's Emerging Markets Data Base).

**Figure 5.5. Bond Markets as a Percentage of GDP, 1998**

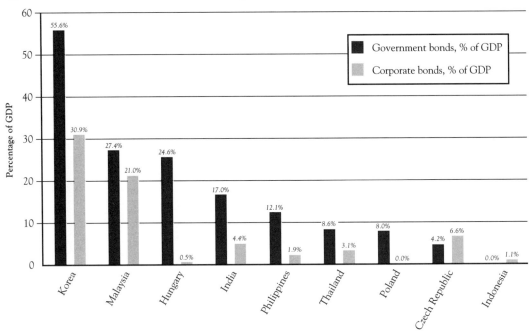

*Source:* World Bank and International Monetary Fund (2001).
Note: Figures for the Philippines are from December 1997.

**Figure 5.6. Bank and Nonbank Financial Assets as a Percentage of GDP**

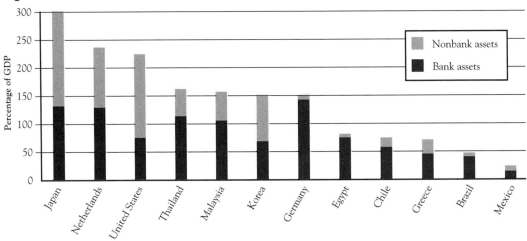

*Source:* Financial Structure and Economic Development Database, created by Beck, Demirgüç-Kunt, and Levine. See www.world-bank.org/research/projects/finstructure/database.htm. The database distinguishes between deposit money banks and other financial institutions (defined in Figure 5.6 as banks and non-banks, respectively). For details, please see Beck, Demirgüç-Kunt, and Levine (1999).

Clearly, the conditions pose challenges for policymakers, and these are discussed later in the chapter.

As shown in figure 5.5, bond markets in developing countries are the younger siblings of equity markets—small and illiquid at this stage. Bond markets in developed countries in 1998 ranged from 61 percent of GDP in the U.K. to 137.7 percent in Japan and 164.2 percent in the U.S.(World Bank and International Monetary Fund, 2001: 366). Compared with bond markets in developed countries, the major emerging bond markets are not very large.

Although the situation varies somewhat from country to country, sovereign issues typically dominate these markets, and the maturities of issues are short term. Similarly, secondary markets are very illiquid, with instruments being held to maturity by their first purchasers, mostly commercial banks.

Although the past decade witnessed the significant development of capital markets, emerging markets remain heavily dependent on banks for business finance. As shown from the sample of countries in figure 5.6, with the exception of Germany, banks typically contribute a much smaller proportion of overall finance in developed financial systems than they do in emerging markets.

## Factors Affecting the Growth of Securities Markets

What accounts for the rapid growth in capitalization and liquidity of emerging markets? The remarkable progress in regulatory standards and institutions as well as market infrastructure is both a cause and a result of the virtuous cycle evident in market depth and breadth. Instilling better regulation and trading infrastructure provides a safety net for investors and thereby promotes market growth. On the supply side, the privatization of state-owned assets and public underwriting of closely held assets lead to the offering of new securities, while the growth of institutional investors—pension funds—creates demand for new investments.

### Improvements in Regulation

Following the Asian banking crisis and the problems identified with opaque banking systems, many countries recognized that wide-ranging reforms were needed in banking and capital markets to ensure that they are able to mobilize and allocate capital efficiently in a market-based system. As a result, in the 1990s policymakers turned their attention to the development of market-based financial markets. A cornerstone of that development was the need for adequate regulation.

During the 1990s, emerging markets made great strides in improving the legal and regulatory frameworks and establishing the institutions required to regulate and supervise their capital markets. In constructing regulatory standards and institutions, developing countries adopted a framework based largely on disclosure—self-imposed market and industry discipline. Implementing this new regulatory model involved the formulation of new or revised securities laws and regulations. In parallel, a large number of countries established and strengthened independent commissions to regulate capital markets. Further, some countries began to foster the development of self-regulatory organizations (SROs), albeit with a modest degree of success.

### New Laws and Regulations

A notable thrust of these efforts was the formulation of revised laws and regulations. The underlying regulatory model was anchored in a three-prong system relying on arm's-length transactions, disclosure, and self-regulation. Initially, legal and regulatory initiatives focused on enhancing market mechanisms through better disclosure. More recently, emerging markets began to focus more on improving corporate governance and minority shareholder rights.

### Clear Mandates

A complementary effort sought to establish dedicated, and sometimes independent, securities regulatory institutions for capital markets rather than continue to rely on ministries of finance or central banks.[3] The underlying rationale was that capital markets require specialized knowledge and skills that are not necessarily found in the civil service and central banks; thus, in order to have credibility, the securities regulatory institution needs to be at arm's-length from political pressures. A large number of markets have established such institutions, although the degree of independence and credibility varies widely from country to country.

---

3. A more recent trend is the transition to integrated regulators. This topic is discussed in chapter 2.

## Market Infrastructure

Market infrastructure comprises the systems and institutions that facilitate the trade, payment for, and custody of securities. The key functions of market infrastructure include exchanges, clearance and settlement, depositories, and custodians.

A dated and unreliable market infrastructure leads to poor execution of trades, long delays in the settlement process, and unsatisfactory performance of the custody of securities, such as the accurate and timely reporting of positions, collection of dividends, and resolution of taxation, all of which discourage investors. One of the more notable initiatives in capital market development during the 1990s—fueled in part by technological advances—was the concerted effort of emerging markets to improve market infrastructure. Tangible results were evident in the following areas: trading systems, clearance and settlement systems, and central depositories.

*Trading Systems*

A large number of emerging markets made considerable investments in replacing obsolete trading with state-of-the-art computerized order-driven matching systems. Computers not only process large volumes of trades in a cost-efficient manner but also, more importantly, capture order flow, transactions, and trade matching. The detailed audit trail leads to improved transparency and rapid dissemination of real-time information. It also improves investor confidence in the fairness of the markets, leads to growth in market trading, and improves liquidity.[4] The automation of exchanges facilitated the modernization of post-trade market infrastructure—the clearance and settlement system, depositories, and custody functions.

*Clearance and Settlement Systems*

The clearance function determines what investors are to deliver and receive when a transaction is completed; the settlement function takes place when

---

4. There is considerable debate regarding the potential disadvantage of computerized order-driven systems in markets with shallow liquidity. A number of studies suggest that there is an important role for market makers as well as for periodic auctions in these markets. The automation of exchanges does not preclude the role of market makers, similar to the Nasdaq trading system.

the transaction is completed and the securities and funds change hands. Most emerging markets have made great progress in improving the clearance and settlement infrastructure for equities, but less progress in doing so for bonds.[5]

*Central Depositories*

A central depository can significantly improve the operational efficiency of the clearance and settlement system. It shortens the settlement cycle and improves reliability by replacing paper-intensive delivery of securities at settlement with a computer (book entry) system. Practically all emerging markets have established a central depository—one of the G-30 benchmarks—and this has significantly shortened the settlement cycle. Depositories also can speed up and increase the reliability of registration, another bottleneck in many emerging markets, since the depository maintains ownership records for market participants.

## Supply Side Factors

In addition to the improvements in market regulation and infrastructure, supply side factors also stimulated the development of capital markets in a number of emerging-market countries. One important development was the widespread privatization of state assets that accompanied the shift from centralized ownership in many transition economies. This created a pool of assets suitable for floating on stock markets.

A second factor on the supply side was the emergence of domestic and foreign institutional investors. The growth of domestic investors is covered in other chapters. The growth of foreign investors followed the trend toward financial integration. From a minimal presence in the late 1980s, foreign investors now own a considerable share of the free float in emerging markets.

---

5. The G-30 clearance and settlement benchmarks were formulated in 1990, and most emerging markets have made progress in achieving them. These benchmarks are directed at reducing transaction costs, including the opportunity cost of delays in settlement as well as the counterparty risk for individual investors and the systemic risk for the market as a whole.

## Contribution of Securities Markets to Economic Growth and Stability

Capital markets are an integral part of the financial system. They mobilize long-term capital efficiently by attracting resources from a large number of savers in a cost-efficient manner and by converting the funds of short-term investors into long-term capital. They provide an alternative intermediation mechanism for mobilizing savings, allocating and managing risk and liquidity, and managing government debt. Capital markets reduce the financial vulnerability of enterprises by increasing their access to equity markets and reducing their dependence on short-term bank debt, by lowering the refinancing risks of governments in a domestic public debt market, and by lowering the banking system's maturity transformation risks.[6] The development of other nonbank financial institutions discussed in this book—insurance companies and collective investment schemes—acts as a catalyst for the development of capital markets by creating a base of institutional investors.

When a country's financial system relies heavily on its banks, systemic vulnerabilities increase. The Asian financial crisis provided ample evidence of the risks associated with the absence of multiple channels of financial intermediation. The message was captured eloquently in Chairman Greenspan's "spare tires" speech at the 1999 meetings of the World Bank Group and the International Monetary Fund: "This leads one to wonder how severe East Asia's problems would have been during the past 18 months had those economies not relied so heavily on banks as their means of financial intermediation….Had a functioning capital market existed, the outcome might well have been far more benign….The lack of a spare tire is of no concern if you do not get a flat….East Asia had no spare tires" (Greenspan 1999b).

There is considerable evidence regarding the beneficial impact of equity markets on economic development. For instance, in a recent study, Bekaert, Harvey, and Lundblad (2001) show that equity market liberalization, on average, leads to a 1 percent increase in annual real economic growth over a five-year period. Their study finds that a large secondary school enrollment, a small government sector, and an Anglo-Saxon legal system amplify the liberalization effect. There is evidence as well that developed capital markets also mitigate the costs of financial crisis. Figure 5.7 presents the fiscal costs of crisis in select countries against the perceived

---

6. McKinnon (1991) emphasizes that the absence of active and open security markets in developing countries places excessive risk on bank-based financial systems.

**Figure 5.7. Fiscal Costs of Crisis Compared with the Perceived Sophistication of the Financial Market**

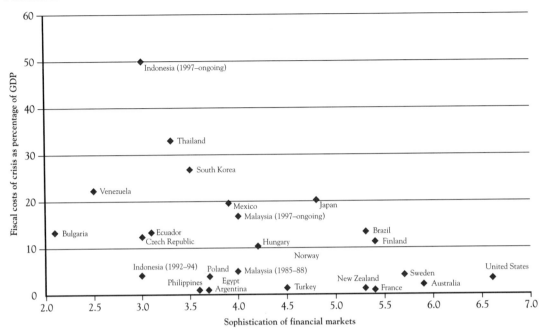

*Source:* World Economic Forum and Center for International Development, Harvard University (2000).

"sophistication of the financial market" as rated by the Global Competitiveness Report 2000.[7] The evidence suggests that diversification, depth, and breadth help financial markets to manage crisis better.

Development of capital markets leads to an open, balanced, and competitive financial system in which capital is allocated transparently and with appropriate consideration of risk. Statistics on financial sector development suggest that, in general, economies that depend too heavily on the banking sector and rely too little on capital markets can lead to corporate excesses such as high leverage and poor profitability. The key ingredients that ensure the success of capital markets—transparency, corporate accountability and governance, and proper pricing of risk through the transmission of market signals—also encourage improved corporate performance.

---

7. Sophistication of financial market: the level of sophistication in financial markets is higher than international norms (1 = strongly agree; 7 = strongly disagree). World Economic Forum and Center for International Development, Harvard University (2000).

Moreover, there is considerable evidence that in countries that rely solely on the banking system for intermediation, compared with countries that have more balanced financial systems with developed equity markets, a high degree of leverage undermines the performance of corporations. The reliance on debt leads to a financial structure that is inherently risky and vulnerable to internal and external shocks.

Although discussions about the benefits of financial deepening usually emphasize equity markets, the benefits of developing private bond markets are also compelling. Bond markets are an essential component of the financial system because they offer key benefits:

- *Balanced corporate financing structure.* Bond markets complement the ability of banks to mobilize short-term working capital and reduce maturity mismatches for corporations and banks alike. They allow corporations to mobilize longer-term funds for projects with long gestation periods such as infrastructure and housing.
- *Reduced cost of capital.* Innovations such as asset-backed securitizations in real estate, credit cards, and receivables increase diversification, reduce risks, and tap into new market segments of issuers and purchasers alike. Therefore, investors demand a lower liquidity premium, thereby reducing the cost of capital. Similarly, liquidity in the secondary market leads to a lower premium. Up to 80 percent of the reduction in interest charges is passed on to the issuers.
- *More resilient financial system.* Bond markets disperse risks across savers and reduce the concentration of risks in the banking sector, thereby enhancing the ability of the financial system to cope with shocks.
- *Higher savings.* Bond markets provide a wider choice of liquid instruments to savers and thereby promote the propensity to save.
- *More efficient resource allocation.* Bond markets perform ongoing and vigilant assessment and monitoring of creditors. Hence, bond issues contribute to heightened scrutiny of issuers, improved disclosure and transparency, and good corporate governance.
- *Better policy instruments.* Deep and liquid bond markets provide the means and instruments for conducting indirect monetary policy. They constitute a noninflationary domestic source of funds for the public sector and reduce the vulnerability associated with reliance on external financing.

5

## Box 5.1. Objectives and Principles of Securities Regulation

Although internationally agreed standards are not new, in the past few years, considerable effort has been made to address the development of internationally recognized standards to provide policymakers with benchmarks of good practice in key areas. The adopted standards (benchmarks of good practice) are designed to offer a roadmap to improve economic policymaking and strengthen the financial system. Standards and codes cover a number of economic and financial areas, including data dissemination; fiscal, monetary, and financial policy transparency; banking regulation and supervision; securities and insurance regulation; accounting, auditing, and bankruptcy; and corporate governance.

Among them are the objectives and principles of securities regulation issued by the International Organization of Securities Commissions (IOSCO), the global forum for securities regulators. In September 1998, IOSCO released 30 principles of securities regulation, which IOSCO members believe form the basis for an effective system of regulation of securities and derivatives markets. The document sets sound prudential principles and practices for the regulation and supervision of securities markets. It provides guidance for securities regulators and a yardstick against which progress toward effective regulation can be measured. The document establishes three objectives of securities regulation: to protect investors, to assure that markets are fair, efficient, and transparent; and to reduce systemic risk.

The 30 principles are grouped into eight categories:

- *Principles relating to the regulator.* (1) The responsibilities of the regulator should be clear and objectively stated; (2) the regulator should be operationally independent and accountable in the exercise of its functions and powers; (3) the regulator should have adequate powers, proper resources, and the capacity to perform its functions and exercise its powers; (4) the regulator should adopt clear and consistent regulatory processes; and (5) the staff of the regulator should observe the highest professional standards, including appropriate standards of confidentiality.
- *Principles for self-regulation.* (6) The regulatory regime should make appropriate use of self-

regulatory organizations (SROs) that exercise some direct oversight responsibility for their respective areas of competence, to the extent appropriate to the size and complexity of the markets; and (7) SROs should be subject to the oversight of the regulator and should observe standards of fairness and confidentiality when exercising powers and delegated responsibilities.

- *Principles for the enforcement of securities regulation.* (8) The regulator should have comprehensive inspection, investigation, and surveillance powers; (9) the regulator should have comprehensive enforcement powers; and (10) the regulatory system should ensure an effective and credible use of inspection, investigation, surveillance, and enforcement powers and implementation of an effective compliance program.
- *Principles for cooperation in regulation.* (11) The regulator should have authority to share both public and confidential information with domestic and foreign counterparts; (12) regulators should establish information sharing mechanisms that set out when and how they will share both public and confidential information with their domestic and foreign counterparts; and (13) the regulatory system should allow for assistance to be provided to foreign regulators who need to make inquiries in the discharge of their functions and exercise of their powers.
- *Principles for issuers.* (14) There should be full, timely, and accurate disclosure of financial results and other information that is material to investors' decisions; (15) holders of securities in a company should be treated in a fair and equitable manner; and (16) accounting and auditing standards should be of a high and internationally acceptable quality.
- *Principles for collective investment schemes.* (17) The regulatory system should set standards for the licensing and regulation of those who wish to market or operate a collective investment scheme; (18) the regulatory system should provide for rules governing the legal form and structure of collective investment schemes and the

*Continued*

---

**Box 5.1 (Continued). Objectives and Principles of Securities Regulation**

segregation and protection of client assets; (19) regulation should require disclosure, as set forth under the principles for issuers, of information that is necessary to evaluate the suitability of a collective investment scheme for a particular investor and the value of the investor's interest in the scheme; and (20) regulation should ensure that there is a proper and disclosed basis for the valuation of assets and the pricing and redemption of units in a collective investment scheme.

- *Principles for market intermediaries.* (21) Regulation should provide for minimum entry standards for market intermediaries; (22) there should be initial and ongoing capital and other prudential requirements for market intermediaries; (23) market intermediaries should be required to comply with standards for internal organization and operational conduct that aim to protect the interests of clients and under which management of the intermediary accepts primary responsibility for these matters; and (24) there should be procedures for dealing with the failure of a market intermediary in order to minimize

damage and loss to investors and to contain systemic risk.

- *Principles for the secondary market.* (25) The establishment of trading systems, including securities exchanges, should be subject to regulatory authorization and oversight; (26) ongoing regulatory supervision of exchanges and trading systems should aim to ensure that the integrity of trading is maintained through fair and equitable rules that strike an appropriate balance between the demands of different market participants; (27) regulation should promote transparency of trading; (28) regulation should be designed to detect and deter manipulation and other unfair trading practices; (29) regulation should aim to ensure the proper management of large exposures, default risk, and market disruption; and (30) the system for clearing and settlement of securities transactions should be subject to regulatory oversight and designed to ensure that it is fair, effective, and efficient and that it reduces systemic risk.

## Regulating Securities Markets

As financial systems are deregulated, the regulatory mandate is shifting away from overseeing the pricing of new equity and determining suitability standards ("merit regulation") and toward ensuring that incentives and market discipline protect investors; that markets are fair, efficient, and transparent; and that systemic risk is minimal (see box 5.1). Emerging markets are converging on a regulatory model for capital markets that is based on arm's-length transactions, disclosure, and self-regulation. Key regulatory functions in this approach ensure full and timely disclosure of all material information that investors need to make decisions, guard against anticompetitive market conduct by market participants, and protect investors from unscrupulous operators and practices.

Ultimately, good regulation is a "win-win" situation for issuers and investors. Recent literature highlights the relationship between good corporate governance and market valuation in the United States and other countries (see Black 2001; Coffee 2001; Gompers, Ishii, and Metrick 2001).

These papers find that investors reward greater shareholder rights, disclosure, and transparency with higher stock price valuations.

This model of good regulation places emphasis on achieving good market conduct by acting as a facilitator of market efficiency rather than as a heavy-handed guide. It has little place for merit-based regulation. The effectiveness of this approach relies heavily on the credibility of the regulator to enforce discipline on those who breach the rules. This requires a wide range of both criminal and administrative sanctions and a commitment on the part of the regulator to use its powers to the fullest.

Although most major emerging markets have the legal and regulatory foundation of a market-based regulatory system, achieving a mature framework is gradual and takes many years. In emerging markets, disclosure, in particular, is a relatively new concept. Two key aspects of disclosure systems are what and how to disclose, and both are of concern in many emerging markets. Regarding the issue of what to disclose, all regulatory systems across the world rely, to a large extent, on the materiality of the information standard, which requires firms to disclose all information that is material to investment decisions. Many industrial-country markets, rather than attempting to define specific standards, rely on market practice and due diligence to ensure the disclosure of all material information. In developing countries, however, market practices and due diligence are not as well developed, and it would benefit the authorities to be more proactive in defining and enforcing specific disclosure and financial reporting standards.

A second challenge confronting emerging markets is enforcement. During this nascent phase, emerging capital markets typically do not have the resources or the self-discipline to enforce and therefore to fulfill their signaling and monitoring functions. Equally important, in many jurisdictions, securities regulators are insufficiently supported by their court systems. Consequently, these regulators are often forced to rely on administrative sanctions to deal with criminal breaches of the law.

## The Policy Agenda: Second-Generation Challenges for Emerging Markets

A task for policymakers is to determine the key priorities for developing capital markets. In essence, the initial focus in the 1990s on establishing market basics—regulatory structure and trading infrastructure—was right.

The countries that are still struggling with these issues need to accelerate their efforts to resolve them. But developing countries need to bear in mind that development of capital markets is a process and not an event and that the rapid evolution of the world will continue to bring new challenges as well as opportunities.

Despite the recent progress, emerging markets still lag behind developed markets in market infrastructure and in the basics of modern regulatory frameworks and their implementation. In this context, emerging markets face a series of second-generation challenges in the new millennium. The most pressing is the need to strengthen disclosure and corporate governance. Also of concern are the links between the corporate sector and capital markets. Equity markets do not exist in a vacuum. Vibrant, financially healthy, and profitable corporations are the core foundation for markets. Unfortunately, the evidence points to poor corporate financial "health" in many emerging markets.[8] Addressing corporate financial health and performance is one of the key challenges confronting emerging markets. A third challenge is to deepen capital markets by developing the bond market and to create more representative equity markets by reducing the concentration of issuers. Fourth, the development of domestic institutional investors remains a challenge. Finally, emerging markets need to develop the capacity for self-regulation.[9]

## Improving Corporate Governance

Corporate governance came to the fore of the international development agenda in the wake of the Asian financial crisis. Unsustainable rapid and excessive investment in fixed assets, financed by excessive borrowing, took place in Asia prior to the crisis. The investment-spending spree resulted in poor profitability, as reflected in low and declining returns on equity and returns on capital employed. Both boards of directors and financial markets

8. Poor corporate performance is linked to poor return on investment in emerging markets. See Pomerleano and Zhang (1999).

9. There are two caveats to this process. Second-generation "intangible" challenges, such as disclosure, minority shareholder rights, and investor protection, probably will take more time to implement; they also are more demanding and require acceptance and ownership from a broader set of stakeholders. The list of issues pending is not inclusive. To name just a few, policymakers also are preoccupied with e-finance, the role and impact of foreign investors in equity markets, the rapidly changing trading platforms, and the changing nature of financial intermediation.

---

**Box 5.2. OECD Principles of Corporate Governance**

In this context, the Organisation for Economic Co-operation and Development (OECD) has formulated principles of corporate governance. Endorsed by the OECD's members in May 1999, the principles are designed to offer countries a benchmark for strengthening their corporate governance processes:

- *The rights of shareholders.* The corporate governance framework should protect shareholders' rights.
- *The equitable treatment of shareholders.* The corporate governance framework should ensure the equitable treatment of all shareholders, including minority and foreign shareholders. All shareholders should have the opportunity to obtain effective redress for violation of their rights.
- *The role of stakeholders in corporate governance.* The corporate governance framework should recognize the rights of stakeholders as established by law and encourage active cooperation between corporations and stakeholders in creating wealth, jobs, and the sustainability of financially sound enterprises.
- *Disclosure and transparency.* The corporate governance framework should ensure that timely and accurate disclosure is made on all material matters regarding the corporation, including the financial situation, performance, ownership, and governance of the company.
- *The responsibilities of the board.* The corporate governance framework should ensure the strategic guidance of the company, the effective monitoring of management by the board, and the board's accountability to the company and the shareholders.

---

conducted poor oversight of these financial excesses, and this was at the core of the corporate crisis. Although many developing countries made rapid and substantial progress in reforming their legal and regulatory frameworks during the 1990s, both corporate governance and disclosure systems remain generally weak.

Following the Asian crisis there has been increasing awareness of the critical role of private sector firms in creating economic well-being and the importance of disclosure and governance in the process. As disclosure improves, outside investors are better able to monitor corporate insiders and hence to monitor and discipline performance. Similarly, a good corporate governance regime helps to ensure that the corporate board is accountable to the company, the shareholders, and other stakeholders. In the process, good disclosure and governance help to maintain the confidence of investors—both foreign and domestic—and to attract more equity capital. Therefore, improving disclosure and corporate governance is critical to improving the efficient use of corporate resources and the efficiency and safety of financial systems (see box 5.2).

## Strengthening Disclosure

The disclosure-based regulatory model is not yet functioning well in emerging markets for several reasons. First, as documented in table 5.1, family control of firms and majority state ownership are still prevalent in the transition economies. In these circumstances, corporations have little tradition of disclosure. Second, because market discipline is weak, firms and insiders do not face sufficient pressure to improve disclosure and corporate governance practices. Third, although there have been improvements "on paper" in the legal and regulatory framework surrounding dis-

**Table 5.1. Ownership of 10 Largest Nonfinancial Domestic Firms by Large Shareholders**

| Country | Ownership by the three largest shareholders | |
|---|---|---|
| | Mean | Median |
| **Africa** | | |
| Nigeria | 0.40 | 0.45 |
| South Africa | 0.52 | 0.52 |
| **Asia** | | |
| Thailand | 0.47 | 0.48 |
| Indonesia | 0.58 | 0.62 |
| Philippines | 0.57 | 0.51 |
| Korea, Rep. of | 0.23 | 0.20 |
| India | 0.40 | 0.43 |
| Malaysia | 0.54 | 0.52 |
| **Latin America** | | |
| Argentina | 0.53 | 0.55 |
| Brazil | 0.57 | 0.63 |
| Chile | 0.45 | 0.38 |
| Mexico | 0.64 | 0.67 |
| **Europe** | | |
| Greece | 0.67 | 0.68 |
| Turkey | 0.59 | 0.58 |
| **Middle East** | | |
| Egypt | 0.62 | 0.62 |
| Israel | 0.51 | 0.55 |

*Source:* La Porta and others (1998: table 7).

closure and corporate governance, these improvements are not yet embedded in the cultural fabric. Finally, both corporate governance mechanisms and disclosure are undermined by inadequate accounting standards as well as lack of deterrence, weak enforcement, and poorly functioning legal systems.

## Protecting Minority Shareholder Rights

One of the key objectives of corporate governance is to protect shareholder rights. In emerging markets, two weaknesses reduce the effectiveness of these legal mechanisms. First, the enforcement capacity of capital market regulators is generally poor. Second, many countries do not provide adequate legal protections to minority shareholders. Overall, these weaknesses undermine the mechanisms of corporate governance. Remedial measures are needed to achieve the following objectives:

- Prevent abusive behavior by insiders (for example, prohibition of loans to directors, rules regarding insider trading)
- Limit the discretion of insiders in key corporate matters (for example, mandatory shareholder approval of fundamental decisions)
- Ensure adequate disclosure and transmission of information (for example, mandatory disclosure of connected interests of board members)
- Facilitate shareholder control and monitoring (for example, provisions for proxy voting, including by mail)
- Permit "oppressed" minority shareholders the option of walking away from a company or seeking judicial remedy if they object to a majority decision.

Emerging markets can create an effective legal and regulatory framework that promotes good corporate governance by embedding appropriate mechanisms in company and securities legislation and in exchange listing rules (see table 5.2). Although by no means exhaustive, the measures include provisions regarding the duties of insiders (directors and corporate officers), the rights and remedies of shareholders, disclosure and use of information by insiders, and takeovers and new issues.

Inextricably linked to the effective implementation of a disclosure-based regulatory system is the requirement for credible financial information. Therefore, stronger accounting and financial reporting standards and prac-

**Table 5.2. Corporate Governance in Asia and Latin America**

| Region and country | Investor protection[a] | Creditor protection[b] | Judicial enforcement[c] |
|---|---|---|---|
| **Asia** | | | |
| India | 2 | 4 | 6.1 |
| Indonesia | 2 | 4 | 4.4 |
| Malaysia | 3 | 4 | 7.7 |
| Pakistan | 4 | 4 | 4.3 |
| Philippines | 4 | 0 | 4.1 |
| Sri Lanka | 2 | 3 | 5.0 |
| Thailand | 3 | 3 | 5.9 |
| Average | 2.9 | 3.1 | 5.4 |
| **Latin America** | | | |
| Argentina | 4 | 1 | 5.6 |
| Brazil | 3 | 1 | 6.5 |
| Chile | 3 | 2 | 6.8 |
| Colombia | 1 | 0 | 5.7 |
| Mexico | 0 | 0 | 6.0 |
| Venezuela | 1 | — | 6.2 |
| Average | 2.0 | 0.8 | 6.1 |

— Not available

a. An index of how well legal frameworks protect minority shareholders. It aggregates four variables and a measure of how easy it is for shareholders to call an extraordinary meetings of the shareholders. See La Porta and others (1997).

b. An index of the rights of secured creditors in liquidation or reorganization of a corporation that ranges from 0 (lowest) to 4 (highest).

c. An index equal to the average of five judicial enforcement variables presented in La Porta and others (1996). The enforcement variables are measures of the efficiency of the judicial system, rule of law, corruption, and risks of expropriation and contract repudiation. The index ranges from 0 (worst) to 10 (best).

*Source:* La Porta and others (1996, 1997).

tices are urgently needed. Overall, emerging markets have improved their accounting and auditing standards, but they still need to adopt accounting standards that are consistent with those issued by the International Accounting Standards Committee.[10]

10. For summaries of international accounting standards, visit the website of the International Accounting Standards Committee: www.iasc.org.uk/cmt/0001.asp.

## Improving the Performance of Corporations and Corporate Equities

The performance of emerging-market equities, as well as their risk-return profile, has proved to be disappointing to investors and issuers compared with the performance of equities in the more developed markets (Pomerleano 1998). It begs the question, Why? In part, the under-performance of developing countries is attributable to the volatile settings of their economies, which are subject to more frequent and larger shocks than industrial countries. However, there also is substantial evidence that, in some countries, very little, if any, effort is made to focus on corporate performance. As a result, corporate return on assets and on equity is not competitive with that in other markets (Pomerleano and Zhang 1999).

## Developing Bond Markets

A common challenge across developing countries is to accelerate the development of domestic sovereign and corporate bond markets alike. Although some developing countries were able to strengthen government bond markets in the 1990s, the size and liquidity of their corporate bond markets continue to lag significantly behind (Dalla and Khatkhate 1996; World Bank and International Monetary Fund 2001). These weaknesses in domestic bond markets limit the financing options available to corporations and may contribute to excessive foreign borrowing (World Bank 1998).

The authorities need to address the major impediments to bond market development. The first constraint is market infrastructure, including trading, clearing and settlement, and custody systems. A second constraint is the legal and regulatory framework, where bond markets are facing difficult problems in moving toward a market-based system. Third, weaknesses in credit rating agencies need to be addressed. Finally, government benchmarks are needed to price securities with different risk profiles.

*Trading, Settlement, and Depository Infrastructure*

Trading and settlement infrastructure in bond markets currently lags well behind that in equity markets:

- *Clearance and settlement.* In many developing countries, there are no standard settlement procedures for corporate bonds or central depositories, and settlement is accomplished through certificates. As a result, settlement can experience long delays, and failures are common.
- *Trading systems.* Trading systems, particularly for corporate paper, are mostly over-the-counter, dealer-based systems with weak transparency. Information on trading volumes, quotations, and prices is not disseminated to the market, which undermines transparency and confidence in secondary markets.

The lack of market infrastructure increases transaction costs and discourages trading.

*Regulatory and Legal Framework*

As in the case of equity markets, the authorities need to develop, adopt, and enforce a disclosure-based regulatory system for debt markets. Weak disclosure, financial reporting, and accounting practices undermine the quality of the information available to potential investors and the capacity of credit rating agencies to conduct due diligence. Similarly, the weakness of bankruptcy regimes, coupled with the poor functioning of the court system, undermines the legal protection of creditors.

*Credit Rating Agencies*

Credit rating agencies monitor the creditworthiness of issuers and thereby assist both issuers and investors in the bond market. Credit ratings help investors to estimate the risk premiums required to compensate them for default risk. Ratings also benefit issuers, since they help to instill credibility and assist investors in differentiating appropriately between instruments and issuers. Both the ratings of new issues and the ongoing monitoring of outstanding issues are particularly important in emerging markets, where credit analysis skills are scarce (Pomerleano 2001). The development of credit rating agencies also benefits the investment community and other financial institutions by attracting skilled professionals. In summary, rating agencies help to reduce the information asymmetries between issuers and

5

investors and improve the efficiency and liquidity of the primary and secondary bond markets.

*Benchmarks*

The need for benchmarks is the final impediment. Government securities, when issued and traded in competitive markets, have traditionally served as the benchmark for the price discovery process and as a hedging vehicle for private issuance. Market-based sovereign benchmarks are needed to price securities subject to varying degrees of risks. They also can be used to assess market expectations of inflation and changes in the interest rate. Benchmark securities have various desirable characteristics. First, they are liquid, which implies large and regular issues of instruments with similar characteristics. In addition, benchmark securities that cover the whole range of the yield curve are useful for pricing longer-term securities.

## Fostering the Development of Domestic Institutional Investors

Emerging markets also need to foster the development of domestic institutional investors. Domestic institutional investors play a beneficial role in capital market development by providing depth and liquidity to markets as well as by improving corporate governance. Institutional investors can be a strong force for better disclosure and a source of demand for credit ratings. In this context, the most widely cited example of the impact of institutional investors is the development of the private pension industry in Chile and its favorable impact on capital market development. Given the diversity of institutional investors, including venture capital, mutual and pension funds, and insurance companies, all of which are discussed in other chapters, suffice it to say here that measures are needed to foster the development of institutional investors.

## Strengthening Self-Regulatory Organizations

The implementation of a new regulatory model based on arm's-length disclosure and self-regulation requires the strengthening of self-regulatory organizations (SROs), including exchanges, professional organizations, and clearing and depository institutions. The underlying premise is that SROs bear much of the responsibility for regulating and monitoring securities markets: they develop rules for their members and ensure compliance with those rules and with the securities laws. The common challenge confronting emerging markets is to develop SROs with the institutional capacity and incentives to oversee both market development and regulation. All developing countries are struggling with how to strengthen these institutions, as well as with key decisions, such as which regulatory responsibilities should be transferred to SROs and when.

In many developed markets, SROs bear much of the responsibility for regulating and monitoring securities markets, subject to regulatory oversight. SROs develop rules of behavior for their members and ensure compliance with the securities laws and regulations. The most visible SROs are stock exchanges, which oversee market rules and regulations. Similarly, broker-dealer associations license broker-dealers, determine capital and probity requirements, and set ethical codes for their members. SROs often regulate clearing and depository institutions. Equally important are professional and industry associations for analysts, accountants, lawyers, and the mutual and pension fund industries.

The benefits of self-regulation are, in many situations, compelling. First, the expertise and first-hand knowledge of practitioners are conducive to the formulation of rules that are relevant to the regulatory task. Second, the information required for effective monitoring, such as information on transactions, generally is more readily available to market participants than to regulators. Third, information usually travels faster within markets than between markets and regulators, and market participants generally respond more promptly than regulators to adverse developments.[11] Fourth, it is human nature to accept self-imposed rules more readily than rules imposed by outsiders, especially where those outsiders are believed (rightly or wrongly) to lack adequate understanding about how markets really work. Finally, SROs enable official regulatory agencies to leverage their limited public resources through their expertise and oversight. This aspect is especially relevant where the regulatory responsibilities cover several large institutions or sectors, as well as a vast array of small operators. Delegating some responsibilities to SROs can enable the agency to avoid having its limited resources dispersed widely on minor matters, in return enabling the agency to focus its resources where the risks are greatest.

---

11. There is ample evidence that interbank credit lines are one of the first warning signals of distress.

Despite its attractions, self-regulation is not without pitfalls. The most obvious of these is self-interest. Although industry and professional organizations have a reputation to uphold through tough regulatory standards, such standards often have a negative impact on profits, which may compromise their pursuit. In this respect, delegating regulatory responsibilities to SROs is sometimes regarded as equivalent to "putting the fox in charge of the hen house." Self-regulation is also predicated on the assumption that ethically strong members will enforce discipline on recalcitrant members within their ranks. The implicit assumption is that developing fair and efficient markets is in the enlightened long-term self-interest of the securities industry. This is certainly true up to a point. However, if the industry is cartelized, and potential new participants are not able to enter it, the SRO might become a vehicle for extracting rents. Indeed, markets with a small number of dominant participants rarely are good candidates for self-regulation. Finally, self-regulation can only work where the industry has the requisite expertise to set appropriate regulations and is willing to commit the resources needed to enforce them.

Clearing corporation SROs illustrate the advantages as well as the drawbacks of self-regulation. In the case of a clearing corporation, counterparty settlement risk is likely to encourage members to police each other closely as well as to establish safeguards to protect themselves and the system from the failure of a member to settle. At the same time, members of the clearing corporation have an interest in keeping membership limited, both for security and profit reasons. Provided membership can be restricted to those in the club, there is an incentive to establish regulatory burdens that are as low in cost as possible to members.

Using self-regulation in a way that extracts its benefits, without endangering the stability and integrity of the financial system, challenges both emerging and developed nations alike. The stage of development is itself a primary determinant of the extent to which SROs can be relied on. The reality for emerging-market countries is that the essential prerequisites for the self-regulatory model rarely are well developed:

- Market participants may not place high value on the long-term benefits of controlling abusive practices and enhancing confidence, when compared with the short-term gains afforded by market abuse
- Market structures are often highly concentrated

- Unless corporate governance concepts are well developed, the expertise and commitment needed to establish sound regulatory principles may not be available in the market.

The experience of the United States in pioneering the SRO model in securities regulation is a useful reminder of the difficulties posed by self-regulation and the time that can be required to balance the inevitable conflicts. Although SROs were established in the United States as far back as 1929, concurrent with establishment of the Securities and Exchange Commission (SEC), the governance arrangements of SROs were still being questioned as late as the 1990s.[12] In 1995, following an SEC inquiry, the U.S. National Association of Securities Dealers significantly reformed its governance bodies. More recently, the demutualization of the New York Stock Exchange once again threw into question the appropriateness of its being an SRO.

Emerging-market countries considering the selective use of SROs need to address the following questions: Is the institutional and human capital required for SROs adequate? Does the lack of competition undermine the incentives for market participants to self-police? Is the corporate governance structure adequate to mitigate conflicts of interest? How can SROs be nurtured? Is there a natural process for transferring responsibilities to SROs as markets develop?

The following are some measures that can support development of the prerequisites for self-regulation in securities markets:

- *Nurture the development of key professions.* Regulators can play an active role in developing the base of skills required for SROs. In the first place, they can develop these professions by creating a sound regulatory structure to ensure that practitioners have high levels of competence, diligence, and integrity and that clients can rely on their expertise and judgment. Concurrently, regulators can nurture the development of skills through the outsourcing of government contracts.

---

12. The most visible experiment with—and failure of—financial self-regulation in recent decades took place in the United Kingdom. After a decade in which the powers and effectiveness of the complex structure of SROs were repeatedly challenged and found wanting, the structure was folded back into a more conventional official regulatory agency, the Financial Services Authority.

- *Encourage competition.* To reduce the possibility that established firms can limit entry into the industry, regulators should formulate clear and transparent licensing criteria and, where appropriate, open markets to foreign participants.
- *Facilitate the adoption of new technology.* Information improves transparency. In some cases, regulators can provide information directly; in others, they can assist markets to identify and implement relevant technological advances related to the provision of data. Efforts to upgrade information systems, such as market trading data systems, can greatly improve transparency and, in the process, pave the way for self-regulation.
- *Improve governance standards.* Regulators can help to establish the foundation for SROs by improving governance in both the industry and, ultimately, the SROs themselves, when they are established.
- *Improve regulation.* The higher are the regulatory standards set by official regulatory agencies, the more relevant are the benchmarks against which SROs can be judged.

On balance, the development of SROs in emerging markets is desirable. At the same time, it should be seen as a process rather than an event. The process should involve a graduated delegation of powers in response to the emergence of the necessary conditions for successful implementation of self-regulation and an active contribution by the official regulatory agencies to the establishment of those conditions.

## Epilogue

As this book is being written, watershed changes are taking place in the structure of capital markets and the definition of markets and exchanges. Most significant among these are the demutualization of stock exchanges and the growth of cross-border listings and markets.

Demutualization involves the reformation of stock exchanges as listed companies. This process, which started with the Sydney Stock Exchange in Australia, has some wide-range implications for the conduct and regulation of exchanges:

- First, demutualization introduces greater competitive pressure and efficiency into the affected exchanges by breaking the long-standing—and in most cases, extremely conservative —"club mentality" of the old mutual exchanges.
- Second, Demutualization introduces the need to satisfy the demands of shareholders for profits, pressuring the exchanges to reduce their costs and expand their services.
- Third, demutualization creates a situation in which the exchanges may list in their own boards, thereby exposing them to the same governance and disclosure requirements that they have imposed on other listed companies.
- Fourth, listing on their own boards exposes a conflict of interest between the exchange as a company and the exchange as a self-regulatory organization. In effect, it is difficult for a market participant to regulate the market in which it operates. Some countries are addressing this conflict by reorganizing the exchange and creating a separate, independent regulatory arm. Others are addressing it by returning most of the regulatory oversight to the market conduct regulatory agency involved.

5

The future of demutualization is still unclear. On the one hand, economic pressures and the temptation to unlock capital value mean that it will be difficult to reverse course. On the other hand, the governance and conflict issues raised by demutualization are still being resolved.

The second significant issue emerging in world capital markets is the growth of cross-border listings and cross-border markets. The pressures of globalization in all areas of commerce and finance have made some developments in this respect inevitable. Cross-border listings and dual listings of companies (in which a company registers multiple units in different countries and links them by a shareholder agreement that effectively creates a single entity) have been around for several years. What was perhaps least expected in recent years was the emergence of global markets spanning more than one country (such as Euronext) in which exchanges go beyond simple cooperation agreements and form a genuine transnational exchange.

Again, these developments have interesting regulatory implications. In the case of dual-listed regulated institutions, host regulators appear to be favoring joint supervisory arrangements, with one or the other as the lead agency in the event of difficulties. These may prove inadequate as the cross-border structures become more complex. The emergence of multinational markets is even more demanding. The challenge for regulators is to develop a multijurisdictional approach to regulation that parallels the development of institutions and markets. If nothing else, the creation of multinational markets will pressure international regulators to harmonize their policies and procedures and to coordinate their activities to a much greater extent than has been the case in the past.

5

# Chapter 6

# Specialized Financial Institutions

*Specialized financiers play a range of roles in both developed and emerging markets. In developed markets, their roles are driven primarily by the benefits that accrue to specialization and, in some cases, by tax incentives. In emerging markets, they often play a broader role in deepening financial markets and overcoming legal and regulatory shortcomings.*

*This chapter concentrates on just two of the range of specialized financial institutions: leasing financiers and real estate financiers. These two groups are among the best established of the specialized financial institutions and serve to illustrate most of the issues involved with this group. The chapter also offers some comments on cooperatives.*

## Leasing Finance

Leasing is a contractual arrangement that allows one party (the lessee) to use an asset owned by the other party (the lessor) in exchange for specified periodic payments (this section draws heavily on International Finance

Corporation 1996). In practical terms, a lease is almost indistinguishable from an asset purchase, where an external financier provides the finance, the asset user makes periodic repayments against the loan, and the purchased asset secures the loan. What distinguishes the lease from the leveraged purchase is that ownership of the asset resides with the financier, rather than with the asset user; that is, legal ownership of the asset is separated from its economic use.

There are many variants of the basic lease structure. Under a financial lease, the lessee is responsible for maintaining the asset and has an obligation to purchase the asset (in some cases, this may be an option to purchase or an option to refinance) at the expiry of the lease at a prearranged residual value. In many cases, the lease payments are structured to fully amortize the lessor's capital costs over the term of the lease. Under an operating lease, the lessor is responsible for maintaining the asset and assumes full risk for its residual value.

Leases also can be fully financed by the leasing company or leveraged through the introduction of an external financier, whose recourse is usually limited to the lessor. Cross-border leveraged leases, which became fashionable in the early and mid-1990s, involve complex structures in which both the lessor and lessee may be financed externally, with the liability for future lease payments being fully pledged to one of the external financiers. These more elaborate structures are designed largely to arbitrage different tax jurisdictions (in particular, differences in depreciation regimes) and bear little resemblance to the basic structure of financial or operating leases. Hire-purchase arrangements are a hybrid instrument in which both the user and the financier of the asset share equity and in which ownership of the asset transfers progressively to the user.

Sale/lease-back arrangements involve existing, rather than new, capital equipment. Under a sale/lease-back arrangement, the lessee sells the asset from its balance sheet to the lessor. The lessor, in turn, leases the asset back to the lessee in return for long-term lease payments. Where the assets are dedicated to the uses of the lessee, such as electricity-generating plants and railway tracks, the asset usually reverts to the lessee at the end of the lease contract, for a nominal amount. Sale/lease-back arrangements can be a useful means of raising liquidity from existing assets.

In financial terms, leases are structurally comparable with other financing transactions in that the provider of the finance seeks to recover its capital outlays plus interest on the funds tied up for the period involved. The cost of this finance to the asset user varies according to who bears the various risks involved (such as obsolescence and maintenance) and the financier's cost of funds (including any tax or other benefits involved).

The range of assets suitable for leasing is extensive. Large-scale, durable, nonportable assets, such as commercial real estate, are ideal candidates for leasing. The absence of these ideal characteristics, however, is not insurmountable, and leases are extended to cover virtually all forms of capital equipment, from aircraft and heavy earth-moving equipment to mobile telephones.

Leasing has a long history, although its popularity has increased greatly in the past 40 or so years in developed markets and over the past 20 years in emerging markets. In its early stages in the nineteenth century, leasing emerged primarily as a technique to help manufacturers sell their products, by providing administratively simple, and in some cases relatively cheap, finance. The industry evolved beyond this narrow focus in the 1950s with the formation of independent leasing companies in the United States. The industry extended to Japan and Europe in the 1960s, and, by the mid-1990s, leasing had become established in over 80 countries, including more than 50 emerging markets.

It is estimated that $500 billion of capital equipment are financed by lease every year (Fleming 2000). This figure represents about an eighth of the world's private investment. In Organisation for Economic Co-operation and Development (OECD) countries, up to a third of private investment is financed through leases. In terms of volume, the United States dominates the world market, accounting for around 40 percent of worldwide leasing. Although leasing has been growing very rapidly in emerging market economies, the extent of penetration of private investment finance is still relatively low in all but a few of these countries.

The most spectacular growth in leasing among the emerging market economies has been in the Republic of Korea. By the mid-1990s, Korea's leasing market had become the fifth largest in the world (at over $13 billion, it represents about a fifth of private investment). Colombia, Indonesia, Mexico, and South Africa are other emerging market economies that rank highly in the world in their use of leasing finance.

## Real Estate Finance

Real estate finance refers to financing the acquisition of real property. Borrowing for the purpose of acquiring real estate typically is secured by a

165

mortgage (that is, a claim or lien) over the property being purchased. Although the lender demands additional collateral, the use of the property itself as the primary collateral is what distinguishes real estate finance from most other types of finance. Real estate finance usually is divided into commercial and residential, and both areas have been fertile grounds for financial innovation. In many countries, real estate finance is one of the most dominant forms of finance in the economy, often accounting for between one-quarter and half of bank lending.

The traditional model of real estate finance involves lending from the balance sheet of a financial institution, which takes responsibility for all stages of the lending process. Although banks and insurance companies have been a major source of on-balance-sheet lending for real estate, specialized financial institutions also have emerged to carry out the same function. Specialized real estate financing institutions are called savings and loans (or thrifts) in the United States, building societies in the United Kingdom and countries with a British commonwealth background, and mortgage banks in Europe.[1] The origins of building societies and thrifts and some comments on their regulation are taken up further in the section on cooperative financial institutions.

Under this traditional model, the financial institutions involved provide all the services associated with the financing process:

- They originate the loans from their client base, taking responsibility for the paperwork involved and assessing both the capacity of the borrower to repay and the quality of the real estate taken as collateral.
- They fund the loans from their balance sheets.
- They service the loans by collecting loan repayments and by pursuing overdue payments.
- They manage the risks involved in providing real estate finance.

The traditional, or full-service, model of real estate finance includes two basic forms of mortgage. The most common is the amortizing mortgage, in which the borrower makes regular repayments of sufficient size to cover the periodic interest commitments as well as to reduce the outstanding principal. Over the term of the loan, the payments fully amortize the principal. The second is the interest-only loan, in which the payments are only suffi-

---

1. To a lesser extent, in some countries credit unions and housing cooperatives provide real estate finance.

cient to cover the periodic interest commitments. Under this form, the principal liability remains intact and is due for repayment in full at the termination of the loan period. Each of these types of basic mortgages can be issued either as fixed rate, in which the interest rate is set in advance for the entire term of the loan, or as variable rate, in which the rate is adjusted in line with movements in market interest rates over time, either at the discretion of the lender or according to a predetermined formula.

In recent years, the range of repayment and interest rate options in mature mortgage markets has expanded to include many variations:

- Balloon mortgages, which repay part of the principal over a relatively short term (for example, three to five years) and then the balance at the end of that term
- Canadian rollovers, which require refinancing every few years
- Graduated payment mortgages, which start with low repayments in the early years and graduate to a plateau in the later years (in some cases, the early payments are lower than the costs of interest servicing, with the result that the principal increases as interest is capitalized during the early years)
- Growing equity mortgages, in which initially low payments increase in line with a prearranged index
- Shared appreciation mortgages, which offer low interest rates in return for part equity participation by the lender
- Convertible mortgages, which are convertible from fixed-rate mortgages to variable-rate mortgages
- Reverse amortization mortgages, in which the homeowner draws an annuity income to be repaid on the sale of the property or on the death of the borrower.

The risks in real estate lending are dominated by credit exposure to the borrowers. Mitigating these risks is the value of the real property that collateralizes the loan. Historically, default rates on residential real estate lending have been relatively low. Further, residential real estate generally has provided stable or increasing collateral value for these loans.[2] The picture is quite different for commercial real estate, where changes in property values due to changes in market prices and vacancies are much more volatile.

---

2. The relatively low-risk nature of residential mortgage lending is reflected in the concessional risk weight allocated to these loans under the Basle Committee's Capital Accord.

For example, in Thailand in the late 1990s, commercial properties accounted for only one-quarter of the total value of real estate, yet, in the aftermath of the Asian crisis, commercial properties accounted for around three-quarters of the loss in wealth resulting from the collapse in real estate values.

The other major risk in real estate lending relates to funding. Real estate finance is inherently long term. Where funding is provided predominantly from short-term sources, as is the case with bank and most specialized institution financing, the lender is exposed to market risk arising from changes in the shape and position of the yield curve and to liquidity risk arising from the possible loss of short-term funds. The market risk is compounded by the tendency in most countries for mortgage lending to offer the borrower an option for early repayment. This creates some ambiguity about the maturity of the loans and increases the difficulty for the lender in trying to match the maturity of its assets and liabilities. Where banks and insurance companies provide real estate finance, they manage these risks within the context of their overall portfolios. Specialized real estate financiers usually manage these risks in a much narrower context.

The traditional model of real estate financing tends to be relatively high cost, because one institution performs all functions and manages all risks. This, combined with the relatively homogeneous nature of mortgage loans, creates an incentive for financial innovation to make the process more cost-effective. Innovation has resulted in unbundling of the various stages of the credit process, securitization of mortgages, and even to unbundling of the various components of claims against the borrowers. Although this new model of real estate financing has been active in the United States for decades, its emergence in other countries is much more a product of the 1990s.

Unbundling the credit process has occurred through specialized service providers managing each of the separate stages. Under this model, specialized real estate loan originators focus on marketing the loans, processing applications, underwriting the initial extension of credit, and, in some cases, warehousing the loans temporarily until they are on-sold to longer-term investors. Unlike full-service real estate financiers, these service providers do not take the mortgages onto their balance sheets other than in a warehousing role. In many cases, banks, insurance companies, and specialized real estate lending institutions still perform some of the functions in this delivery chain, either in loan origination, in mortgage insurance, or in loan servicing and foreclosures.

Unbundling the service chain in real estate finance has introduced new sources of competition and eroded margins. The full-service institutions have, nevertheless, been reasonably supportive of this process to the extent that it provides a degree of liquidity, not only for new mortgage loans but also for existing loans on their books.

The process through which full-service real estate lending institutions transfer the loans and the associated credit and market risks off their balance sheets is known as securitization. Securitization refers to the process of endowing otherwise illiquid assets with the qualities of a security. In practice, this involves packaging income-yielding assets into standardized bundles and issuing them in tradable form as highly rated securities secured by the underlying assets. In many cases, the quality of the securities is improved by the addition of enhancements from third parties. These enhancements include insurance over the timing of payments and over certain default events.

The purchasers of the securitized instruments provide the ultimate finance for the real estate loans and absorb the residual credit and market risk. By packaging the loans in this way, the market is able to reduce some of the risks involved, for example, by better matching the maturity profile of the assets and liabilities involved.

Securitized mortgages are marketed in three main forms: pass-through securities, mortgage bonds, and collateralized mortgage obligations (CMOs). The most developed of these markets is that for pass-through securities.

A pass-through security involves establishing a trust, into which the mortgage assets are sold, with beneficial ownership assigned to the holders of the securities that are issued against them. The trustee pays interest and principal on the mortgages to the managing financial institution, which passes them to the holders of the securities, less any management and insurance fees.

Mortgage bonds are securities issued by a financial institution and collateralized by mortgages or mortgage-backed securities. In this case, the assets stay on the institution's balance sheet.

Collateralized mortgage obligations take the process of specialization one step further by breaking the underlying obligations into maturity tranches. Holders of the first tranche receive priority for the return of their principal from early repayments. Thus, if a high percentage of borrowers exercise their early repayment option, holders of the higher-priority tranches may be paid out quite early. As is the case with mortgage bonds, CMOs

6

usually remain on the institution's balance sheet. Real estate mortgage investment conduits (REMICs) take this process even further by stripping CMOs down into principal-only and interest-only components.

The real estate finance industry not only has been innovative in creating debt instruments but also has generated innovative equity instruments. Real estate investment trusts (REITs) emerged in the United States as far back as the 1960s. These trusts are formed as corporations and registered with the Internal Revenue Service as REITs for tax benefits—primarily the ability to issue dividends before tax rather than after tax. In order to qualify for the tax concessions, REITs must satisfy certain income tests (for example, 75 percent of the company's income must come from rents, mortgage interest, and capital gains from real property sales) and asset tests (for example, 75 percent of the company's assets must be in real estate). REITs provide real estate investment opportunities to small investors by increasing the divisibility and diversification benefits through pooling.

## A Note on Financial Cooperatives

Cooperative societies may be formed for a wide array of purposes, ranging from the marketing of primary produce to the provision of community services such as the supply of water, electricity, and transport.[3] Most cooperatives have their philosophical roots in the self-help movement that emerged in Victorian England and spread to Europe and elsewhere during the nineteenth century. Cooperatives traditionally are founded on the principle of mutuality and are operated as clubs. Over time, the role of cooperative societies has expanded to encompass the field of finance. The three dominant forms of financial cooperatives throughout the world are building societies, credit unions, and friendly societies.

Early building societies were formed by small groups of people, usually with similar occupations or beliefs, who pooled their resources to provide housing finance to members. When the loans were fully repaid, the societies terminated. A variation of these terminating societies, Starr Bowkett societies, was distinguished by the feature that their members were entitled to low-interest or no-interest loans allocated by ballot. Terminating building societies evolved into permanent building societies or thrifts, which spe-

3. This section draws on Committee of Inquiry into Non-Bank Financial Institutions and Related Financial Processes in the State of Queensland (1990).

170

cialize in housing finance. Other than their specialization in housing finance, modern permanent building societies are almost indistinguishable from other deposit-taking institutions such as banks. Most countries allow permanent building societies to raise equity capital, raise deposits from the public, and invest in a wide range of assets beyond residential mortgages.

According to the World Council of Credit Unions, credit unions (societies) are described as cooperative financial institutions, owned and operated on a not-for-profit basis by their members according to democratic principles. The original self-help philosophy of credit cooperatives provided for ownership of the society by its members and for operation of the society for their benefit. Credit union members traditionally were drawn together by a common bond encompassing occupational, industrial, religious, or ethnic links. Although modern credit unions have retained their mutual origins to a much greater extent than have permanent building societies, they too have evolved. In most countries, the concept of common bond has been interpreted loosely to incorporate almost any characteristic short of local nationality. In many cases, credit unions have evolved into community-based financiers rather than common-bond financiers. Like permanent building societies, they have many similarities with banks, raising deposits from the public and specializing in unsecured consumer lending.

Friendly societies traditionally provided insurance against a wide range of contingencies, including death, sickness, and unemployment. As with other cooperatives, their origins lay primarily in the provision of welfare benefits and social activities. During the past century, a small percentage of friendly societies have grown into substantial financial enterprises specializing in insurance and contractual savings.

In most countries, the cooperative sector is relatively small. Of the three groups, credit unions have been the most successful at establishing an international spread of a relatively homogeneous model. Permanent building societies and friendly societies are less widely established, although in some jurisdictions they have a substantial presence.

Where cooperatives have remained small and not-for-profit in orientation, they have created few regulatory concerns and in most cases have been subject to fairly light regulation. In some cases, however, cooperatives have been able to exploit favorable tax treatment or lax regulatory regimes to establish themselves as significant players in the financial system. In these cases, they have been capable of generating both systemic concerns and moral hazard problems for government.

A fundamental principle of good regulation is that institutions offering similar promises should be subject to the same type and intensity of regulation. Modern building societies and credit unions are indistinguishable from banks in the promises they make. Similarly, modern friendly societies are indistinguishable from insurance companies in the promises they make. Notwithstanding their mutual origins or not-for-profit orientation (although the relevance of this stated objective is highly questionable in modern financial systems), there is a strong case for regulating these institutions in the same way as comparable conventional financial institutions.

There may be a case in emerging market economies for implementing this level of regulation in a staged manner. Cooperatives can be a healthy source of growth for community-based nonbank financial institutions (NBFIs) in areas and among communities where larger institutions find the scale of operation uneconomic. The fact that they are community based and not-for-profit makes them ideal for small communities. It also makes them fertile ground for fraud and abuse. During the early stages of financial development, there is a case for focusing regulation primarily on governance requirements to minimize abuse. As the industry grows, there should be a natural progression from focus just on governance to a wider range of prudential requirements, leading eventually to regulation as ordinary deposit-taking institutions.

The one signal that regulators need to be conscious of in a staged regulatory evolution is unexpectedly rapid growth. Not only is rapid growth of a financial business a normal source of prudential concern, in the case of emerging markets, it also is likely to be a signal that the institutions have identified a weakness in the regulatory structure and have grown beyond their original charter to exploit the weakness.

## Factors Affecting the Growth of Specialized Financial Institutions

Ultimately, the growth of specialized financial institutions is a product of two main factors: the natural market for particular forms of specialized finance and the net outcome of incentives and impediments imposed by governments.

**Leasing Finance**

The fact that leasing finance has grown as strongly as it has in recent decades suggests a natural base of strong demand for this type of financing. This natural base arises from a number of advantages that leasing offers to both the lessee and lessor.

*Separation of Ownership and Use*

The main natural advantage of leasing in emerging markets lies in its separation of ownership from economic use. For the lessor, ownership provides stronger security. In countries where collateral laws are not well developed or enforced by courts, secured lending of the type offered by banks can involve considerable collateral risk. Leasing offers the advantage of simpler procedures for repossession, because ownership of the asset already lies with the lessor.

Advantages also can accrue to the lessee. Many small- and medium-size enterprises have limited access to capital for investment and, due to the nature of their balance sheets and business histories, often find conventional sources of finance difficult to obtain. Since ownership of the asset remains with the lessor, collateral requirements for leased assets often are waived or minimal. Documentation also typically is simpler and therefore less expensive because the lessor holds direct title to the asset in question. In some emerging markets, leasing may be the only source of finance available for small enterprises.

Leasing also can benefit the lessee to the extent that it enables the lessee to leverage off the purchasing strength of specialized lessor companies. Not only do leasing companies typically have more concentrated purchasing power with manufacturers than do small- and medium-size enterprises, but they also often have better access to scarce foreign exchange resources and to import licenses (where the equipment is imported). The lessee benefits to the extent that these cost reduction factors pass from the lessor through to the lessee in the form of lower leasing charges. The lower cost structures, in turn, support the demand for leasing.

*Use of Existing Assets*

Not only has leasing proved to be a relatively cheap and efficient source of funding for new capital investment, but sale/lease-backs also have provided a rich source of funds from existing capital. This has been an important source of funds for privatized industries, where governments often leave newly privatized firms asset rich but liquidity poor. By selling dedicated assets and leasing them back through long-term arrangements, these firms have been able to increase their liquid assets for working capital, for capital expansion, and even for corporate acquisitions. Thus privatization tends to provide a natural boost to the demand for sale/lease-back arrangements.

Some semi-government agencies and charitable organizations also have used sale/lease-back arrangements as an alternative means of raising finance. Since these agencies usually are exempted from tax, the sale/lease-back enables them to share in the tax deductibility of capital expenditure from which they would not benefit otherwise. It also provides them with greater flexibility in their finances and, in some cases, enables them to circumvent government restrictions on their capacity to raise conventional debt and equity finance.

*Government Incentives*

In many jurisdictions, governments provide net incentives that support the natural advantages of leasing. The most fundamental of these incentives are taxation concessions. The conventional tax treatment of leases is to permit the lessee to expense the full amount of lease payments. As the owner of the asset, the lessor is required to treat the lease payments as income, against which it can deduct depreciation and other associated costs, including the interest cost on its own sources of finance. Provided the two parties to the lease are subject to the same tax burden, the net impact is largely neutral. However, where their tax burdens are different, either because of timing or because of their ability to access deductions, the impact can be significant. For example, in a start-up situation, the lessee may be unable to take advantage of tax deductions for several years. Where depreciation rates are high in the early years of an asset's life, leasing usually increases the combined after-tax value of the asset purchase (measured as the combined value to the lessor plus the lessee).

The scope for extracting tax advantages from leasing is greater in situations in which the lessee and lessor reside in different tax jurisdictions. Although cross-border leasing has grown significantly in the past decade, it is still relatively uncommon in emerging financial systems because of the additional cross-border jurisdictional risks involved.

*The Role of Insurance*

Another factor that can influence the growth of leasing is the availability of insurance. Most leased items are exposed to loss of capital value through destruction, loss, or theft, as well as through normal wear and tear in the everyday business of the lessee. Since the lessor has little or no control over these events, the ability to insure leased assets through third-party insurers is a precondition for the development of a deep and active market for leasing.

Finally, as with most forms of finance, a sound legal system is conducive to the growth of leasing. In particular, a supportive legal system provides for different forms of leasing contracts, assigns clear property rights, and, in the event of economic failure, provides for the timely establishment of default and enforcement of rights for collection and disposal of leased assets.

## Real Estate Finance

6

The dominant factor behind the overall growth of the real estate finance market has been demographic patterns. The relative growth rates of the providers of real estate finance, however, relate more closely to differential regulatory burdens.

*Demographic Factors*

Demographic trends exert a strong influence on the demand for residential real estate and real estate finance. Where population growth is high, the demand for new residential housing follows. On a global scale, the world's population has almost tripled since 1930, from around 2 billion to around 5.7 billion in 1995 (Famighetti 1995). The growth of population and wealth has been accompanied by an increase in urbanization and housing investment. Thus there has been a natural and growing demand for real estate finance.

This natural base of demand does not guarantee that there is a natural base of demand for specialized financial institutions in the provision of real estate finance. Real estate finance, both residential and commercial, is a relatively straightforward process and is well suited to banks and life insurance companies. Banks have ready access to cheap sources of funds through retail deposits and have the infrastructure to process real estate loans efficiently and the skills to manage the risks involved. Insurance companies are equally well suited to providing real estate finance because of their stable base of funding and the natural long-term nature of their liabilities.

Historically, the main competitors for banks and insurance companies in the field of real estate finance have been specialized institutions, such as savings and loan associations, mortgage banks, and building societies. These institutions do not appear to bring any particularly innovative financing techniques or cost-efficiencies to the business. In many ways, they share the same advantages and disadvantages of full-service banks. In some areas, such as specialization and focus, they have potential advantages, but in other areas, such as diversification, risk management expertise, and access to cheap funding, they normally operate at a disadvantage relative to banks. This arguably modest natural base of demand for their services has, however, been supplemented by regulatory advantages in many countries.

*Regulatory Influences*

The impact of differential regulatory burdens on competing financial institutions can be significant. During the 1960s and 1970s, most banking regulators approached safety and soundness in the banking system largely by limiting the activities that banks could undertake and by imposing interest rate ceilings on both deposits and lending. The result was loan rationing and sluggish growth in banking systems. In contrast, regulation of specialized real estate finance institutions was relatively light; in some countries, such as the United States, it was lax and heavily prescriptive, while in others it was simply lax. The result was a regulatory imbalance between banks and specialized financial institutions, despite the fact that they offered essentially the same products to both depositors and real estate borrowers.

The experience in Australia provides a good example of pressures that were felt in many countries. During the 1960s and 1970s, Australian banks were constrained to maintain the growth of their lending within limits set by the central bank.[4] They also were required to hold prescribed deposits with the central bank and to hold a prescribed minimum ratio of their assets in the form of liquid assets and government securities (this ratio varied over time but was generally between 15 and 20 percent). In addition, their ability to compete for deposits was constrained by an interest rate prohibition on deposits for less than 90 days and by interest rate ceilings on deposits

---

4. The description and numbers cited in this section for Australia draw heavily on Edey and Gray (1996), and Lewis and Wallace (1993).

longer than 90 days. Life insurance companies were required to hold 30 percent of their assets in the form of government securities, at least two-thirds of which had to be commonwealth government securities.

Finance companies and building societies competed with banks and life insurance companies in providing mortgage lending in Australia.[5] The latter two did so, however, without the lending, pricing, and balance sheet constraints of the former. Indeed, banks established many of the finance companies as subsidiaries in order to circumvent these regulations.

With economic conditions generally stable throughout most of the 1960s, the tension between market forces and the prescriptive regulations facing banks and insurance companies remained latent. During the 1960s, bank assets as a share of total financial institution assets declined from around 46 percent to around 41 percent. The share of building society assets in this total increased from around 3 percent to around 4.5 percent, the share of insurance company assets increased from 20 percent to 23 percent, and the share of finance companies increased from 7.5 percent to a little over 9 percent.

The impact of regulatory differences was much more pronounced in the 1970s. With many lending rates capped and inflation rising sharply, the demand for debt to finance real asset acquisitions (often at negative real rates of interest) increased sharply. In this environment, nonbanks such as specialized real estate finance institutions found it attractive to bid depositors away from banks and to on-lend funds at unregulated interest rates. Against this background, the share of bank assets in the total declined further to 38 percent by the end of the 1970s. The share of insurance companies fell from 23 percent to around 17 percent.

Both building societies and finance companies, in contrast, won market share from the regulated sector and increased their market share to around 8 percent and almost 12 percent, respectively. Although figures are not available for residential housing lending on a consistent basis for this period, the impact of differential regulatory burdens on the housing finance market was much more dramatic than these aggregate numbers suggest. For example, in 1980, while building societies accounted for only 8 percent of the total assets of the financial system, they accounted for closer to 40 percent of the market for residential housing finance.

The importance of differential regulatory burdens on the growth of specialized real estate financial institutions was further highlighted by the peri-

----

5. Finance companies also were major competitors for banks in the area of leasing finance.

od following sweeping deregulation in the late 1970s and early 1980s. By 1990, Australian banks and insurance companies had both rebuilt their market shares almost to their 1960s levels. In contrast, building societies had declined back to their 1960s market share of 3 percent, and finance companies had slipped almost 2 percentage points below their 1960s level to a market share of only 3 percent. This trend away from specialized real estate finance institutions continued over the past decade.

*Technological Innovation and Legislative Facilitation*

Technological advances have played a role in the emergence and growth of specialized nonintermediary service providers in the real estate financing process. The high cost of providing full-service mortgage lending has created an incentive for service providers to specialize in different aspects of the delivery chain. Unlike the specialized full-service real estate financiers, these service providers do not take the mortgages onto their balance sheets other than in a warehousing role.

Technological advances, especially those associated with computerized software for managing back-office functions, such as allocating membership rights in pooled assets and for marking asset values to market, have paved the way for this process of unbundling to make inroads into the real estate finance market.

In some cases, technological advances have not been sufficient by themselves to generate unbundled finance as an alternative to the traditional full-service model. Depending on the nature and scope of securities law, special provisions may need to be legislated to enable securitization to take place. At a minimum, the law should provide the necessary protections for the investors in securitized pools of mortgages, by defining their rights relative to those of other members, the pool manager, and the scheme promoters.

*Other Government Incentives*

In addition to their influence through the regulatory system, governments have influenced both the growth of real estate finance generally and the structure of the industry through their welfare policies.

Governments often have viewed residential housing as a key area of welfare policy and, in many cases, have sought to implement their policies through financial institutions. In this area welfare policy focuses primarily on the provision of housing to low-income groups and the difficulties they have obtaining loans from conventional sources.

Some governments have sought to support low-income housing by offering cash payments and tax incentives to the purchaser. In other cases, the incentives are offered to the welfare recipient indirectly through a financial institution. This may take the form of required lending targets (a prescriptive approach) or financial subsidies and incentives for lending to specified groups within society. The third form of support for low-income housing occurs where the government establishes public financial institutions specifically for the purpose of subsidizing housing finance.

Each of these approaches has the potential to stimulate the growth of the real estate market and the demand for real estate finance relative to other forms of economic and financial activity in the community. Only the first does so in a way that is relatively neutral across the industry. Because the first approach provides the subsidy directly to the welfare recipient, it does not distort the recipient's decision with respect to competing sources of finance.

The second approach, in which housing finance incentives are offered through financial institutions, has the potential to distort the pattern of real estate finance unless the incentives are offered uniformly across all providers of real estate finance. For example, the granting of tax-exempt status to providers of mutual housing finance, as has been the case in some Anglo-Saxon countries, confers a competitive advantage on these institutions.[6] Similarly, mortgage banks in Europe have been used historically to provide subsidized housing consistent with the government's welfare policies.

The third approach—the provision of government-supported deposit guarantee schemes, such as the Federal Savings and Loans Insurance Corporation scheme (and its successor) in the United States—is yet another way in which these subsidies can be provided indirectly through the institution rather than directly to the welfare recipient. Although tax and other incentives often are accompanied by restrictions aimed at concentrating the financing activities of these institutions among lower-income groups, markets are notoriously creative at exploiting differential financial incentives. This approach has the greatest potential to influence both the growth of real estate finance and the structure of the industry. The leading example of this approach has been the United States, where the strength of the

---

6. For example, the terminating building societies and cooperatives housing societies that are found in a number of countries with a British commonwealth heritage.

**Box 6.1. Government-Sponsored Financial Enterprises:
The Cases of Fannie Mae and Freddie Mac**

The U.S. Congress created government-sponsored financial enterprises (GSEs) in response to the perception that private financial markets were not adequately meeting the credit needs of certain market segments such as housing and agriculture. The Federal National Mortgage Association (Fannie Mae), the Federal Home Loan Mortgage Corporation (Freddie Mac), and the Federal Home Loan Bank System (FHL Bank System) are all GSEs that seek to facilitate the channeling of credit into homeownership (U.S. General Accounting Office 1997). Their legislated mission is to enhance the availability of mortgage credit by creating and maintaining a secondary market for residential mortgages. In 1992, the Office of Federal Housing Enterprises Financial Safety and Soundness required the Department of Housing and Urban Development (HUD) to establish affordable housing goals and directed Fannie Mae and Freddie Mac to finance housing for low- and moderate-income families and housing in central cities and other underserved areas.

Fannie Mae and Freddie Mac borrow funds in the capital markets and use them to purchase residential mortgages from lenders such as banks and thrifts. Although they retain some mortgages in their portfolios, they place most mortgages in a pool to create mortgage-backed securities (MBS). These are sold to investors in the secondary mortgage market. Fannie Mae and Freddie Mac have grown to become two of the largest financial institutions in the United States, and together they own or guarantee roughly 40 percent of outstanding U.S. residential mortgages. The debt obligations that they have issued or guaranteed amount to nearly $2.5 trillion in liabilities and mortgage-backed securities, roughly the same size as the insured deposits of the U.S. commercial banking system. Both GSEs are stockholder-owned corporations listed on the New York Stock Exchange. However, the government's presence is reflected in the composition of their boards of directors, which are made up of 13 members elected by stockholders and five appointed by the president of the United States.

The activities of these GSEs are restricted by their public missions; in return, they receive financial and other benefits from the government that help them to carry out those missions. For example, Fannie Mae and Freddie Mac securities are exempt from state and local taxation and from registration requirements of the Securities and Exchange Commission. Each also has a backup line of credit with the U.S. Treasury.

The government sponsorship of GSEs poses a serious policy dilemma that has, in recent years, led to a vigorous debate between their proponents and opponents. By statute, securities issued or guaranteed by Fannie Mae and Freddie Mac must expressly state that they are not guaranteed by the United States. However, rightly or wrongly, there is a perception among investors that the securities benefit from an implicit government guarantee. Those who argue that the role of these agencies should be wound back cite government involvement in board appointments and credit support as grounds for investors to assume, wrongly, that a government guarantee exists; they also cite the small risk premium on their debt relative to government debt as evidence that the financial markets treat the liabilities of Fannie Mae and Freddie Mac as implicitly backed by the government.

The opponents of the GSEs also argue that financial system efficiency requires that markets be able to discipline risk taking through the pricing mechanism. The benefits of market discipline are maximized when all risks are fairly priced. For example, increased risk taking by private sector firms would necessarily result in higher borrowing costs. In the case of Fannie Mae and Freddie Mac, however, the perception of implicit government guarantees makes market discipline ineffective. In their case, an increase in their assumed credit and interest rate risks would be unlikely to translate into higher borrowing costs. Thus opponents of the GSEs argue that the favorable funding arrangements and other government-related benefits provide a subsidy to homeownership and allocate a disproportionate amount of economic resources to the housing sector.

Proponents argue that the benefits of providing liquidity and stability to the secondary mortgage markets and of providing greater overall access of the

*Continued*

---

**Box 6.1 (Continued). Government-Sponsored Financial Enterprises:
The Cases of Fannie Mae and Freddie Mac**

population to mortgage credit need to be weighed against the distorting effect of the government subsidies. Another subtle consideration is that many private financial institutions, such as banks and thrifts, also benefit from explicit government guarantees, because their deposits are federally insured.

In 1992, in an effort to mitigate the effects of weak market discipline on these GSEs, the U.S. Congress established the Office of Federal Housing Enterprise Oversight (OFHEO) to oversee the safety and soundness of Fannie Mae and Freddie Mac. The OFHEO required Fannie Mae and Freddie Mac to abide by regulations comparable to those governing private financial institutions, including holding capital commensurate with the risks they undertake. OFHEO's oversight responsibilities include the following:

- Developing and implementing a risk-based capital standard
- Issuing regulations concerning capital and enforcement of the standards
- Making quarterly assessments of capital adequacy
- Conducting on-site examinations of Fannie Mae and Freddie Mac
- Undertaking necessary enforcement actions
- Prohibiting excessive executive compensation.

OFHEO is funded through assessments levied on Fannie Mae and Freddie Mac. Although it is not clear that these initiatives fully substitute for effective market discipline, they at least provide a mechanism for imposing some financial discipline.

---

**6**

securitization market has been closely linked to the presence of government institutions established primarily for the purpose of providing finance for low-income housing (see box 6.1).

This market was supported in its early stages by creation of the Federal National Mortgage Association (known as Fannie Mae). Fannie Mae began operations as a government-owned and -operated agency in 1938, with the purpose of purchasing, and thereby guaranteeing a market for, the new Federal Housing Administration loans. A similar institution, Freddie Mac, began operations in 1970 as a wholly owned subsidiary of the Federal Home Loan Bank System. Both institutions were created to subsidize the residential mortgage market by creating a secondary market for mortgages issued by federal housing schemes and by savings and loan associations, respectively. They both operate with substantial financial and regulatory concessions from the government and are required to meet the government's objectives by providing housing finance to certain income and geographic groups. In 1996 the U.S. government estimated that the total subsidy conveyed to Fannie Mae and Freddie Mac was in excess of $5 billion annually.

In 1968 Fannie Mae was divided into two separate corporate entities:

- The Government National Mortgage Association (known as Ginnie Mae), chartered to provide a secondary mortgage market for government-guaranteed mortgage loans
- Fannie Mae, recreated as a privately owned corporation, charged with providing a secondary market for nongovernment-guaranteed mortgage loans.

Freddie Mac also was rechartered along the same lines as Fannie Mae under the Financial Institutions Reform, Recovery, and Enforcement Act of 1989. In the process, its scope was broadened to provide a secondary market for mortgage loans originated by all lenders, not just savings and loan associations.

Fannie Mae and Freddie Mac are classified as government-sponsored enterprises, which are hybrid public/private enterprises. Although they are owned and operated by the private sector, they are chartered by the U.S. government and operate with public missions. The government mandates that certain percentages of their mortgage purchases must be from low- and moderate-income families as well as from geographically underserved areas. As government-sponsored enterprises, they must balance the profit motive against their statutory requirements to perform their public mission.

The residential real estate loans purchased by Fannie Mae and Freddie Mac are either held on balance sheet or grouped together into pools and securitized. As an indication of their position in the U.S. financial market, the combined on-balance-sheet portfolio of these two institutions stood at around $850 billion at the end of 1999; their combined securitized debt stood at a further $1.2 trillion. These two institutions are among the largest financial institutions in the world, and the combined size of their issues is larger than that of all but the most developed financial systems in the world. Although it is difficult to estimate their contribution to the development of the U.S. financial system, they have been pivotal in the development of the securitized debt market.

# The Contribution of Specialized Financial Institutions to Economic Growth

The contribution of specialized financial institutions to economic growth arises in large part from the same factors that underpin the natural base of demand for their services: namely, cost and scale efficiencies and the ability that they give to small- and medium-size enterprises to tap finance where they might otherwise be unable to do so.

## Leasing

The greatest contribution that a strong leasing market can offer to economic growth is its ability to finance small- and medium-size enterprises. Leasing offers cost efficiencies to these enterprises and sometimes is the only avenue of finance available to these firms to fund capital investment. This contribution can be significant where collateral laws are not well developed or enforced. It also can be important in start-up operations, where the firm has no track record and normal banking facilities are difficult to obtain. With start-up operations, the tax benefits of leasing, and therefore the potential cost savings from leasing, tend to be the greatest.

The specialized nature of leasing companies, combined with their scale, also can lead to efficiencies in accessing foreign products and the foreign exchange to pay for them. They can offer efficiencies in dealing with government bureaucracies to negotiate and secure investment incentives, import licenses, and other investment-related government benefits.

A strong leasing market also can benefit financial sector development more generally by broadening the financial markets. In the early stages of development, it is typical for leasing companies to raise their funding from wholesale sources such as banks, insurance companies, and pension funds. As they develop in sophistication, however, they can issue paper—in the form of commercial paper or bonds—directly into the securities markets. Once they have a sufficient credit history, they also can tap the equity markets by going public. At a higher level of sophistication, leasing companies may securitize their lease receivables, thereby tapping a larger pool of funding and assisting in deepening and developing the securities markets.

6

### Real Estate Finance

A supportive market for real estate finance is conducive to economic development and welfare. Further, to the extent that real estate finance markets are fertile ground for financial innovation, they may contribute to the overall efficiency and vibrancy of the financial system. In particular, they can help to stimulate development of the securities market by providing a ready pool of standardized instruments ideal for securitization.

Unlike the case for leasing finance, however, specialized full-service real estate financing institutions do not bring any immediately obvious advantages to the financial system that are not available through banks or insurance companies. The advantages noted for the development of securities markets are more a product of the specialized service providers than of the specialized intermediaries. The one area where they may contribute is through competition with the larger institutions in dealing with retail borrowers who otherwise might have difficulty dealing with larger institutions. To the extent that they produce a better outcome for retail customers, they add to social welfare. This case is far from convincing, however, particularly if the banking and insurance markets are reasonably competitive.

## The Appropriate Form of Regulation

Although there may be a case for variations in the details of how individual groups of specialized financial institutions might be regulated, they have much in common at the broad philosophical level. Like all financial institutions, specialized financiers warrant regulation for market failure associated with competition and market integrity. Indeed, since one of the major professed benefits of the types of finance that are conducive to specialization is the potential cost saving for small- and medium-size enterprises, a highly competitive market in this area is fundamental to achieving those benefits. Thus a priority of competition regulation should be to ensure that these markets remain contestable.

The key issue to be considered in designing a regulatory framework for specialized financial institutions is the extent to which the particular institutions involve market failure associated with asymmetric information, thereby warranting prudential regulation. In most cases, analysis of the promises that these institutions make provides very little support for a strong market failure of this type. The notable exception is where the institutions involved offer deposits to the public. This distinction is a useful reminder that the regulatory attention in financial markets should be focused very clearly on the liability side of the balance sheet.

## Specialized Deposit-Taking Institutions

Where specialized institutions solicit deposits directly from the public, the potential for asymmetric information failure is greatly increased. The one group that tends to fit this model in most countries is the group of specialized real estate intermediaries, such as building societies, mortgage banks, and savings and loan associations. The situation is exacerbated when the deposits of these institutions are guaranteed, either implicitly or explicitly, by the public purse. In these cases, there is a very strong case for regulating specialized institutions at least to the standard of banks. Indeed, a case can be made that their regulation should be more exacting, given that their risks are greater than those in banks, which have more diversification in their balance sheets.

6

For these institutions, the form of regulation is critical. The lessons from failures such as the U.S. savings and loan crisis and Australia's Pyramid Building Society (see box 6.2), both products of inappropriate regulation in the late 1980s, are many and include the following:

- The potential for balance sheet restrictions to increase rather than mitigate risk
- The dangers of overly prescriptive regulation that bears little or no relationship to the risks being taken by the institutions involved
- The dangers of regulatory forbearance (if an institution is already insolvent, it faces an asymmetric incentive structure that encourages it to take on almost unlimited risk; although there is nothing further to lose, a favorable outcome on one gamble may be sufficient to restore the institution's fortunes)
- The potential dangers involved in deposit insurance when regulation fails to counteract the moral hazard problem that insurance introduces.

The modern approach to banking regulation has done much to remove these pitfalls and is more risk based in its application. Applying this framework to specialized financiers that solicit deposits from the public is essen-

## Box 6.2. The Cost of Inappropriate Regulation:
## The U.S. Savings and Loan Crisis and Australia's Pyramid Building Society

The collapse of the savings and loan industry in the United States in the late 1980s and early 1990s and the failure of Pyramid Building Society in Australia are sharp reminders of the need to shape the form of regulation to the nature of the market failure.

The causes of the widespread failure of U.S. savings and loans were many and have been covered in detail in many places. They include fraud, risky lending, insider loans, and falling real estate prices. But poor regulation was one of the most important contributors to the crisis.

In the 1980s, the savings and loan regulatory system was a fragmented and inconsistent combination of state and federal regulators with three basic flaws:

- Regulatory standards were lax and overly prescriptive. Little attention was paid to capital or solvency, accounting standards were weak and oriented primarily toward achieving tax concessions, and there was virtually no focus on risk management.
- The prescriptive nature of the regulations included two inherently contradictory requirements: savings and loans were restricted to lending almost exclusively against mortgages (thereby limiting their ability to reduce risk through diversification), and they were restricted to making long-term, fixed-rate loans (despite the fact that their natural funding base was through short-term deposits).
- Savings and loans were able to issue deposits backed by deposit insurance without facing any effective supervision to manage the risks they were taking.

The combination of these flaws meant that savings and loans faced a material maturity mismatch on their balance sheets and were effectively insuring borrowers against interest rate rises. They were, in turn, being insured by a deposit insurance scheme that took no account of the risks involved in the maturity mismatch.

When short-term interest rates rose in the early 1980s, many savings and loans became technically insolvent. Recognizing the conflict posed by the balance sheet restrictions, the Garn St-Germain Act of 1982 loosened these restrictions and allowed savings and loans to take on greater risks in lending, at a time when many of them should have been closing down. As a result, in some states savings and loans became heavy investors in junk bonds and other low-grade investments in an effort to trade their way out of insolvency.

The ultimate result was the collapse of around one-third of the savings and loan associations, leaving U.S. taxpayers with a bill of around $132 billion—making it one of the biggest and best-known financial crises since the Great Depression of the 1930s.

Although the total cost of the failure of the Farrow Group of Building Societies (known popularly as the pyramid crisis, named after Pyramid Building Society, the major society in the group) in Victoria in 1991 was much smaller than that of the U.S. savings and loan crisis, it was sufficient to prompt a major overhaul of the regulatory structure for nonbank deposit-taking institutions in Australia. The pyramid crisis contained many of the same features present in the savings and loan crisis (the material in this case study relies heavily on Lewis and Boyd 1993).

In early 1990, the three building societies in the Farrow Group experienced a sharp outflow of deposits. At the time, Australia had a history of unjustified runs on building societies that had been stopped by state politicians who had reassured depositors that their governments stood behind the societies, absent any legislative requirement to do so. This experience encouraged the Victorian government to step into the situation and issue a statement to the effect that the state had investigated the societies and found them to be financially sound. This action subsequently proved costly to both depositors and the state.

Within four months, the run on deposits resumed at an unsustainable rate, forcing the state regulator of building societies (the Registrar of Building Societies) to freeze the group's activities and appoint an administrator.

*Continued*

**Box 6.2 (Continued). The Cost of Inappropriate Regulation:
The U.S. Savings and Loan Crisis and Australia's Pyramid Building Society**

The resulting investigation revealed a litany of irresponsible practices within the societies and total regulatory failure. The Farrow Group had built its high-growth strategy around unacceptably poor practices:

- Offering interest rates on deposits that were usually 1 percent and often 2 percent above market
- On-lending these funds to high-risk commercial real estate developments (contrary to the Victorian Building Society regulations that required at least 50 percent of building society assets to be invested in mortgages for owner-occupied housing)
- Current-period profits that were generated by high up-front fees on commercial loans, leaving the resulting asset/liability income streams commercially unviable
- Loans that were typically for 100 percent of construction costs plus capitalized interest for the period of the development
- Lending based on inflated and unrealistic selling prices
- Nonperforming loans that were hidden by creative rescheduling of loans
- Substantial fees that were siphoned off from the societies to management companies owned and operated by the two principals of the Farrow Group.

The final resolution of the group's problems registered losses of around $1 billion—almost 50 percent of the group's assets. Unfortunately for the Victorian government, the losses had increased significantly between their initial reassuring public statement and the eventual administration of the group. More than 200,000 depositors were affected. The extent of individual losses was mitigated by a government "guarantee," which was an inevitable outcome of their intervention throughout the crisis. The guarantee consisted of 25 cents on the dollar up-front plus a bond that offered repayment of the balance owing over an unspecified period (which in practice ranged from one to five years). The bonds did not pay interest and did not cover interest arrears on deposits. As a result, those depositors who elected to accept the government's offer lost around 30 percent on average of their claim against the Farrow Group, while those who chose to pursue their own remedy in the courts lost closer to 50 percent on average.

As with the U.S. savings and loan crisis, the failure of the Farrow Group exposed weaknesses in the Victorian regulatory structure. The regulations were overly prescriptive and deficient in allowing 100 percent ownership of a financial institution by private companies. The failure of the regulator to enforce the regulations was an even greater concern. Despite clear regulatory violations and repeated warnings from others in the industry, the Victorian regulator failed to act, despite the fact that the Farrow Group represented more than one-third of building society assets under its jurisdiction. Under the circumstances, a crisis was inevitable.

6

tial if these institutions are to meet their promises under a wide range of possible circumstances.

It is probable that applying such an onerous regulatory framework to these institutions would remove much of the incentive for their existence. Historically, they have flourished best where they have enjoyed a regulatory advantage relative to banks and other real estate financiers. Regulatory arbitrage, however, is a poor justification for a permanent place in the financial system. To warrant such a place, these institutions need to establish a natural role for themselves in the absence of such distortions. The ability of nondeposit-taking institutions and service companies to decompose real estate finance into its component parts and to compete effectively at each stage in advanced financial markets indicates that the future of specialized deposit-taking real estate financiers may be quite limited.

### Nondeposit-Taking Specialized Financial Institutions

With the exception of specialized real estate intermediaries, most specialized financial institutions raise funds from wholesale markets. Where they do tap retail markets, they tend to do so through marketable securities rather than through retail deposits. Consequently,

- Their promises are much less onerous than those of deposit takers and insurance companies.
- Their corporate structures are less complicated than those of banks and insurance companies.
- The social cost of their failure to honor their promises is relatively modest, in the sense that it usually is localized to the immediate debt and equity holders of the company.

Further, competitiveness should be a priority in these markets. Since prudential regulation is, by its nature, partly anticompetitive, the net social cost of imposing a prudential regime on specialized financial institutions could be very high.

The very fact that specialized financial institutions do not rank highly in terms of the three key characteristics of their promises, and therefore do not justify the high cost of prudential regulation, is one of the factors that makes them cost competitive. Thus specialized financial institutions should, in general, be restricted by law from taking deposits from the public and from making any other promises that warrant prudential regulation. This limitation is consistent with their role as specialized sectoral financiers.

The conclusion that the majority of specialized financial institutions do not warrant prudential regulation is not equivalent to concluding that they should not be regulated at all. As argued earlier, there is a case for very strong competition regulation to ensure that the cost efficiencies offered by these institutions are passed through to their customers. The need for a competitive market in these forms of finance suggests that the competition regulator should seek to ensure that entry into the market is as contestable as possible for new firms.

## Systemic Considerations

Provided that the market is competitive and that adequate disclosure and governance are imposed through market conduct regulation, specialized financial institutions are, in general, unlikely to pose a systemic threat.

This is not to imply that these institutions are low risk. On the contrary, some specialized financial institutions involve substantial risk. Their very nature as specialized institutions means that their risks may be highly concentrated. Leasing companies, for example, often have large exposures to a small number of industries, such as construction or mining, in which they choose to focus their expertise. This can leave them exposed to the swings in fortune of those industries. To compound their risks, the resale value of specialized capital equipment usually is positively correlated with the fortunes of the industries in which it is used. In assessing the problems experienced by leasing companies in emerging markets, the International Finance Corporation (1996) finds that over-concentration of risks by sector or client and general vulnerability to adverse macroeconomic changes are major contributors to financial failure.

Specialized financial institutions also are exposed to the balance sheet risks that face all financial institutions. For example, real estate loans are usually long term in nature. Leasing contracts are usually medium term in nature. Unless the institutions providing this finance have access to matching maturities in their liabilities or to derivative products for managing the risk, they can be highly exposed to shifts in the shape and position of the yield curve. This can be a particular problem in emerging markets, where wholesale sources of funds often are limited and derivative markets are underdeveloped.

Systemic issues can nevertheless arise when any industry becomes very large and concentrated. This risk increases where the institutions rely heavily on short-term liabilities to fund longer-term assets. The disruption caused by large-scale failure of these institutions is borne mainly by the investors and creditors of the companies involved, although price bubbles and institutional failures can retard the development of the financial system more generally. Flow-on problems can occur where these institutions are established

6

as subsidiaries of banks, are not subjected to consolidated regulation, and are used to circumvent the effects of regulation on banking activity.

The most reliable signal of impending problems is when one industry group grows far more rapidly than other sectors of the financial system. In some cases, the differential growth rate may reflect nothing more than the emergence of a natural source of demand or the response to the removal of previous impediments. In other cases, abnormal growth can reflect exploitation and abuse of incentives. Excessive growth often masks poor business practices and mispricing, as industry participants scramble to exploit short-term opportunities. Once conditions stabilize, the poor practices are exposed to competitive pressure and declining demand, and failures often follow.

The regulatory challenge for specialized financial institutions is to balance the positive contribution to economic growth that can follow from light regulation against the possible disruption that might occur from financial failures. Although these institutions can have systemic implications under certain circumstances, the impact of institutional failure falls mostly on groups that should be competent in assessing the risks. Provided these institutions are adequately quarantined from high-prudential-risk institutions such as banks, and provided the industries are subjected to adequate competition and market conduct regulation, these considerations point more to a monitoring role than to any direct regulation of specialized financial institutions on either prudential or systemic grounds.

Although a broad monitoring function should be adequate for assessing systemic risks among most groups of specialized financial institutions, the main exception to this rule arises where a particular institution or group of institutions takes on risk that has recourse to the public purse. The need for some form of regulation to protect the public liability in these cases is increased when the institutions involved are substantial in size.

The most striking example of the potential risks involved is in the U.S. mortgage market. Fannie Mae and Freddie Mac have a combined balance sheet of around $850 billion of mortgages. Together, they guarantee a further $1.2 trillion of mortgages. Although the securities of these institutions are not technically guaranteed by the U.S. government, because of their unique relationship to the government and the extent of the subsidies that they administer, the market treats them as though they are. The failure of either of these would create not only a potentially enormous liability for

U.S. taxpayers but also systemic risk by disrupting the markets for housing and housing finance.

The case for regulating specialized institutions in these unusual circumstances is supported by their systemic significance, the extent of government subsidies that they enjoy, and the fact that, as government-sponsored institutions, they are not subject to the normal disciplines of the market. In 1992, in the face of the burgeoning cost of rescuing the savings and loan industry, the U.S. government created the Office of Federal Housing Enterprise Oversight to regulate these two institutions.

## Regulatory Tools and Techniques

The following subsections present the key regulatory tools and techniques that address deposit takers and other specialized nondeposit-taking institutions.

### Deposit Takers

In terms of tools and techniques, the key regulatory requirements for deposit takers are summarized in a series of standards and guidance notes issued by the Basle Committee.[7] The broad categories are summarized very briefly in chapter 2; the following are the most important for deposit takers:

- Licensing requirements
- Capital adequacy requirements for credit risk and market risk
- Loan loss provisioning guidelines
- Operational risk guidelines.

At present, the Basle Committee's standards distinguish between internationally active banks and domestic banks, with the more rigorous of its requirements applying only to the former. Discussions are currently under way to update the capital requirements of banks and to extend coverage to all banks. This latter proposition has met with considerable support internationally. In view of this likely development, there is a very strong case for

---

7. The Basle Committee was created in 1974 by the Committee of G-10 Central Bank Governors, from its forerunner the Basle Committee on Banking Regulation and Supervisory Practices.

applying the same international standards to specialized financial institutions that raise funds through retail deposits. Not only does this approach minimize regulatory arbitrage, but it also reduces what can be a substantial risk to consumers of financial services.

Although full harmonization of regulatory standards between banks and specialized deposit-taking institutions is conceptually straightforward, it is considerably more difficult in practice. It requires a major commitment from governments to overhaul what is often outdated legislation covering the nonbank deposit-taking sector. In the process, care needs to be taken to treat all deposit takers equally, so as not to perpetuate regulatory differences inadvertently.[8] It also requires cooperation between the bank and nonbank regulators (where these are not the same agency).

Although the case for regulatory neutrality is very strong, whether or not regulation of the nonbank deposit takers is pursued to the point of full harmonization is a matter of judgment. The essential point is that institutions that take deposits from the public must be regulated to the point where the likelihood of their failing to honor their promises is acceptably small. In practice, this should be achievable without the need to attain full regulatory harmonization of all deposit takers. In making such a decision, governments need to weigh the adjustment costs involved against the efficiency benefits of full regulatory neutrality.

## Systemic Risks

In regulating for systemic risks among specialized financial institutions, the primary tool, consistent with the low level of risk generally involved, is to have a monitoring role over the whole industry. In general, such a surveillance role would fall to the central bank. In the event that the central bank was concerned about the growth or behavior of a particular industry group, it could refer the matter to the government for regulatory consideration. Since abnormal growth also can arise as an unintended consequence of gov-

---

8. For example, most countries have separate legislation covering banks and nonbanks. Those acts usually refer to the institutions by their industry groupings, thereby establishing differences by definition. Creating a single act for licensed deposit takers, as was done in Australia in 1998, is a useful first step. In Australia, rewriting the prudential standards to remove all discriminations was a second step that took a further two years after the new legislation was enacted. Even then, a number of old prudential conditions had to be grandfathered in so as not to cause some institutions unnecessarily costly short-term readjustments.

ernment incentives, this monitoring role for the central bank could serve as an early warning of industry abuse of incentives or of unintended consequences and the need for remedial action.

The exception to this general principle arises in those unusual circumstances where a financial institution enjoys substantial government benefits or is of sufficient size as to create a serious systemic risk. In either case, the risks to the taxpayer should be protected by regulation. The appropriate form of regulation should be tailored to the situation.

Where the risk to taxpayers arises from a government subsidy or tax concession, there is a strong case for reviewing the objective of the subsidy/tax concession. Where the benefit is intended for certain targeted groups in the community, the most efficient way to distribute the benefit usually will be directly to the ultimate recipient. Administering subsidies through financial institutions not only opens up greater opportunity for abuse but also adds the cost of regulation to the cost of the subsidies. It also can confer on a select group of financial institutions a competitive advantage that may interfere with industry efficiency.

Where direct payment of benefits to intended recipients is impractical or excessively costly to monitor for abuses, care should be taken to minimize the competitive impact of the subsidies. In particular, efforts should be made to ensure that the benefits are passed on to the intended recipients and that the prudential requirements imposed on the institution are no less stringent that those imposed on other institutions making essentially the same promises.

## Other Specialized Nondeposit-Taking Institutions

For the majority of specialized financial institutions, where retail deposit taking and systemic issues are not involved, competition and market conduct regulation should be sufficient to meet society's needs.

### Entry Requirements

Normally, the competition regulator would encourage low barriers to entry into these sectors by ensuring that there are minimal restrictions on the corporate form and ownership structure of these institutions, freedom of entry for foreign firms, and strong antitrust conditions to prevent excessive concentration in the industry. The only structural restrictions that are consistent with this objective are those that prohibit these institutions from accepting deposits from the public and from participating in the payments system. The competition regulator's natural desire for minimal licensing requirements may need to be balanced against any concerns that the market conduct regulator may have.

### Disclosure

Since these institutions typically raise finance in wholesale markets, the market conduct regulator should, in principle, be able to meet its concerns through strong disclosure requirements and corporate governance principles as applied through general corporate law.

Where these institutions are the beneficiaries of government tax incentives, subsidies, or privileges such as import licenses or currency convertibility, there is a case for imposing reporting requirements, additional disclosures, and even inspection or audit requirements to ensure that the incentives and privileges are not subject to abuse.[9] Whatever the motivation for additional market conduct regulation, its impact should be weighed carefully for its anticompetitive implications. It is important to avoid a situation in which a small group of institutions is granted access to government incentives and privileges, while at the same time being protected from competition by an overly protective regulatory regime. Such situations often lead to abuses of privilege, exploitation of consumers, slow growth in the very areas of finance that the government is attempting to promote, and appropriation of the economic rents involved by the protected firms.

### Associations with Other Institutions

In general, the desire for healthy competition among specialized financial institutions militates against heavy restrictions on associations with other institutions. That said, where government incentives, subsidies, and concessions are involved, corporate associations may need to be monitored closely to prevent abuses. The surest way of managing these risks is, wherever possible, to pay the benefits directly to the intended recipients.

The second situation where associations may need to be monitored closely is where specialized institutions are established as subsidiaries of reg-

---

9. This possibility is more likely in the case of leasing institutions than it is in the case of specialized real estate finance institutions.

ulated institutions as a means of circumventing the impact of the regulations. The dangers of excessive growth in unregulated subsidiaries were highlighted in a number of Asian countries, including Japan, during the recent Asian crisis.

Consolidated supervision is one way of ensuring that regulatory requirements are met on a group-wide basis. An alternative approach that separates the institutions a little more strongly is to require a nonoperating holding company structure for groups involving some companies that are prudentially regulated and some that are not. Some group-wide requirements may still be imposed on such groups.[10]

*Additional Forms of Regulation*

Where corporate law is well developed and supported by the courts, there is less need for additional regulation. In practice, the need for stronger licensing conditions and restrictions such as minimal capital requirements still may arise in countries where general corporate laws are not sufficiently strong to prevent exploitative behavior on the part of the specialized institutions or in industries particularly prone to such behavior.

The need for some additional form of regulation is more likely in emerging markets, where corporate laws often are still evolving. In these situations, the following conditions can support market conduct:

- Licensing requirements, with evidence of skills among the directors and company management, and restrictions on directors or management with criminal convictions
- Minimum capital requirements, commensurate with the minimum scale of operations necessary for the business involved
- Accountability requirements including auditing requirements and some restrictions on accounting practices
- Risk conditions consistent with the risks involved (for example, evidence of risk diversification).

---

10. The appropriate regulatory approach to conglomerates is still a matter of intense discussion around the financial world, and there is no consensus about the best way to minimize the risks involved. It is nonetheless widely agreed that the structure of a nonoperating holding company offers some safeguards that other structures do not.

Whatever additional conditions are imposed, they should be weighed carefully against any anticompetitive impact that they may have. Additionally, they should be reviewed frequently in the context of developments affecting the overall legal framework.

**6**

# Chapter 7

# Issues for Emerging Markets

*The nonbank regulatory issues facing emerging markets are, by and large, the same as those facing developed markets. Every country can benefit from a healthy sector of nonbank financial institutions (NBFIs) that provide a sound basis for economic growth. The regulatory structure for NBFIs is not only a critical factor in ensuring that these institutions perform their functions efficiently but also an important factor in stimulating or retarding their growth and development as part of the financial system. Excessive regulation can stifle their emergence. Equally unhelpful, a poor incentive structure can encourage growth for the wrong reasons and in the wrong forms, leading ultimately to problems, if not crises.*

*The objective should be to provide a sound regulatory framework that enables NBFIs to flourish to the mutual benefit of all involved—neither forced to grow beyond the economy's needs nor prevented from playing their natural role of increasing financial efficiency.*

*Although many issues are relevant to NBFI regulation, most of the general issues have been covered in the preceding chap-*

*ters. This chapter focuses on issues that are particularly relevant to emerging markets, including the importance of legal infrastructure, the role of financial sector professions, the role of incentives for the growth of NBFIs, the role of foreign competition, the role of government provision of financial services, the importance of public sector governance, and the importance of sequencing reforms.*

## The Importance of Legal Infrastructure

The general legal framework is arguably the single most important determinant of a sound NBFI sector. Legislation underpinning the specific regulatory framework for NBFIs is the foundation stone of good regulation. This includes both the acts creating and giving powers to the regulator and the acts underpinning the legal existence and behavior of the entities being regulated. It is critical that these acts specify clearly the powers of the regulator and the extent of the regulator's coverage. There should be no ambiguity as to the meaning of terms such as securities, deposits, insurance, mortgages, and leases.

Equally important are the supporting laws, such as those governing accounting rules, property rights, and contract enforcement. In a recent study of the relationship between legal infrastructure and financial development, Levine, Loayza, and Beck (1999: 28) find that "Countries with (a) laws that give a high priority to secured creditors, (b) legal systems that rigorously enforce contracts, and (c) accounting standards that produce comprehensive and comparable corporate financial statements tend to have better-developed financial intermediaries."

Of particular interest, Levine, Loayza, and Beck examine the impact of legal origin on legal effectiveness. Following the convention of legal scholars, they separate legal systems into four major legal families: English, French, German, and Scandinavian. Although all four descended from Roman law, they evolved in different ways and, through colonization and conquest, spread throughout most of the world, providing the bases for most modern legal systems. Levine, Loayza, and Beck find that differences in legal origin explain differences in the legal rules covering secured creditors, contract enforcement, and the quality of accounting standards.

Their main finding on legal origin is that countries with a German legal origin have better-developed financial intermediaries, countries with a French legal origin have less well-developed intermediaries, and those with English or Scandinavian origins lie in between. They suggest that these results can be explained partly by the following characteristics of the four legal traditions (see also Laporta and others 1998):

- The English tradition emphasizes the rights of creditors more than the other three (the French tradition protects creditors the least).
- The German and Scandinavian traditions are the strongest at enforcement (again, the French is the weakest).
- Countries with an English tradition tend to have better accounting standards than the others.

A well-balanced prudential framework is one that seeks to implement the best of these systems, with strong and predictable rights for creditors, strong but fair enforcement, and a reliable system of accounting and disclosure.

Although legal infrastructure is the critical foundation stone of a sound regulatory system, the skills needed to implement and enforce the infra-structure must be available as well. This requires well-trained and independent professionals such as auditors and actuaries, an independent and ethical judiciary, and an adequate depth of skilled private sector personnel capable of implementing legal, accounting, and risk management principles.

## Critical Financial Sector Skills and Professions

The development of NBFIs requires a solid base of human capital.[1] One of the most pressing challenges confronting emerging markets is the limited availability of financial sector skills and the urgent need to develop human capital by establishing a base of capable professionals such as bankers, accountants, lawyers, appraisers, analysts, and insolvency experts. The development of these professions will foster the sophistication of financial markets and the development of nonbank financial institutions.

One set of available data covers employment in the financial services sector as a percentage of total employment (see table 7.1). Despite the dif-ficulties in measuring the differential in skills across countries and adjusting

1. This section draws extensively on Pomerleano (2001).

**Table 7.1. Employment in Finance, Insurance, Real Estate, and Business Services as a Percentage of Total Employment in Select Countries, 1997**

| Country | Share of total employment |
| --- | --- |
| Indonesia | 0.754 |
| Philippines | 2.442 |
| Malaysia | 5.219 |
| Japan | 8.769 |
| United States | 11.399 |

*Source:* United Nations (1997).

for productivity, there is evidence that financial sector services play a small role in many emerging market countries. Employment in finance, insurance, real estate, and business services as a percentage of total employment is much lower in Indonesia, for example, than in the United States. In the Tiger economies, the former growth model emphasized production and exports and did not promote services.

Functioning, complete markets require a base of professional financial skills. However, recognition of the need often grows only out of crisis. In the United States, for example, the savings and loan debacle in the 1980s, discussed in chapter 6, prompted creation of the certification process for appraisers just 10 years ago. The regulation was in direct response to evidence of appraisal problems and misconduct inside U.S. financial institutions. According to evidence brought to light in the U.S. Congress, fraud and self-dealing by officers, directors, and insiders caused or contributed to half of all financial institution failures. Faulty or fraudulent real estate appraisals were used systematically to overvalue collateral and to make unsafe real estate loans. In response, the Appraisal Subcommittee of the Federal Financial Institutions Examination Council (ASC) was created to oversee appraisers and to ensure that they are sufficiently trained and tested, are competent, independent, and ethical, and use uniform, high professional standards. The United States is not perfect; it just experienced and responded to its crisis earlier than other countries.

Critical professions that are lacking and whose absence impedes the development of NBFIs include insolvency experts, lawyers, accountants, appraisers, financial analysts, and actuaries (see table 7.2). The following paragraphs discuss some of these professions in detail.

7

**Table 7.2. Appraisal, Actuarial, and Insolvency Professionals in Select Countries**

| Country | Appraisers Number per million population | Number | Insolvency experts Number per million population | Number | Actuaries Number per million population | Number |
|---|---|---|---|---|---|---|
| Argentina | — | — | 0.92 | 34 | 4.54 | 168 |
| Australia | — | — | 31.57 | 606 | — | — |
| Austria | — | — | 2.84 | 23 | — | — |
| Belgium | — | — | 0.68 | 7 | — | — |
| Brazil | 29.39 | 5,000 | — | — | 2.40 | 408 |
| Canada | — | — | 34.89 | 1,071 | — | — |
| Czech Republic | 535.37 | 5,500 | 1.56 | 16 | — | — |
| China | 10.64 | 13,420 | 0.01 | 8 | 0.01 | 8 |
| Finland | 28.96 | 150 | — | — | 18.73 | 97 |
| France | 29.74 | 1,750 | 2.53 | 149 | 21.78 | 1,282 |
| Germany | 97.38 | 8,000 | 0.99 | 81 | 20.22 | 1,661 |
| Hong Kong (China) | 159.46 | 1,084 | — | — | 29.27 | 199 |
| Hungary | — | — | 2.20 | 22 | 12.87 | 129 |
| India | 0.34 | 350 | 0.03 | 33 | 0.11 | 111 |
| Indonesia | 6.665 | 1,400 | 0.02 | 4 | 0.03 | 7 |
| Israel | — | — | 0.16 | 1 | — | — |
| Italy | — | — | 0.80 | 46 | — | — |
| Japan | 44.96 | 4,700 | 0.04 | 5 | 6.73 | 853 |
| Korea | 36.47 | 1,724 | 0.02 | 1 | 0.23 | 11 |
| Lithuania | 126.01 | 466 | — | — | — | — |
| Malaysia | 21.50 | 500 | 1.12 | 26 | — | — |
| Mexico | 30.62 | 3,000 | 0.02 | 2 | 1.95 | 191 |
| New Zealand | — | — | 49.86 | 191 | — | — |
| Nigeria | — | — | 0.03 | 4 | — | — |
| Norway | — | — | 2.00 | 9 | — | — |
| Pakistan | — | — | — | — | 0.10 | 14 |
| Philippines | — | — | 0.01 | 1 | 0.90 | 68 |
| Poland | 77.62 | 3,000 | 0.28 | 11 | 0.10 | 4 |
| Romania | — | — | 0.62 | 14 | — | — |
| Russia | 27.48 | 4,000 | — | — | — | — |
| Singapore | 129.17 | 519 | 2.74 | 11 | 20.41 | 82 |
| South Africa | — | — | 7.13 | 305 | — | — |
| Spain | — | — | 0.30 | 12 | — | — |
| Sweden | 56.38 | 500 | 1.58 | 14 | 27.74 | 246 |
| Switzerland | — | — | 0.84 | 6 | 48.05 | 345 |
| Thailand | — | — | 0.13 | 8 | 0.21 | 13 |
| United Kingdom | 334.79 | 20,000 | 27.02 | 1,614 | 79.75 | 4,764 |
| United States | 284.14 | 80,000 | 6.54 | 1,841 | 53.16 | 14,968 |

— Not available

*Source:* For insolvency, INSOL membership database; for appraisers, the International Valuation Standards Committee; for actuaries, the International Actuarial Association.

## Insolvency Experts

Insolvency practitioners are needed to analyze the business and financial viability of a real estate project or a company and to choose between restructuring and liquidation. They require expertise to negotiate approval of, implement, and monitor the restructuring plan and to manage operations of the company. If liquidation is needed, insolvency practitioners arrange for the orderly disposition of the company's assets and the creditor's claims. Their expertise and integrity must be above reproach.

The International Federation of Insolvency Professionals (INSOL) is a worldwide federation of national associations for accountants and lawyers who specialize in insolvency. The members are engaged in formal insolvency proceedings, advise creditors and businesses, and restructure businesses in financial difficulty. INSOL International currently has 29 member associations worldwide with more than 8,000 professionals. The quantitative data in table 7.2 indicate the disparity of skilled professionals available in Japan (five members), Canada (1,071 members), and the United States (1,841 members).

With regard to qualifications and regulation, the requirements vary among local organizations and from country to country (see table 7.3). For instance, in the United Kingdom, any of seven recognized bodies can authorize an insolvency practitioner to act. INSOL International is the international umbrella organization for member associations from 26 countries. Memberships in the local associations typically are made up of qualified accountants or lawyers. In general, accountants tend to take insolvency appointments in the common law system, and lawyers tend to lead in the civil law system and in the United States. However, overall, there are considerable differences in the training and licensing of insolvency professionals. In very few nations (United Kingdom, Canada, Australia, and some others) are insolvency practitioners examined, licensed, and regulated either by their professional bodies or by the state. In other countries, such as France, the list of court-approved liquidators and administrators is very restricted. In the vast majority of nations, however, accountants or lawyers who also provide other services carry out insolvency work. Some may specialize in insolvency work, but not possess distinct formal qualifications or accreditation.

In many countries, any remotely qualified person—whether an accountant or a notary—is eligible to be a court-appointed liquidator, as long as the person is a disinterested party. Often the appointed "expert" lacks ability,

**Table 7.3. Qualification Requirements of Insolvency Experts in Select Countries**

| Country | Qualification requirements | Source |
|---------|---------------------------|--------|
| Canada | Membership requirements include the association's standards of admission, prescribed course of study, and passage of required examinations. In 1997 the National Insolvency Qualification Program was created to harmonize qualification requirements. | Canadian Insolvency Practicioners Association (CIPA) |
| New Zealand | Government is opposed to occupational registration, so there is no registration of insolvency practitioners. The following cannot qualify for appointment: persons under 18 years of age and creditors, shareholders, directors, auditors, or receivers of the company. | INSOL New Zealand |
| Switzerland | Insolvency is not a specialized profession. Activities are performed mostly by other specialized professions (lawyers, accountants). | Swiss Bankers' Association (SBA) |
| United Kingdom | Insolvency experts are licensed and regulated by one of eight recognized professional bodies (for example, the Institute of Chartered Accountants in England and Wales plus the Secretary of State for Industry). | Association of Business Recovery Professionals |

**7**

independence, or both. For instance, in the People's Republic of China the draft of a new insolvency law only requires the administrator to have not been struck off as a lawyer or accountant within the last five years. The administrator does not even have to be an accountant or a lawyer.

## Appraisers

Appraisers are needed to value property, including commercial property (office buildings, retail, shopping centers), industrial property (manufacturing plants, warehouses), residential property (apartment houses, single-family homes), and machinery and personal property. Appraisers reduce the risk involved in property transactions by assigning credible values to property based on a standard method: all participants recognize the methodology, and the valuation is consistent. In many emerging markets, standards of certification are lacking. Therefore, it is important to establish and promote minimum uniform standards of appraisal and minimum qualifications. Professionally recognized training and certification programs can ensure the professional expertise, integrity, and responsibility of appraisers.

The International Valuation Standards Committee (IVSC) is an association comprising professional valuation associations from some 50 countries. A brief look at the quantitative data in table 7.2 indicates wide differences in the availability of appraisal services in select markets. The frequency ranges from 335 appraisers per million population in the United Kingdom to 0.3 appraiser per million population in India.

The standard methodology for appraisals relies on the market, income, and cost approaches. Perhaps the most striking point is that not all countries abide by appraisal based on market value—for example, the use of comparable transactions in order to establish market value. For instance, in Japan valuations rely on the cost approach. Appraisals of property often are based on the value of land (land price index) and, rarely, the sales comparison and income approach. The reliance on cost basis is due to the lack of data: market data are scarce due to lack of information disclosure and the failure to collect transaction data. Further, property appraisers tend to be architects and engineers, and their bias is to use cost basis for appraisals. Therefore, the real estate market is not transparent.

Moreover, there is no consistent treatment across countries of the appraisal and valuation profession with respect to training and regulation. Similarly, in many countries—for example, Argentina—there are no uniform standards of valuation. In others—for example, France and Mexico— there is no state-appointed or self-regulatory body for the supervision of real estate valuation. In many countries, the regulation and development of the profession usually have followed a crisis of some sort—the savings and loan crisis in the United States, the property crash in the 1980s in Europe, the reform of the centrally planned economies in Eastern Europe, and the recent financial crisis in Asia.

Similarly, the U.K. experience with instilling training and licensing requirements for surveyors is instructional of best practices. The Royal Institution of Chartered Surveyors (RICS) is the premier global professional body that represents, regulates, and promotes chartered surveyors and technical surveyors. In order to become either a technical or professional member of RICS, candidates are expected to complete an approved academic qualification followed by at least two years of structured training in the workplace. On completing the minimum training period, candidates are assessed via submissions and an interview. Successful assessment allows members to be upgraded to technical or professional membership. After they have been full members for a minimum of five years, they can apply to become a fellow. The members are bound by the rules of conduct and bylaws outlined in the RICS charter.

Countries in the process of establishing a mortgage lending market and introducing mortgage-based instruments in their capital markets need to improve the standards of valuation. Clearly, appraisal standards should be correctly applied and regulated. This can be accomplished by establishing professional standards of valuation, educational requirements, methodology, ethics, and oversight in developing real estate markets.

## Financial Analysts

Disciplined financial decisionmaking demands expertise. Such financial analysis is employed in a variety of functions—securities analysis, portfolio management, and the budgeting process. Financial analysts practice in a variety of industries, including investment management, banking, and insurance.

Expert financial analysis requires education, standards of professional conduct, and standards of practice. The Association for Investment Management and Research (AIMR) was created to educate and certify investment managers and analysts and to sustain high standards of professional conduct. However, 82 percent of its members practice in North America, while only 8 percent practice in Asia and less than 1 percent practice in Latin America.[2]

## Actuaries

Actuaries traditionally work in the insurance and employee benefits industries and the health and retirement benefits sectors. They make it possible to share and disperse risks and, in a market economy, help to stabilize the financial system. Nevertheless, actuaries are scarce in developing countries. The International Actuarial Association (IAA) brings together the actuaries in member countries, and its members are actuarial associations worldwide. The IAA is dedicated to the research, education, and development of the profession and of actuarial associations. It reviews and implements the rules for the accreditation of individual members and recommends educational guidelines and a syllabus for an internationally recognized actuarial

---

2. A caveat with respect to the AIMR is that analysts in other regions might choose membership in domestic organizations.

**Table 7.4. Qualification Requirements of Actuaries in Select Countries**

| Country | Qualification requirements |
| --- | --- |
| Argentina | Examinations, university courses |
| Brazil | University degree program |
| Finland | Examinations by industry bodies, government examinations |
| Germany | Examinations, university courses |
| Hungary | University degree plus 18 months of practice |
| India | Examinations by industry bodies |
| Japan | Examinations by industry bodies |
| Mexico | University degree program |
| Singapore | Examinations by industry bodies, university degree programs |
| Sweden | University degree program |
| Switzerland | University degree plus at least three years of qualified professional experience, in line with international guidelines of ASTIN (International Actuarial Association) |
| United Kingdom | Examinations, university courses |
| United States | Examinations by industry bodies |

*Source:* International Actuarial Association.

qualification. Table 7.2 indicates the wide disparity in the availability of actuaries in the sample countries, while table 7.4 shows the rigor of training required of them.

Some economies have professions that are properly trained and regulated and have commonly accepted standards of business that produce a strong institutional structure. But the facts regarding the proliferation of the professions raise intriguing questions. Specifically, why do Hong Kong and Singapore have more financial sector professionals per capita than Japan and Korea? Does that make their economies more flexible?

Some economies have a better professional infrastructure than others because of their legal traditions—common law versus civil law. Common law countries, including Australia, Canada, Hong Kong, Singapore, and the United States, are former British colonies and rely on independent judges and juries and legal principles supplemented by precedent-setting case law to respond to evolving circumstances. Civil law countries, which include Indonesia, Japan, Korea, and Latin American nations, rely on legal codes that contain very specific rules. Therefore, civil law countries are not adept at responding to the changing needs of the economy. They have to pass new rules regarding property valuation and regulation of new financial products such as insurance. Legal traditions affect the development of professions to a remarkable degree. According to La Porta and others (1998), there is a robust negative correlation between the civil law tradition and lack of professions, and there is also a supporting and beneficial impact of professions on the rule of law.

What can be done? Effort is required along three dimensions: regulations to facilitate the growth of the financial services professions, incentives to induce individuals to enter these professions, and opening of the financial sector to foreign competition. Governments need to play an active role in all three areas.

The regulatory regime is intended to ensure that practitioners have appropriately high levels of competence and skills, that practitioners have integrity and independence, and that a procedure is available for dealing effectively with enforcement. An effective regulatory regime instills credibility in these professions.

Leadership is needed as well to foster professional associations for appraisers, actuaries, and insolvency experts, among other professions. In the meantime, governments can encourage skills development by outsourcing contracts to licensed professionals in the private sector.

## Incentives for the Growth of NBFIs

Chapter 1 establishes the contribution that NBFIs make to economic growth. They complement banks by filling gaps in the range of banking services and providing either services that are inappropriate for banks to engage in or services that banks produce inefficiently. By specializing in particular products and sectors and in information processing, NBFIs compete with banks, forcing them to be more efficient and responsive to the needs of their customers. Strong NBFI sectors historically have been associated with strong financial and economic development. The issue is to determine the factors that cause the development or underdevelopment of NBFIs.

Vittas (1997), Levine, Loayza, and Beck (1999), and Demirgüç-Kunt and Levine (1999) each provide some answers to this question.[3] The com-

3. The first three subsections draw mainly on Vittas's work, while the final section draws on all three studies.

bined wisdom of these studies suggests that the following four factors are the dominant determinants of NBFI growth:

- The level of income and wealth
- Macroeconomic performance
- Social security
- Regulation.

Some of these factors, such as the influence of public social security on the growth of the private contractual savings sector, are canvassed in earlier chapters. Others are relatively self-explanatory. For example, among very poor countries, low income and low wealth are likely to be the dominant factors inhibiting the emergence of strong NBFIs. The biggest issue for many emerging economies is whether there is a case for additional incentives to stimulate the growth of NBFIs or whether the design of the regulatory system itself is a help or a hindrance to this growth. This section concentrates on issues associated with regulatory and tax incentives.

## Regulatory Incentives

Regulation can influence the growth of NBFIs in two main ways: (a) repressive regulation can retard NBFI growth, and (b) inappropriate regulation or poorly designed regulatory structures can stimulate NBFI growth for the wrong reasons, often creating incentives for regulatory arbitrage and the emergence of unanticipated systemic problems.

### Repressive Regulation

Repressive regulation can have a negative influence on the development of NBFIs, especially where it taxes (either directly or indirectly) the earnings of the regulated institution more heavily than those of its competitors, or where it imposes balance sheet restrictions that constrain risk management. Balance sheet restrictions, often imposed in the name of prudence, can be particularly inhibiting to the growth of NBFIs. For example, regulation historically has restricted pension funds and insurance companies in many continental European countries to investments in debt-type promises, predominantly sovereign debt. Similarly, until the 1980s, Australian insurance companies were a captive market for government bonds. Ironically, in some developing countries where investment restrictions are less debt-oriented, the scope for wider investment is still constrained by the regulation of investment in foreign assets for balance-of-payments reasons.

Repressive regulation in this context includes not only excessive licensing, capitalization, and investment regimes but also situations where related regulations discriminate against NBFIs. For example, many countries restrict investments and the purchase of transactions services by government departments, legal trust funds, and other agencies to products and services offered by banks.

### Inappropriate Regulation and Regulatory Arbitrage

Inappropriate or poorly designed regulation can stimulate the growth of NBFIs for the wrong reasons. During the 1970s, high inflation, coupled with excessive regulation of banks, stimulated the growth of nonbanks around the world as a means of avoiding banking regulations. One of the greatest incentives for growth during this period was the widespread use of interest rate lending ceilings on bank loans. With lending rates capped and inflation rising sharply, the demand for debt finance (often at negative real rates of interest) ballooned. In this environment, nonbanks found it attractive to bid depositors away from banks and to on-lend funds at unregulated rates.

Not only did financing shift to nonbanks during this period, but many banks also established nonbank subsidiaries as a means of circumventing the regulations themselves. One consequence of the incentive structure imposed by interest ceilings was the shifting of higher-risk lending to nonbank subsidiaries. In the absence of compensating prudential regulation of these subsidiaries, prudence was often ignored in the search for higher returns. The need for NBFIs to take further risks was heightened as banks were progressively deregulated and began recapturing their lost market share.

The problem of financial conglomeration and the scope that arises for regulatory arbitrage within conglomerates have been issues of concern for emerging and developed markets alike. The best way to regulate conglomerates has been a topic of debate among national regulators, the Basle Committee, and the Joint Forum of Banking, Securities, and Insurance Regulators. Indeed, as pointed out in chapter 2, the issue of conglomerates has been one of the factors driving the recent trend toward integrated regulation.

Many adverse experiences among developed financial systems have prompted this interest:

7

- The collapse of Barings Bank as a result of unauthorized trading by a subsidiary in Singapore
- The weakening of Japanese banks through losses sustained in finance company subsidiaries
- The problems created for Deutsche Bank by losses in its British securities subsidiary Morgan Grenfell
- The loss of Australia's last state bank, the State Bank of Victoria, through losses sustained in its investment banking subsidiary.

The problem in every case was that a regulated institution was placed in difficulty because of losses in subsidiary or related companies that were either unregulated or poorly regulated.

Problems associated with regulatory arbitrage and conglomeration in emerging markets have been similar to those in developed markets, but, in many cases, the consequences for systemic instability have been greater. Specific incidents include the following:

- The growth and failure of leasing companies in Korea (see chapter 6)
- Also in Korea, the growth of life insurance companies as a secondary banking system in the 1990s
- The growth during the 1990s of the pre-need industry in the Philippines outside the regulatory system[4]
- The failure in the late 1990s of finance company subsidiaries of banks in Thailand.

At the heart of the regulatory arbitrage problem—whether it arises through conglomerates or through competing institutions providing essentially the same services under different regulatory regimes—is the pressure on every financial institution to manage its capital efficiently in order to maximize returns to shareholders.

This pressure is not inherently undesirable, since profitable institutions are a comfort to regulators as well as to shareholders. Where conflict can arise is in the different risk profiles that the regulator and shareholders may be willing to accept in pursuing profitability. This poses a dilemma for regulators. On the one hand, regulators typically prefer to impose regulations that are simple to implement and easy to understand. On the

---

4. The pre-need market in the Philippines covers a range of products that ensure that funds are available when they are needed, such as for education and funerals.

other hand, simple rules inevitably create distorted incentives for the regulated institution.

At the most basic level, regulatory prohibitions on certain transactions or types of business always create an incentive to circumvent the regulations, provided the prohibited business is potentially profitable. This conflict was one of the motivations for the Basle Committee on Banking to introduce the Capital Accord in 1988. The accord shifted the regulatory focus in banking away from prescribing the business that banks could undertake and toward allowing banks to choose their own business, with the regulator then imposing regulatory capital minimums according to the assessed risk of the business chosen. However, as banks became more sophisticated in assessing the risks associated with different types of business, the crude risk classifications of the accord again opened up opportunities for regulatory arbitrage, as internally assessed capital requirements and regulatory imposts diverged. This conflict, in turn, motivated the major revision of the Capital Accord that is currently under way.

The one reassuring feature of this process is that, as financial institutions have become more sophisticated, regulators have been better able to rely on the internal risk management processes of the institution as a substitute for mechanical regulatory rules. This process already has been applied by banking regulators and by some insurance regulators in assessing market risk. Under this approach, the regulator shifts its focus from assessing the risks in the institution to assessing the quality of the institution's own risk management systems. Although this trend eventually may resolve the conflict between the objectives of the regulators and the regulated, it is likely to be a long way from the immediate problems of regulators in emerging markets.

The main lesson from these experiences for emerging markets is that NBFI growth that is stimulated by regulatory arbitrage is potentially dangerous for systemic stability and potentially costly in terms of financial failure. Until financial institutions develop their own sophisticated risk management, there is a strong need to undertake the following:

- Ensure that financial institutions that provide essentially the same products are regulated in essentially the same way
- Ensure that the regulatory framework is sufficiently flexible so that new institutions and products are not able to avoid regulation simply by their choice of label

7

211

- Ensure that the regulation of various components of conglomerates are consistent and supportive
- Create a regulatory structure in which at least one regulator has over-all responsibility for financial conglomerates.

## Tax Incentives

Growth of NBFIs is particularly responsive to discriminatory tax treatment. In Australia, for example, friendly societies had a long history as mutual self-help societies. Most were socially oriented and involved largely in the pharmacy industry. Those that were involved in finance limited themselves largely to minor areas of insurance, such as funeral benefits. As a consequence of their mutual structure and social focus, they enjoyed tax-exempt status. In the 1970s, with the growing demand for finance outside the heavily regulated banking sector, a number of these institutions began offering financial products that exploited their tax exempt status to give them a competitive edge over their more conventional competitors. Within a short period of time, they became substantial members of the contractual savings industry, offering tax-free savings bonds in competition with other taxed investments. Their rationale for existence as financiers, however, contracted severely when the government eventually removed their preferred tax status.

Tax incentives also exert a strong influence on the growth of private pension funds and insurance companies. Most governments offer at least some tax concession for long-term savings through these vehicles. In many cases, the incentive acts, as intended, to stimulate savings and to provide for long-term capital formation. In some cases, however, the incentives also are abused. For example, in countries where the registration of private pension schemes and associated governance rules are relatively lax, individuals may exploit the tax incentive without losing control of their funds by investing in the pension plan and then borrowing the funds back for other purposes. Although these activities are not necessarily damaging to systemic stability, they can promote a false impression of savings and growth of the NBFI sector. At the same time, the forgone tax revenue can be costly to the government's budget.

The main lesson from experience is that tax incentives can be genuine incentives for growth of NBFIs. To achieve their purpose, however, without undesirable side effects, the tax incentives need to be accompanied by strict regulations designed to prevent abuse.

## The Role of Foreign Competition

The appropriate role for foreign competition in the development of the financial sector is a widely debated subject. The positive features of permitting foreign entrants into various parts of the financial system are many:

- *Access to foreign expertise.* This is particularly important in highly technical areas where local skills are not yet well enough developed. Indeed, lack of expertise is one of the main hurdles to financial development in emerging markets. Foreign participants not only help to bridge the expertise gap but also help to train and upgrade skills in the local population.
- *Access to foreign capital.* This is often another major hurdle to developing a sound NBFI sector. Emerging markets often lack a wide base of investors to capitalize NBFIs. With local capital often tightly held by a few companies or wealthy families, the alternative to foreign capital is usually excessive concentration in the ownership of financial institutions. This, in turn, can create problems associated with insider manipulation, lack of arm's-length transactions with the industry, and corruption.
- *Risk sharing with foreign participants.* If problems arise in the financial system, foreign equity shareholders can share any losses involved.
- *Competition.* In many emerging markets, shortages of capital and skills often result in a high degree of market concentration, especially among the larger institutions. The fact that domestic institutions take time to grow means that, in many situations, foreign entry is the only source of effective competition among financial institutions. In some cases, for example in the Australian banking industry in the early 1980s, the very threat of foreign entry can be sufficient to increase competitiveness in the domestic market.

Although there are many positive features in encouraging foreign entry into the financial system of emerging markets, there also are some draw-

7

backs. The greatest concern of most governments is that foreign competitors will be so far advanced over local institutions that the local institutions will never achieve the market size needed to be competitive. There is also a concern that foreign firms may employ largely foreign residents, with the result that employment of local residents in the industry may fall and the intended transfer of skills may not occur. These concerns are legitimate and need to be balanced against the benefits associated with foreign competition. Notwithstanding these concerns, a number of countries, including New Zealand and Argentina, have embraced foreign dominance of certain sectors of the financial system, where local expertise or capital was inadequate to provide the financial services needed by the economy.

The appropriate mix of foreign and domestic competition can vary across industry sectors. There is a strong case for allowing foreign entrants to the insurance industry even before a domestic industry emerges. The need for foreign participants arises partly because of the important role that risk transfer plays in the efficient conduct of commerce and partly because of the specialized skills needed to carry out this role effectively.

In general, however, the timing and extent of foreign entry into various industries of the NBFI sector are a matter of judgment. The greater is the desire for economic development and financial efficiency, the greater is the case for foreign entry. Nevertheless, it generally is in the country's interests to ensure that foreign participation occurs in an environment conducive to the development of a domestic industry capable of competing on equal grounds with foreign firms.

## The Role of Government Provision of Nonbank Financial Services

The case for government provision of nonbank financial services is similar in many respects to that for foreign participation. Where there is a shortage of private sector capital for the establishment of domestic financial institutions of efficient scale, the government may provide this capital on behalf of the population at large. This case also exists where private capital is available but is owned too closely to satisfy the requirements for independence from the commercial sector with which the financial institutions will do business. In this way, the government is an alternative to foreign institutions as a source of capital. This case for government ownership, which often is rejected very quickly in the case of commercial enterprises, can be sustained more readily with respect to the financial sector because of its importance to economic growth and welfare. The implications of public ownership are, however, significant.

Unlike foreign participation, government ownership of financial enterprises does nothing to resolve the shortage of financial skills within the local community. Indeed, publicly owned enterprises are notoriously inefficient. Without pressure from shareholders, they rarely develop the skills or performance efficiencies of privately owned enterprises. More important, if there are problems in the industry, government ownership does nothing to spread the burden of loss with nonresidents. On the contrary, it spreads the cost of failure across the entire community. Public ownership confers an implicit public guarantee over the products that it provides. In the case of financial services, this not only destroys the natural spectrum of risk among financial products but also confers an unfair advantage on publicly supplied financial services that can inhibit the development of a viable private sector alternative.

It sometimes is seen as politically attractive to use government ownership of financial institutions as a vehicle for social policies, such as subsidized homeownership and business loans. The attractiveness lies in the fact that these subsidies remain off-budget. The attractiveness, however, is purely political. There is no efficiency gain from delivering social objectives through government-owned financial institutions, relative to other more transparent methods. Indeed, the potential for social policies to interfere with the normal costing and pricing of competitive financial services creates an efficiency loss.

These distortions and the efficiency losses associated with public ownership of financial institutions have long been regarded as a source of potential systemic damage. In a study for the International Monetary Fund, Garcia (1996) examines the role of public ownership in 18 banking failures in a range of countries, including both developed and emerging markets. Of the 18 failures, 13 were in countries with a high level of state ownership and control of financial institutions. Although these failures occurred for a variety of reasons, including regulatory failure, lack of competition, and deficiencies in governance, state ownership contributed to the problems in each case and was the common factor shared by most.

For these reasons, public ownership of financial institutions has, at best, a limited role to play in the development of NBFIs. Where it does have a

7

role to play—for example, in an embryonic insurance industry where there is insufficient local capital and foreign capital is unwilling to accept the risks involved until the economy is better established—there is a powerful case for replacing public ownership with private ownership as quickly as the market can sustain.

## The Importance of Public Sector Governance

A key component of a sound regulatory system is a strong foundation of corporate governance. One of the major tools of market integrity regulation is the institution of corporate governance rules to minimize the likelihood of insider trading and market manipulation. Similarly, prudential regulation relies heavily on strong internal governance to prevent fraud and to ensure that difficult promises can be met. However, another aspect of governance is equally critical for the effective functioning of the financial system: public sector governance. It is surprising that this important area has only recently begun to receive the attention it deserves.

The suggested importance of public sector governance rests on two fundamental propositions: first, that weak public sector governance leads to economic and financial underperformance and, second, that without strong public sector governance, effective corporate governance in the financial sector will be unattainable. The evidence on these issues is still largely subjective, but it is growing, and that which is available lends strong support to both propositions.

### Governance and Performance

According to Kaufmann, Kraay, and Zoido-Lobaton (2000: 10), public sector governance can be defined as

> the traditions and institutions that determine how authority is exercised in a particular country. This includes (1) the process by which governments are selected, held accountable, monitored, and replaced; (2) the capacity of governments to manage resources efficiently and formulate, implement, and enforce sound policies and regulations; and (3) the respect of citizens and the state for the institutions that govern economic and social interactions among them.

A wide range of international and commercial organizations, including risk-rating agencies, multilateral organizations, think tanks, and non-governmental organizations, produce qualitative measures of governance. Some of these measures are based on surveys of outsiders (from those who do business with the countries involved to those who simply observe from afar), while others are based on surveys of insiders (individuals, businesses, and experts within the countries involved). Most recently, the World Bank, in cooperation with the European Bank for Reconstruction and Development, the Inter-American Development Bank, and the Harvard Institute for International Development have commenced a worldwide survey of firms that has begun to produce much more quantitative data.

Existing measures focus mainly on six broad aspects of governance: voice and accountability, political instability and violence, government effectiveness, regulatory burden, rule of law, and control of corruption. As Kaufmann, Kraay, and Zoido-Lobaton note, despite the wide range of sources, the measures produced are surprisingly consistent in their assessments about governance. In particular, they point to the striking consensus between the assessments of risk-rating agencies and those of businesses and citizens within countries.

Using an "unobserved components model" to analyze the various measures of governance, Kaufmann, Kraay, and Zoido-Lobaton conclude that good governance is strongly correlated with better economic development. They also find a causal effect running from improved governance to better development outcomes. This causal relationship runs counter to the frequent suggestion that good governance is a superior good; that is, richer countries can better afford the luxury of good governance.[5] Although their work is still in its early stages, the size of the effects they find are significant. For example, they suggest (Kaufmann, Kraay, and Zoido-Lobaton 2000: 12),

> An improvement of one standard deviation in the rule of law from the low level prevalent in Russia to the "middling" level in the Czech Republic or, alternatively, a reduction in corruption from the very high level prevalent in Indonesia to the lower level in Korea leads to between a twofold and fourfold increase in per capita incomes, a decline in infant mortality rates of similar magnitude, and an improvement of 15–25 percentage points in literacy levels.

5. Had this been the case, the causal relationship would have run from better economic development to better governance, not the reverse.

Even if the dividend from improved public sector governance is only a fraction of these estimates, the economic case for improvement remains compelling.

### The Relationship between Public and Corporate Governance

The primary case for asserting that poor public sector governance inhibits good private sector governance rests primarily on the logic that the private sector will take its lead from the public sector. More to the point, for a corrupt public sector to profit from its actions, the payments must be provided by the private sector. It would defy logic to suggest that the corporate sector could behave corruptly in its dealings with the public sector, while remaining incorruptible in its internal dealings. The mere existence of tough corporate governance laws is unlikely to deter firms that are used to "purchasing" legal outcomes from a corrupt public sector. The same line of thinking suggests that it would be illogical for corruption to be rampant in the nonfinance sector, while leaving the finance sector untainted. Ultimately, corruption starts at the top and breeds corruption throughout the system.

In a recent study, Hellman, Jones, and Kaufmann (2000) analyze the relationship between firms and governments in transition economies. They argue that there is a need to move beyond the traditional, one-dimensional view of corruption in which public officials monopolize the returns to corruption. They suggest an alternative form in which firms seek to capture the officials and share the returns from collusion with them. They distinguish three types of corrupt relationships between firms and government: first, state capture, in which the firm controls legal and regulatory reforms to its own benefit through illicit payments to government; second, influence, where the firm achieves the same outcomes without the need for illicit payments, simply because of its size or special relationship with government (for example, ownership or repeat business); and administrative corruption, in which the firm makes illicit payments to public officials to distort the intended outcome of public rules and policies (for example, legal outcomes).

They find that influential and captor firms grow at a "substantially faster rate than other firms" (Hellman, Jones, and Kaufmann 2000: 4). However, they also find that the returns to these forms of corrupt behavior are only significant in highly corrupt countries. In other words, where governments have a low level of corruption, the returns to corrupt behavior by firms are, on average, zero or negative.

This work has several implications:

- Corruption is a two-way process; it requires complicity on the part of both the public and private sectors.
- The gains for the firms involved in corrupt behavior are greatest where there is both a high level of public sector corruption and significant potential benefits from controlling the formation of regulations or their implementation, which suggests that the financial sector is highly unlikely to be free from corruption in countries where public sector corruption is high.
- Improving public sector governance is a critical foundation stone if there is to be any hope of implementing a system of strong corporate governance.

## The Importance of Sequencing Reforms

The recent Asian crisis highlighted the importance of the sequencing of reforms. The prevailing wisdom is that financial opening in many of the affected countries ran ahead of the regulatory reforms needed to support systems with a substantial exposure to outside markets. The question is whether there is also a need to sequence the regulatory reforms themselves.

There is arguably no unique best sequence of regulatory reforms. Although it may be possible, in theory, to map out an ideal sequence for a country starting from a zero base, in practice no country has a zero base. Every country has an existing regulatory structure and faces a particular set of regulatory issues at every point in time.

Although every situation has its own unique features, prioritizing the various elements of regulation can provide a useful guide to any country looking to sequence its own particular reforms, whether they are financial sector reforms in general or NBFI reforms in particular.

The following subsections present some general principles and priorities that should be relevant to most situations.

### Supporting Regulations Should Come First

Supporting regulations provide the base-level foundation, without which higher-level regulations often fail to operate effectively. Thus regulatory reforms that focus on the regulatory agencies before establishing these foundations may result in disappointed expectations. Paramount among these supporting regulations are accounting rules and legal infrastructure, including those that establish the powers of the regulators, as well as property rights and contract enforcement.

Although in some countries the market integrity regulator administers both accounting rules and disclosure rules, they are conceptually quite distinct. Disclosure rules determine what information is to be provided to the community; accounting rules determine the nature and quality of that information.

The importance of legal foundations is emphasized earlier in this chapter. In many areas of financial regulation, the emphasis is on forcing institutions to honor the promises they make to those who do business with them and hold their claims. Without sound laws governing property rights and enforcement of contracts, the regulator's intentions can be thwarted. One of the most important pieces of supporting legislation is a strong corporations law, setting out principles of good corporate governance and heavy penalties for their violation across the entire corporate community.

Strong supporting legislation is particularly important to the effectiveness of prudential regulators. For example, regardless of the efforts of the prudential regulator, the safety and soundness of deposit-taking institutions ultimately depend on the safety and soundness of the businesses to which they extend credit. If the supporting legislation does not provide a legal and ethical framework that encourages prudent and honest business practices, protects property rights, and imposes open disclosure of meaningful information, both the financial institutions and the regulator effectively have their hands tied.

Finally, prudential regulation typically requires the regulator to operate within the legal framework established by the individual pieces of legislation covering the institutional groups being prudentially regulated. Flaws in these industry acts, especially inconsistencies between them and the act giving powers to the regulator, can weaken the effectiveness of the regulator.

## Regulatory Skills and Commitment Are Critical

Regulatory skills and commitment matter more than regulatory structure. Notwithstanding the recent emphasis that has been placed on reforming regulatory structures, without the regulatory skills and commitment, even the best-designed structure can fail.

One of the greatest challenges facing regulators is to keep pace with the innovations that occur in financial markets and the consequent demands that are placed on staff to approve certain actions or adjust the rules to cope with change. Being able to understand the difference between an innovation that increases risk or circumvents the intent of an existing regulation and one that increases market efficiency often requires advanced financial skills. Being able to sift through partial data, whether on-site or off-site, and detect problems before they arise are skills that every regulator needs. Being able to put aside territorial conflicts with other regulators and personal difficulties that may arise with the staff of regulated institutions and to remain focused at all times on the broad objectives of regulation requires a level of commitment that every regulator aspires to, but few ever attain.

The point is that people make regulators work. Regulatory structure can help greatly, by reducing incentive conflicts and removing gaps and overlaps. But, ultimately, the success of a regulator in achieving its objectives will depend most critically on the quality of the people it employs.

**7**

## Do Not Extend the Prudential Net Too Widely

Drawing the boundaries around the institutions that warrant prudential regulation is one of the most important steps in designing an efficient regulatory system. As discussed in chapter 2, prudential regulation is fundamentally different from other forms of regulation. Prudentially regulated financial institutions are almost always more stable than unregulated institutions (provided the regulation is effective). At the same time, they are almost always less efficient and less innovative than unregulated institutions. This outcome is an inevitable consequence of the intrusive and preventative nature of prudential regulation.

Development of a vibrant, innovative nonbank financial sector demands that the net of prudential regulation be drawn around as few of these institutions as possible. Where the institutions make financial promises that rank highly in all three of the promise characteristics (difficult to understand, difficult to assess, and causing great adversity in the event of failure), prudential regulation must be considered. Few would dispute, for example, that some form of prudential regulation is warranted in the case of insurance promises. Beyond insurance, however, the case becomes less compelling.

Extending the prudential net further than is warranted can be costly. Not only is prudential regulation resource intensive, but there also can be a further cost if explicit or implicit safety nets are extended to these institutions. This imposes a potential future liability on the government and can reduce efficiency if the safety net is poorly designed (and fails to deal with the problem of moral hazard).

Strong market integrity and competition regulation should provide sufficient regulatory oversight for most noninsurance NBFIs.

## No One Regulatory Structure Fits All

It is critical when reforming a regulatory structure that the framework be appropriate to the particular situation. There is much to learn from the experiences of others. At the same time, each country's situation is at least a little different from that of others, whether the difference results from a cultural background that encourages or discourages a particular type of financial institution or activity or from the particular stage of development.

The regulatory structure appropriate to a financial system in which NBFIs are already growing strongly may be different from that appropriate to a system in which NBFIs are just beginning to emerge. The applicability of foreign entry may be different in a system that has just lost most of a particular set of intermediaries through failure than in one in which those institutions are just finding their feet.

In general, it is preferable to consider regulatory reforms during a period of relative financial stability. Stability permits these issues of appropriateness to the particular situation to be thought through fully. When reforms occur in times of crisis, there is a tendency to seize on the latest regulatory fashion as the solution to last year's problems rather than as a preventative against next year's problems.

## Take Reforms One Step at a Time

Good regulatory systems are not built overnight. Most of the regulatory systems in developed markets are the outcome of several decades or more of evolution. Most of these have undergone periodic reforms as crises have exposed weaknesses in their foundation, approach, or structure. Some of these reforms have taken years to bed down, while others have required continual refinement. These developed regulatory systems have had the luxury of time to build their base of skills and to learn from their mistakes as well as from each other's mistakes. Most of the designers of these systems would concede that there is still much to learn and more reforms to experience.

It is important to be realistic about what can be expected from regulatory reforms and, in particular, about the speed with which regulatory benefits can be achieved. For example, applying a complex, risk-based regulatory approach focused on internal models to an insurance industry that is still in its infancy might be intellectually appealing but would be counterproductive to the development and stability of the industry. A more realistic sequence would be heavily staged and might involve the following steps:

- Initial establishment of the accounting and legal foundations
- Imposition of a simple solvency requirement while the industry develops the actuarial and accounting skills to move to a more complex solvency rule based on actuarial evaluation of liabilities
- Subsequent introduction of risk-based capital requirements for market and credit risk
- Introduction of an internal models option once the industry and regulator are sufficiently skilled to implement and monitor the risks involved.

A sequence such as this could take a decade or more. Although the purists may become frustrated with the apparent lack of progress in a staged approach, it is important that the industry and regulator both have time to come to terms with each stage of development before moving to the next. Ultimately, each reform that strengthens the regulatory system adds another brick to the foundation of a stronger economy over time.

7

# References

The word "processed" describes informally reproduced works that may not be commonly available through libraries.

Advisory Group on Best Practices for Fund Directors, Investment Company Institute. 1999. "Enhancing a Culture of Independence and Effectiveness." Report of the Advisory Group on Best Practices for Fund Directors, Investment Company Institute, June 24. Processed.

Ayala, Ulpiano. 1996. *The Savings Impact of the Mexican Pension Reform.* World Bank Discussion Paper. Washington, D.C.: World Bank.

Balino, Tomas J. T., and Angel Ubide. 1999. "The Korean Financial Crisis of 1997: A Strategy of Financial Sector Reform." Working Paper WP/99/28. International Monetary Fund, Monetary and Exchange Affairs Department, Washington, D.C., March. Processed.

Bateman, Hazel, and John Piggott. 1998. "Mandatory Retirement Saving in Australia." *Annals of Public and Cooperative Economics* 69 (4):547–69.

Beck, Thorsten, Aslı Demirgüç-Kunt, and Ross Levine. 1999. "A New Database on Financial Development and Structure." Policy Research Working Paper 2146. World Bank, Development Research Group, Washington, D.C., June. Processed.

Bekaert, Geert, Campbell R. Harvey, and Christian Lundblad. 2001. "Does Financial Liberalization Spur Growth?" NBER Working Paper 8245. National Bureau of Economic Research, Cambridge, Mass., April. Processed.

Black, Bernard S. 2001. "The Corporate Governance Behavior and Market Value of Russian Firms." *Emerging Markets Review* 2: 89–108.

Catalan, Mario, Gregorio Impavido and Alberto R. Musalem. 2000. "Contractual Savings or Stock Market Development: Which Lead?" *Journal of Applied Social Studies 120* (3):445–87.

Claessens, Stijn, Simeon Djankov, and Daniela Klingebiel. 2000. *Stock Markets in Transition Economies.* Financial Sector Discussion Paper 5. Washington, D.C.: World Bank, Financial Sector Strategy and Policy Group, September.

Claessens, Stijn, and Daniela Klingebiel. 1999. "Alternative Frameworks for Providing Financial Services." Policy Research Working Paper 2189. World Bank, Financial Sector Strategy and Policy Group, Washington, D.C., September. Processed.

Coffee, John C. Jr. 2001. "The Coming Competition among Securities Markets: What Strategies Will Dominate?" Working Paper 192. Columbia Law School, Center for Law and Economic Studies, New York, September. Processed.

Committee of Inquiry into Non-Bank Financial Institutions and Related Financial Processes in the State of Queensland. 1990. "Report of the Committee of Inquiry into Non-Bank Financial Institutions and Related Financial Processes in the State of Queensland." Brisbane, Australia. Processed.

Courtis, Neil, ed. 1999. *How Countries Supervise Their Banks, Insurers, and Securities Markets.* London: Central Banking Publications.

Dalla, Ismail, and Deena Khatkhate. 1996. "The Emerging East Asian Bond Market." *Finance and Development 33* (1, March):11–13.

Demirgüç-Kunt, Aslı, and Ross Levine. 1999. "Bank-based and Market-based Financial Systems: Cross-Country Comparisons." World Bank, Development Research Group, Washington, D.C. Processed.

Demirgüç-Kunt, Aslı, and Vojislav Maksimovic. 1998. "Law, Finance, and Firm Growth." *Journal of Finance 33* (6, December):2107–37.

Edey, Malcolm, and Brian Gray. 1996. *The Evolving Structure of the Australian Financial System.* Research Discussion Paper 9605 (Australia). Sidney: Reserve Bank of Australia, October.

Famighetti, Robert. 1995. *World Almanac and Book of Facts 1996*. New York: St. Martin's Press, November.

Financial System Inquiry (Australia). 1996. *Australian Financial System Inquiry Discussion Paper*. Canberra: Commonwealth of Australia, Australian Government Publishing Service, November.

——————. 1997. *Australian Financial System Inquiry Final Report*. Canberra: Commonwealth of Australia, Australian Government Publishing Service, March.

Fleming, Michael. 2000. Presentation made at the Workshop on Nonbank Financial Institutions: Development and Regulation, World Bank, Washington, D.C., January 31. Processed.

Garcia, Gillian G. 1996. "Deposit Insurance: Obtaining the Benefits and Avoiding the Pitfalls." Working Paper WP/96/83. International Monetary Fund, Monetary and Exchange Affairs Department, Washington, D.C., August. Processed.

Gompers, Paul A., Joy L. Ishii, and Andrew Metrick. 2001. "Corporate Governance and Equity Prices." NBER Working Paper 8449. National Bureau of Economic Research, Cambridge, Mass., August. Processed.

Greenspan, Alan. 1999a. "Do Efficient Financial Markets Mitigate Financial Crises?" Speech given before the 1999 Financial Markets Conference of the Federal Reserve Bank of Atlanta, Sea Island, Ga., October 19. Available at www.federalreserve.gov/boarddocs/speeches/1999/19991019.htm. Processed.

——————. 1999b. "Lessons from the Global Crises." Remarks before the World Bank Group and the International Monetary Fund, Program of Seminars, Washington, D.C., September 27. Processed.

Hellman, Joel S., Geraint Jones, and Daniel Kaufmann. 2000. "Seize the State, Seize the Day: State Capture, Corruption, and Influence in Transition." Policy Research Working Paper 2444. World Bank, World Bank Institute, Governance, Regulation, and Finance Division, and Europe and Central Asia Region, Public Sector Group, Washington, D.C.; European Bank for Reconstruction and Development, Office of the Chief Economist, London, September. Processed.

Herring, Richard J., and Robert E. Litan. 1995. *Financial Regulation in the Global Economy*. Washington, D.C.: Brookings Institution Press.

Herring, Richard, and Anthony M. Santomero. 1999. "What Is Optimal Financial Regulation?" University of Pennsylvania, Wharton School, Philadelphia, September. Processed.

Holzmann, Robert. 1996. "On Economic Usefulness and Fiscal Requirements of Moving from Unfunded to Funded Pensions." Working Paper. University of Saarland. Processed.

Iglesias, Augusto, and Robert J. Palacios. 2000. "Managing Public Pension Reserves. Part 1: Evidence from the International Experience." World Bank, Washington, D.C., January. Processed.

International Finance Corporation. 1996. *Leasing in Emerging Markets.* Lessons of Experience Series. Washington, D.C.

——————. 1999. *Emerging Stock Markets Factbook 1999.* Washington, D.C.

James, Estelle. 1997. "Pension Reform: Is There an Efficiency-Equity Trade-Off?" Paper prepared for the conference Inequality-Reducing Growth in Latin America's Market Economies, World Bank, Washington, D.C., January. Processed.

Kaufmann, Daniel, Aart Kraay, and Pablo Zoido-Lobaton. 2000. "Governance Matters, from Measurement to Action." *Finance and Development 37* (2, June): 10–13.

Kumar, Anjali, ed. 1997. *The Regulation of Non-Bank Financial Institutions: The United States, the European Union, and Other Countries.* World Bank Discussion Paper 362. Washington, D.C.: World Bank, June.

La Porta, Rafael, Florencio Lopez-de-Silanes, Andrei Shleifer, and Robert W. Vishny. 1996. "Law and Finance." NBER Working Paper 5661. National Bureau of Economic Research, Cambridge, Mass. Processed.

——————. 1997. "Legal Determinants of External Finance." *Journal of Finance 52* (3, July): 1131–50.

——————. 1998. "Law and Finance." *Journal of Political Economy 106*(6): 1113–55.

Levine, Ross. 1999. "Law, Finance, and Economic Growth." *Journal of Financial Intermediation (United States)* 8(1/2, January/April): 8–35.

Levine, Ross, Norman Loayza, and Thorsten Beck. 1999. "Financial Intermediation and Growth: Causality and Causes." World Bank, Development Research Group, Washington, D.C. Processed.

Lewis, Steve, and Anthony Boyd. 1993. *Savings: Australia in Crisis.* Maryborough, Victoria: Financial Review Library, John Fairfax Group.

Lewis, Mervyn K., and Robert H. Wallace, eds. 1993. *The Australian Financial System.* South Melbourne: Longman Cheshire.

Matten, Chris. 2000. *Managing Bank Capital, 2d ed.* New York: John Wiley and Sons.

McKinnon, Ronald I. 1991. *The Order of Economic Liberalization: Financial Control in the Transition to a Market Economy.* Baltimore, Md.: Johns Hopkins University Press.

Merton, Robert C. 1990. "The Financial System and Economic Performance." *Journal of Financial Services Research 4* (4, December): 263–300.

OECD (Organisation for Economic Co-operation and Development). 1996. *Ageing in OECD Countries: A Critical Policy Challenge.* Social Policy Studies 20. Paris.

————. 2000. *Institutional Investors Statistical Yearbook 2000.* Paris.

Palacios, Robert J., and Montserrat Pallarés-Miralles. 2000. *International Patterns of Pension Provision.* Social Protection Discussion Paper 9. Washington, D.C.: World Bank, April.

Pomerleano, Michael. 1998. "Performance of Emerging Markets Equity Funds." *Emerging Markets Quarterly 2* (1, Spring):37–43.

————. 2001. "The Morning After: Restructuring in the Aftermath of an Asset Bubble." Paper prepared for the conference Asset Price Bubbles: Implications for Monetary, Regulatory, and International Policies, Federal Reserve Bank of Chicago, Chicago, Ill., October 4–6. Processed.

Pomerleano, Michael, and Xin Zhang. 1999. "Corporate Fundamentals and Capital Markets in Asia." In Alison Harwood, Robert Litan, and Michael Pomerleano, eds., *Financial Markets and Development: The Crisis in Emerging Financial Markets,* pp. 117–57. Washington, D.C.: Brookings Institution Press.

Skipper, Harold D. 2000. "Insurance Worldwide and Its Role in Economic Development." Paper prepared for the second annual Financial Markets and Development Conference: Emerging Markets in the New Financial System: Managing Financial and Corporate Distress, Florham Park, N.J., March 30–April 1. Processed.

Srinivas, P. S., and Juan Yermo. 1999. *Do Investment Regulations Compromise Pension Fund Performance? Evidence from Latin America.* Latin American and Caribbean Studies Viewpoints. Washington, D.C.: World Bank, June.

Swiss Re. 2000. *World Insurance in 1999: Soaring Life Insurance Business.* Sigma 9. Zurich: Swiss Reinsurance Company.

Taylor, Michael W., and Alex Fleming. 1999. "Integrated Financial Supervision: Lessons from Northern European Experience." Policy

Research Working Paper 2223. World Bank, Development Research Group, Private and Financial Sectors Development Unit, Washington, D.C., November. Processed.

United Nations. 1997. *Statistical Yearbook 1997*. New York.

U.S. Attorney General, National Committee to Study the Antitrust Laws. 1955. *Report of the U.S. Attorney General's National Committee to Study the Antitrust Laws*. Washington, D.C.

U.S. General Accounting Office. 1997. *Government-Sponsored Enterprises: Advantages and Disadvantages of Creating a Single Housing GSE Regulator*. GGD-97-139. Washington, D.C., July 9. Available at www.gao.gov/cgi-bin/fetchrpt?rptno=GGD-97-139.

Vittas, Dimitri. 1996. *Pension Funds and Capital Markets*. Public Policy for the Private Sector Note 71. Washington, D.C.: World Bank, February.

———. 1997. "The Role of Non Bank Financial Intermediaries in Egypt and Other MENA Countries." World Bank, Development Research Group, Washington, D.C., November. Processed.

———. 1998. "Regulatory Controversies of Private Pension Funds." Public Policy Research Working Paper 1893. World Bank, Development Research Group, Washington D.C., January. Processed.

World Bank. 1998. *Global Development Finance, 1998*. Washington, D.C.

World Bank and International Monetary Fund. 2001. *Developing Government Bond Markets: A Handbook*. Washington, D.C.

World Economic Forum and Center for International Development, Harvard University. 2000. *The Global Competitiveness Report 2000*. New York: Oxford University Press.